THE BIG ONE

THE BIG ONE

*An Island, an Obsession,
and the Furious Pursuit
of a Great Fish*

David Kinney

Atlantic Monthly Press
New York

All photos are courtesy of the author except: Prologue photo courtesy of
Jen Wlodyka; chapter 7 photo courtesy of Janet Woodcock; chapter 8 photo
courtesy of Kib Bramhall; chapter 10 photo courtesy of Lisa Vanderhoop;
chapter 11 photo courtesy of David Skok; chapter 12 photo courtesy of
Patrick Jenkinson; chapter 13 photo courtesy of Ben Scott.

Printed in the United States of America
Published simultaneously in Canada

ISBN: 978-0-8021-1890-5

Atlantic Monthly Press
an imprint of Grove/Atlantic, Inc.
841 Broadway
New York, NY 10003

Distributed by Publishers Group West

www.groveatlantic.com

09 10 11 12 13 14   10 9 8 7 6 5 4 3 2 1

for Monica, who made it possible

Contents

You might make a curious list of articles which fishes have swallowed—sailors' open clasp-knives, and bright tin snuff-boxes, not knowing what was in them,—and jugs, and jewels, and Jonah.

—*Henry David Thoreau on Cape Cod, 1849–1857*

I caught the thing and I was like, "What the fuck is wrong with this fish?"

—*Lev Wlodyka on Squid Row, 2007*

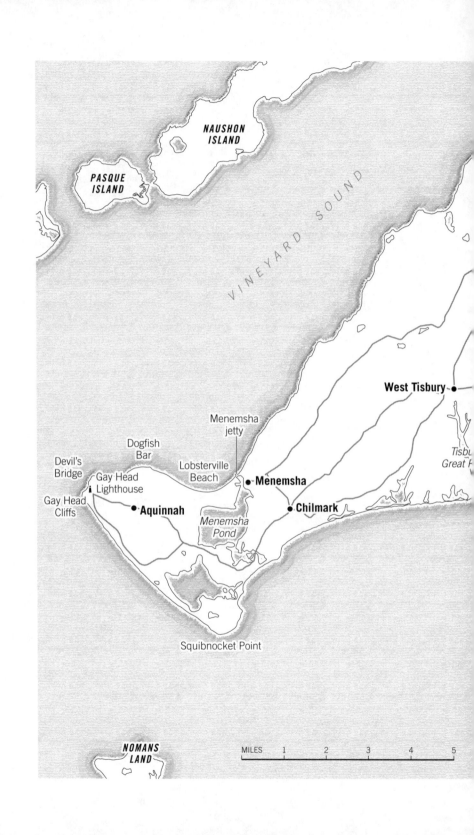

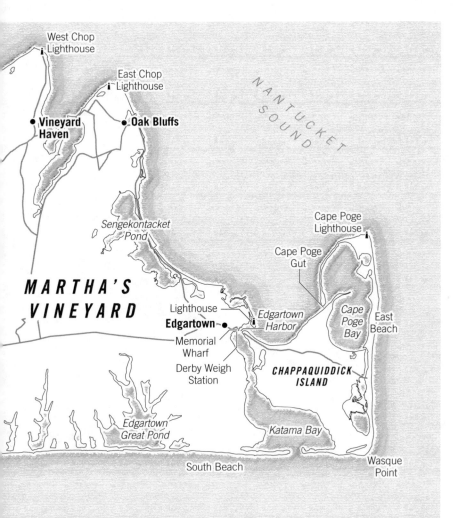

West Chop
Lighthouse

East Chop
Lighthouse

**Vineyard
Haven**

Oak Bluffs

*N A N T U C K E T
S O U N D*

*Sengekontacket
Pond*

**MARTHA'S
VINEYARD**

Cape Poge
Lighthouse

Cape Poge
Gut

Lighthouse

*Edgartown
Harbor*

*Cape
Poge
Bay*

East
Beach

Edgartown

Memorial
Wharf

Derby Weigh
Station

**CHAPPAQUIDDICK
ISLAND**

*Edgartown
Great Pond*

Katama Bay

South Beach

Wasque
Point

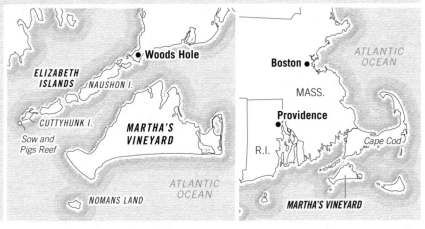

Woods Hole

**ELIZABETH
ISLANDS**   *NAUSHON I.*

CUTTYHUNK I.

*Sow and
Pigs Reef*

**MARTHA'S
VINEYARD**

*ATLANTIC
OCEAN*

NOMANS LAND

Boston

*ATLANTIC
OCEAN*

MASS.

Providence

R.I.

Cape Cod

MARTHA'S VINEYARD

Prologue: The Chase

Lev Wlodyka and "Jelly Belly Nelly."

"You bring beer? If we can't catch a derby winner, at least we can catch a buzz."

Five o'clock on a Sunday afternoon in September and the best young striped bass fisherman on Martha's Vineyard has booze on the brain. This is downtime anywhere else on the planet, but we're in a tiny fishing village called Menemsha—the center of a universe all its own, a weird old watermen's enclave at the far reaches of an island cut off from mainland America by a roiling saltwater river— and work is just beginning for Lev Wlodyka. We're about to head out in his boat to hunt for a giant striped bass, and though beer is not required it comes highly recommended in most quarters of the fishing world. I didn't bring any, but that's no problem. We won't be alone out on the water. Where there are boaters, there are Bud Lights.

It's the eighth day of the five-week Martha's Vineyard Striped Bass and Bluefish Derby, the most celebrated striper fishing tournament on the most storied island on the East Coast, and already a huge bass has been brought to the scale. It's the sort of fish that Lev usually hauls in, the very monster he wanted to get right off the bat, all the better to demoralize the competition and bolster his argument for treating the derby like a job this year: He can jump-start his new charter-fishing business by getting his name in the papers, and while he's at it he can win some loot, maybe even take home one of the $30,000 grand prizes. He fell in love with the derby as a kid, and at twenty-eight he's already won it five times. A year ago, he landed a 57.6-pound bass that ranked among the largest stripers caught on the planet that season, despite the ridiculous name he gave it, "Jelly Belly Nelly." If you were scouting for a franchise player to anchor your fantasy fishing team, Lev would be your man.

This time, though, some other fisherman caught the big one: a thirty-two-year-old house painter named Zeb Tilton. Soon after Zeb pulled the giant aboard, Lev eased up in his boat to see it, and Zeb told him it weighed somewhere in the forties. Then he held it up. "Are you high?" Lev asked. The thing had a head the size of a city block, and it tipped the scales at 56.51 pounds to take the lead in the derby's highest-profile division, striped bass caught from a boat. "I just got lucky," Zeb told *The Martha's Vineyard Times*. His striper wasn't only the largest of this year's derby. It ranked as the fifth-largest fish caught in any derby going back sixty-two years. Beating it would require a historic feat.

Zeb's fish broke spirits all over Martha's Vineyard. "The derby's won," a charter captain took to telling anyone who would listen. But Lev wasn't convinced. He fished forever that Thursday night after Zeb got the beast, and he returned well after midnight with a striper weighing 46.34 pounds that put him into second place. He pounded the water again Friday night.

Now it's Sunday and he's ready to continue the chase for a 57-pound derby winner. "Dude," he tells a friend, "I want to beat that fish so bad."

Lev and I meet on the Texaco gas dock in Menemsha, where vacation homes with picture windows occupy the high ground above a jumbled waterfront scene. Its heyday as a fishing port has passed, but Menemsha still looks (and smells) the part. Traps, buoys, barrels, rope, all the stuff of maritime life is here, lining the docks and settling around decrepit, weathered shacks like washed-up flotsam. Lobstermen and fishermen cruise in and out, a pair of seafood markets do a bustling business, and two rust-streaked offshore boats—the *Quitsa Strider II* and the *Unicorn*—tower over it all. Workboats carry the stench of dead fish to the dockside. Look closely at the tiny plastic skeleton on the pickup parked in front of one shack and you'll notice that some mischievous lobsterman has altered it so it's flipping you the bird. The hood ornament on another truck is a tiny dog taking a dump. The Texaco station next to the dock is home to "Squid Row," a bench where you can sometimes find old-time commercial fishermen commenting on the action in a language all their own. Inside, the station sells fifty-cent coffee, ice cream bars, postcards, fishing lures, derby registrations, and a CD of sensitive acoustic-guitar songs by an angler-musician who graces the cover shirtless holding a bonito. Cell phones don't work well here, which is fine with most people. If Lev wants to make a call, which isn't often, he has to park along the beach, put his flip phone on speaker, and stand it up on the dashboard to get a signal.

The Big One

Lev gasses up his boat, *Wampum*—eighteen feet, ten inches of gore-splattered fiberglass. Duct tape holds together the throttle. The wiring looks jury-rigged. The boat's white-and-powder-blue V-hull could use a paint job. But it's a rugged and reliable craft, and the Wlodykas can't help but regard it with great affection.

Provisioned with crackers, vitamin water, and $40 in fuel we push off the dock. Lev steers through the twin jetties flanking Menemsha channel, pulls his ball cap down over his floppy mop of black hair, and guns the outboard. The green hills and vacation homes recede as he turns into the setting sun. Off in the distance is the string of islands that trace the northern boundary of Vineyard Sound. To the east is Naushon, owned by the Forbes family. To the west is Cuttyhunk, home and namesake to a famous nineteenth-century bass fishing club that hosted the likes of Teddy Roosevelt and William Howard Taft.

The seas off the western end of the island hide boulders the size of Hummers and houses, behemoths dumped by the glaciers more than ten thousand years ago. Every fisherman with a boat and a chart can find the famous rock formations between the Elizabeth Islands and Nomans Land—Sow and Pigs Reef off Cuttyhunk, or Devil's Bridge off the Gay Head cliffs—but there are scores of lesser-known spots and Lev has many of their Global Positioning System coordinates punched into his chart plotter. He pulls *Wampum* to a stop over one of them and starts to set up, tying a new hook onto a fresh stretch of leader, then hanging it over the steering wheel and pulling the line to snug up the knot.

"People think it's over," he says. "I don't think it's over at all." This has become his mantra.

Lev is built like a linebacker: tall and broad-shouldered. He's all movement all the time, and his demeanor shifts like the changing weather, from quiet and aloof to friendly and goofy in five minutes flat. When he gets excited about a story his voice gets barroom-loud, the words tumble out at top speed, and he jumps up to demonstrate before breaking into a high-pitched cackle. His public persona—working-class tough guy—belies an introspectiveness he reveals only to his closest allies.

A handful of eels slither at the bottom of a white bucket, and using an old T-shirt to get a grip he holds one behind the head, hooks it in the mouth, and tosses it over. A windy, cold morning has turned into a pleasant afternoon with a light breeze. The tide is pulling strong and boils on the ruffled waves mark where the water rushes past the rocks. Lev turns the boat sideways to the current and lets it drift over the place where, if he is to be trusted, all the biggest stripers have been caught in this year's derby. But I'm having a hard time believing that he'd brought me to *the* spot, even if the point was to get a bass 57 pounds or bigger. What if I told somebody? What if I came back with a boat of my own?

"This isn't where all these big fish are coming from, is it?" I ask.

"Why else would we be fishing here?" he replies. "This place is going to light up at dark."

The sun is still a hand above the horizon, though, and the fish aren't biting yet. Instead, it's prime time to hunt for beers.

On the way out Lev had hit up a dump-truck driver fishing with his girlfriend on a borrowed boat. The guy couldn't figure out how to use the GPS. "I'll give you whatever you want to show me how to use this," he'd pleaded. Lev jumped on board, fiddled with the device, and climbed back with a couple of bottles. Fifteen minutes later, he spotted four friends crammed onto another tiny fishing boat, their rods bristling in every direction. They looked like refugees about to land on a beach and seek asylum. One of them was fighting a striper. "*Yah boy!*" Lev shouted. "Can we get a beer?" They fired cans from afar. One went in the drink and Lev motored over and fished it out. "Don't waste beers now!" he chided. (He also asked if he could have the bass to give to one of his neighbors, who was dying. They declined, no doubt figuring Lev could just as easily catch one himself.)

Now, Lev returns to the truck driver and arranges another trade. Bait for beers—or, more precisely, live eels for bottled Coronas. With eels running about $1.50 each at the tackle shops, this isn't much of a bargain. It's nothing compared to the time he bartered fifty rubber bands for fifteen lobsters and four packs of smokes during an offshore tuna trip.

"See?" Lev says as we motor back to the spot. "Nothing ventured, nothing gained. Now we can go catch a sixty-five-pounder."

We have good reason to feel confident. During one of our beer runs a guy on the refugee boat mentioned that a charter client got a 60-pound bass today, a possible derby record. Any information shared on the water is of dubious veracity and, as a primary source, this friend is particularly questionable. He likes to screw with people, and he'll let a ruse continue for days. Really, what better way to mess with Lev's head than to tell him that someone else—especially some dude on a fishing charter—got a giant fish today? Lev knew that his friend was not to be trusted. But he wanted to believe.

"Are you serious? Dicky got a sixty?"

A minute later: "Are you kidding me?"

Then: "No shit, huh?"

His friend wasn't backing down from the story, and soon Lev was buying it. "I *knew* there were bigger fish in here. I'm telling you, there are huge bass out here. There are fifty fish out here that are bigger than sixty pounds—probably more. You've just got to get your eel ten inches in front of its face."

When I toss my first eel over the gunwale, I ask Lev how long I should let a striper run with it. Some guys will tell you to wait three seconds before setting the hook, some for as long as ten. Lev has a different kind of answer.

"I imagine them turning."

"Five seconds?" I press. "Seven seconds?"

"Noooooo."

"Not even that quick?"

"Depends on the hit," he says, and like a teacher with a child who's not quite getting it he gives me a brief lesson. "A lot of bass fishing is putting yourself down where your bait is. You've got to visualize your bait drifting around through the rocks, over through the eddies, then the bass coming up behind it and grabbing it. Feel him hit it. He's just swallowed it and then he's turning to go back where he was. You've got to see him with your bait. That's why a lot of people miss. They're just on the surface. You've got to be three-dimensional about it."

This high-def visualization of feeding stripers is the sort of image most fishermen get from *Stripers Gone Wild,* a popular DVD of underwater fishing scenes. (As the name implies, it counts as fish porn among compulsive anglers.) Lev's picture comes from years spent fishing with abandon. For a few weeks every July and August the state of Massachusetts permits the sale of bass, and Lev and a group of twenty-something friends bomb out of the harbor in little powerboats at ungodly hours. Some years, they're fishing day and night, coming in only briefly for fuel, bait, food, and sleep, in roughly that order. They're all but hallucinating, walking around like zombies, and the tourists who flock to Menemsha for a taste of the quaint old harbor must watch these dudes in wonder—unshaven, smelly, wild men materializing off the water like a band of latter-day pirates. They have no use for sleep after a while, and soon everything seems very hilarious. Things that shouldn't be funny have them roaring. One of the guys told me he wishes he had pictures of the things he's seen: the orange moons rising out of the sea in the dark, the sunsets and sunrises, thunderstorms that made their rods hum with electrical energy. One night he watched bass chasing a huge ball of baitfish in seas teeming with bioluminescent microorganisms that light up when they're disturbed. The stripers looked like lightning bolts, and the school of fleeing menhaden looked like a comet exploding around the boat.

Mostly, the commercial bass fishing scene is just ballbusting work. After two months of handling baitfish and big bass, their hands are covered with cuts and scrapes and their fingers are too swollen to bend. For the ones without wives, their personal lives are in disarray: their homes are wrecks, their laundry piles up, their refrigerators go empty. "Your brain actually hurts," one of them told me. "You can't complete a sentence." Then, when the entire fishing fleet catches the limit—one million pounds in 2007—the state closes the season and the guys can sleep. A few weeks later, the derby arrives and they do it all again, maybe not as hard but still a lot harder than normal people.

Admission into their circle—known variously as the Night Crawlers, the Boys of Summer, the Menemsha Kids, and the Mosquito Fleet—is more or less closed. They've been fishing together forever. You'd have to have grown up with them, fished with them since you were a kid, been in on all their jokes. It would take too long to explain. Like brothers, they know one another's flaws, they remember all their fights, and yet they remain loyal. They look out for each other. Some of them have had a reputation for being rough-and-tumble, a bit wild, and some of them are still growing out of it. During this year's derby one fisherman had his face pummeled in a scrap. Another night, after a house party broke up, some of the guys moved the celebration to the beach and started shooting off firecrackers, and two fly fishermen got freaked out and called the cops and they had to talk their way out of there. It wasn't that long ago that one of them owned a boat named *Itchy Scrotum*.

The older generation of island anglers is still trying to adjust to the fact that the Menemsha Kids are grown up. The untamed boys who skateboarded or biked down to the harbor with their fishing rods, who won the derby junior divisions, who went out in all sorts of weather in tiny boats and came back loaded down with fish—those kids now have jobs and real boats and even, in a couple of cases, children of their own. Lev and his wife, Jen, welcomed their firstborn to the world a few months before this year's derby. Lev found himself watching the baby in their cramped rental house while Jen worked. "I still feel like a kid," he said one morning in his truck while we watched for fish. "But I'm not."

They are all good fishermen, and they know it. The bass grounds off the west end of Martha's Vineyard have become as familiar as their own backyards. They've spent years figuring out the boulders and dropoffs that produce the biggest fish, and they are secretive about them to the point of paranoia. "They don't talk about spots," said Jennifer Clarke, a charter fishing captain and derby champion. They'll go out of their way to keep rivals from finding out where they're fishing. They might skip a good daytime tide at a spot if there are other boats around. Then they'll go back out at midnight, turn out their running lights, and fill their boats. "Lev doesn't say anything about anything," she added. "Lev and I have never had a conversation about where he caught what."

Lev has established himself as the best of the Mosquito Fleet. "It's the Mosquito mafia," said an old family friend, "and Levie's the godfather." His friends acknowledge this, with some qualifiers: that he has luck on his side and he's had the privilege of growing up fishing and spending months on the water every year. But it's hard to believe that good fortune alone explains his five derby victories and his consistent hauls every summer.

Consider: One night before this year's derby started, he'd been in bed spooning with his wife under the covers. Then his eyes blinked open and the next thing Jen knew he was off into the night to hunt for bait. "I was thinking about that the other night," Lev said.

"There's no support group for me. There's no FA—no Fisherman's Anonymous. I need help." He's always watching, always thinking, always searching for a trend that will explain where the fish are and what will entice them to bite. Maybe it's a daily event, a tide that works. Maybe it's something you notice only after paying attention for years. He's tried to make a science out of it. Another son of a fisherman who hunts for stripers during the commercial season marvels at how Lev does it. "Things make sense to him more than others."

Out on the water the sun starts to go down, an orange ball dropping into the ocean, the kind of daily finale the tourists applaud at Menemsha in August. Lev watches it appreciatively, and suddenly prime time has arrived. The monofilament peels off my reel, and as I wait for the moment to set the hook Lev starts to coach.

"Hit him, hit him, hit him!"

I close the bail and lift and the rod arcs. With a jolt I'm on. The striper holds in deep water for thirty seconds, sulking, then begins to pull out line against the drag—one, two, three broad-shouldered hauls. It swims west and Lev ducks underneath my line and I move with the fish to the other side of the stern.

"That's a good fish," Lev says, his thoughts turning immediately to how we will split the grand-prize Chevy Silverado he imagines me winning. "Fifty percent, right?"

I suggest 75 or even 95 percent for him—it's his boat, his bait, his know-how. All I've really done is show up and hold the rod.

"I'll take that action," he says.

While we fantasize, a problem arises.

"You're on a rock," Lev says. "Feel the rock?"

No, I don't.

The striper has wrapped the line around a boulder below us, and I can envision it rubbing the line against the rock, trying to saw itself free. Lev springs into action, firing up the engine and steering around in a circle to undo the damage. In a minute, the fish is off the rock and I'm reeling it to the boat.

Lev pulls the fish up on the gunwale by its lower lip and works the hook free of its jaw.

"Thirty-pounder," he estimates. "Thirty-something."

"You should take it for your neighbor," I tell him.

"Nah, it's too big. You want to weigh it?"

He holds up the fish. It's motionless in his hands, and I admire the dusky lines shooting down its flanks. Big stripers have always looked majestic to me out of the water, with their sharp dorsal fins standing up like a crown. I think for a few seconds. This is close to the largest bass I've ever caught. At the same time, the leaderboard fish run between 45 and 56 pounds. A 30-pounder is nothing. I'm thinking like Lev, who has caught too many fish to be sentimental about one this size. "Nah," I say finally. I don't even ask to hold the fish or get a picture for my wife and daughter back home. We're out here for fifties, right?

Back in the water it goes, and as we return to the spot Lev tells me to stay sharp. "It's going to be nonstop. This place is stacked!" Our beers go untouched for another half hour as we stand at attention and get hit after hit. Lev puts one foot in front of the other, his rod held out to the fish. He pulls a few feet of line off the reel and holds it in his fingers like a bowstring, so that if a fish hits he has an extra second to react before the line peels out. A bass yanks at his eel, and he lets it run until he senses that the fish has it. Then he rears back and he's on. But it's nothing huge. We end up with a couple of stripers each and a bluefish. We spot a bass thrashing on the surface of the water and Lev pilots *Wampum* over to check it out. The striper is on its side, and Lev sinks the hook of his gaff into its flank and pulls it onboard. The pig had choked to death on a baitfish known as scup— one that was too large to fit down its throat.

11

Then, with that omen, the spot turns off. "Come *on!*" Lev protests. He tries hailing his friends. "*Speakeasy, Speakeasy,* howbout-cha?" he calls over the radio. Silence. He smacks the steering wheel and lets out a frustrated bark. We reel up and he jams the throttle down and points the boat back toward Menemsha.

Lev has enough experience on the water to know when a spot isn't happening, and tonight it isn't happening. There will be other nights. Just about everybody would agree that Zeb Tilton didn't catch the biggest bass in the ocean. (Neither did Dicky's client; the 60-pounder that got Lev excited is a hoax.) But of the three thousand people who will fish the derby, Lev is probably the only one who believes he can find it. "I wouldn't be out here if I didn't think I could catch something huge. Most years if somebody caught a fifty-six I'd fold her up. I know there's bigger fish out here."

Two weeks later he would prove himself right—and somehow, at the same time, wrong. He'd get a fish that would land on the front pages of the papers, uncover once and for all a secret fishing tactic, thrust islanders into a contentious debate, and throw the tournament into turmoil.

Before it was all over Lev couldn't help but wonder: Would he have been better off just throwing the cursed fish back in the ocean?

1

838 Hours

The weigh station.

Grown men have cried over the derby. They have ignored their wives for week after week, sleepwalked through work day after day, stayed up all night long, skipped out on their jobs altogether, drawn unemployment, burned through every last day of their vacation time, downed NoDoz and Red Bull and God knows what else. They have spied on their rivals and lied to their friends. They have told off strangers and cheated like lowlife bums. If you believe the conspiracy theorists, they have prosecuted bogus charges of rules breaking to get their adversaries tossed from the competition. People have *died* fishing the derby. In 1993, four anglers—two fathers and their young sons—drowned when their boat sank in heavy swells on the second-to-last day of the contest. In 1947, a Boston businessman crashed his plane trying out a contemporary fad: spotting schools of bass from the air, then landing on the beach and casting away at them. A nearby fisherman rushed to give first aid but couldn't save the man. "All that," he lamented, "for an old striped bass."

An old striped bass, yes, but it's not only that. Catch a winner in the Vineyard's beloved annual fishing contest and they'll etch your name on the all-time roster of champions. You'll earn a spot in a tournament history book that starts during the Truman administration. It's something like taking the green jacket at the Masters. "I'm after derby glory," says Dave Skok, a professional fly tier and two-time derby winner. "That's what it's all about for me." For a certain class of Vineyarder (and aspiring Vineyarder), for those who haven't already made their millions and plunked them down on the massive trophy mansions so fashionable on the island today, winning the derby is as close to immortality as they're likely to get.

The conventional wisdom about modern-day Martha's Vineyard goes something like this: popular summer tourist destination; propelled into the national consciousness when U.S. senator Edward Kennedy drove off Chappaquiddick's Dike Bridge in 1969; backdrop for the movie *Jaws;* presidential vacation spot for Bill and Hillary Clinton; one-time address of Jacqueline Kennedy Onassis; host to A-list cocktail parties, yachting regattas, and presidential campaign fund-raisers; land of multimillion-dollar mansions; playground for the fabulously rich and famous, whose ranks of visitors and residents (past and present) have included James Cagney, Ted Danson, James Taylor, Carly Simon, Billy Joel, William and Rose Styron, John Updike, Art Buchwald, David McCullough, David Letterman, Diane Sawyer, Mike Wallace, Walter Cronkite, and Lady

Di. All of that is true, as far as it goes. But the place is not quite so flashy as its press would suggest. The island's moneyed class has traditionally been low-key—this is not the Hamptons; one writer called its vibe "reverse-chic"—and after the summer is over these ranks seem to be outnumbered by the middle class and the working class and the anonymous.

To hang around in the fall is to see the off-hours Vineyard, the place as the year-rounders know it. The island morphs back into an isolated, tightly knit community where everyone knows just about everything about everyone else. It feels as if someone has released a pressure valve. The tourists and glitterati are (mostly) gone. The lines are shorter, the crowds thinner, the days cooler. If you're a Vine-yarder earning most of your annual income during the summer season, September means the mortgage is paid, the bank account is full, you're secure for another winter. It's time to blow off steam, and for a good number of islanders that means it's time to fish the derby.

This year, the contest runs through October 13, but from the very beginning, at 12:01 a.m. on September 9, hundreds of men, women, and children are out on the water chasing the four fish of the derby: striped bass, bluefish, false albacore, and bonito. They have good reason to start early. A quarter of a million dollars in prizes are at stake in thirty-two divisions, eight each for adults, fly rodders, juniors under age fourteen, and children under age eight. The biggest catches each day earn anglers fish pins—cherished mementos people wear on their hats or hang on their walls—and, in the adult divisions, $5 to $20 in cash. The top three finishers in each class at the end of the contest take home rods, reels, and shopping bags filled with lures, line, sunglasses, and other fishing accessories. The anglers who catch the biggest of the four species from the shore and from a boat are "grand leaders," and they win $500, a heavy-duty outdoor jacket, a framed print of fishermen at the Gay Head cliffs painted by island artist Ray Ellis—and a shot at the grand prizes: a nineteen-foot Boston Whaler and the Chevy Silverado, each worth about $30,000. For hardcore fishermen, the most sought-after titles are the shore and boat "grand slam" awards for heaviest combined weight of the four species, a feat that demonstrates complete mastery of the fishery. Win one of those and you get $500, a bag of high-end fishing gear, and the undying respect of the derby world.

Three thousand people—half of them islanders, half visitors—will enter the competition by the time it ends next month, and I'm one of them, Badge No. 402. I'm here to see whether the Great Fish Gods hold me in their favor, since I'll be fishing almost every day, and winning the derby is half-luck anyway. But mostly, I'm here to see what happens when an island full of the fish-addled have 838 hours to feed their passion. Among the many people who are possessed by fish during the derby are a high school teacher, a chef, a painter, a rhythm-and-blues singer, a real estate agent, a gas station attendant, and just about every plumber, carpenter, and electrician on the island. They are men and women, fathers and mothers, teenage boys and girls. They are businessmen, doctors, and blue-collar workmen. They are fly-fishing specialists in their twenties with new high-tech gear and salty old-timers in their seventies using lures and techniques that have changed little in the past half century. The derby invades people's dreams. Fishermen have subconscious premonitions about a particular fish at a particular spot. Gangs of mainlanders—many from fishing clubs with long histories of their own—show up to fish for a weekend, two weeks, a month, the whole contest. Two fly rodders come from Italy. Teachers show up at school on an hour's sleep, and students show up carrying stinking fish they killed the night before. "It's the only time," says taxidermist Janet Messineo, "that you can walk through town and you're covered with squid gook and you smell bad and you look awful, and everybody's smiling at you. 'Oh how you doing? How's the derby?' The whole community sort of rallies behind derby fishermen." Contractors fail to show up at job sites and don't answer phone calls. One fishing hero talked his wife into including the competition in their wedding vows. He promised to put up with her allergies and she promised to put up with his constant pursuit of a winning fish. "It's a lifestyle on this island," Lev's father, Walter, says. "It's a sacred kind of thing."

The derby is a lottery ticket, an ego boost, a chance to die happy, a shot at island renown and modest riches, a chance to *win*. Here are all of life's amorphous pursuits boiled down into something you can hook, kill, lug into town, mount, and hang on the wall. "Lives change during those five weeks," one derby fisherman told me when I first called around to ask around about the competition. I laughed, but the man didn't join in.

"I'm serious," he added, and I stopped chuckling. His voice was flat and steely, as if we were discussing something truly grave.

This little fishing contest? This is no joke.

At 4:30 on the first morning of the derby I drive into Menemsha, park at the beachfront, turn off the engine, and sit, waiting and watching. The Texaco is shuttered and dark. Fishing boats bob in the harbor. I roll down the passenger-side window and hear the faint *clang-clang* of the bell on the green buoy out in the Vineyard Sound. I can just barely make out the beach and the waves and the twin jetties along the inlet to the harbor. The moon is a sliver of a crescent.

After all I've heard and read about the competition, I almost expect to see a mob converging on the parking lot: para-anglers appearing in the sky to storm the jetties like something out of a grainy war movie, or men ducking out from around every corner, derby badges pinned to their hats and fishing rods brandished like weapons. But what I see is more like the aftermath of an all-night party. One guy is lying on the beach under a blanket, his head on a sand-sculpted pillow. His partner is sprawled in the front seat of their pickup. A fly fisherman is asleep on the sister jetty across the channel in Lobsterville. They were all working the beaches for stripers at the official midnight start of the derby, because it can pay to start early. Some years, the winner has caught the big bass on the first day, and once a guy landed it in the first ten minutes. But none of these guys had that kind of luck this morning, and they trickled into the harbor in the darkness to wait for dawn—the time when other derby fish are known to storm the jetties.

I watch from the car for a while, then the sky starts to lighten, imperceptibly at first and then quickly, with each blink. As if an alarm has gone off, the sleepers stir. The fisherman on the beach jumps up and shakes out his blanket and walks over to the truck and wakes up his friend. The guys speed-walk out to the jetty, and when it's just light enough to see I gather up my rod and tackle bag and follow.

We're after two derby species this morning. One is the false albacore (the hipsters call them "'cores" but to everybody else they are "albies") and the other is the bonito (or "bones"). The fish are drawn to the inlet to feed on baitfish—scup, peanut bunker, silversides—sucked in and out every six hours by the tides. On the end of my line is a lure called a Maria, a slug of metal encased in a hard, translucent plastic with a treble hook hanging off the end. I start casting into the roiling water.

The jetty is an L-shaped stack of boulders that runs parallel to the beach for a stretch, then juts out into the Vineyard Sound. At the tip is a navigational aid tower, rusty but solid, that marks the port side of the inlet with a square green sign and the number 3. The tower doubles as a rod holder, tackle-bag rack, and beer stand.

On a post at the foot of the jetty is a weathered white sign with a warning scrawled in black marker. It reads:

WALK

ON

ROCKS

AT

OWN

RISK

Slipping on the rocks is a hazard, but only one of many on this particular jetty. I've been warned that Menemsha can be a tough place. With so many hooks being thrown around in such a confined spot, fights are bound to break out. Guys down shots from miniature liquor bottles, chase them with beer, and smash the empties in the rocks. They jockey in front of you and cut off your casting angle. They fire their lures from point-blank range at the cormorants paddling by the rocks. Some otherwise rugged fishermen are unwilling to brave the crowd.

Before long I see Lev's friend and fishing partner, Geoff Codding, pull up to the Texaco station in the huge Titan he won in last year's derby. Geoff got a college degree in environmental policy and aspires to be a commercial fisherman, but for now he earns a living mowing lawns and harvesting scallops. Not much gets in the way of fishing the tournament every day. Geoff—wearing his derby uniform of waterproof boots, blue jeans, and Red Sox cap—gets out of the truck and talks to some buddies filling up their boat at the gas dock, then returns to his pickup and drives over to the spot on the beachfront where cell phones work. One of his friends might call with reports of fish someplace else. From the front seat of his truck he can watch the water and decide whether it's worth fishing. He sees what looks like a few albies breaking the water's surface at the end of the jetty. Then he spots the telltale sign of fish: everybody on the rocks is bent at the waist, reeling as fast as they can. He grabs his rods and his bag of lures and falls in, casting languidly.

Within minutes, the harbor is teeming with people. A dozen fishermen line the Lobsterville jetty across the water, and more are pouring onto the beach beside it. Boats slide through the inlet and take up stations just off the beach or rumble off to spots unknown. By the time the albies begin their assaults on the baitfish hugging the rocks, I find myself behind fishermen three deep. The men on the rocks are all business. There is little of the usual chatter, and nobody's touching the alcohol tucked under the tower—a six-pack of Coors longnecks and a plastic twenty-ounce bottle of Pepsi spiked with Yukon Jack. The group seems to move as a single life-form: whipping casts, changing directions on a dime, doing whatever it takes to get lures in front of fish. I am forced to stand back and watch in awe. I couldn't fit a cast between them if I tried. When the jetty fishermen are at work, it can either be a symphony of coordinated motion, with one or two guys hooked up and dancing from rock to rock and going under and over each other's rods, or it can be a tangled mess. The pros know how to keep out of each others' way. It would take me a few weeks to figure out how to fish the tip without screwing up the works.

Anglers have an easier time of it on the Lobsterville jetty just a short cast across the inlet. The fishing is comparable but the two spots may as well be different worlds. I never saw a fly fisherman on Menemsha, where they are regarded as pompous hotshots who are overly fastidious about their gear. (People who fish lures and bait using regular spinning reels have a hard time figuring out the fly guys. Why do they spend so much time tying flies and perfecting their casts when they are practically assured of catching smaller fish

20

than everybody else? The answer: even catching a smaller fish is more challenging on a fly rod.) Some disagreements span the inlet. If fish are running in or out of the channel, people are often casting directly at each other. When it works it's like music. Everybody casts and retrieves in rhythm, lures returning to their owners in perfect time. Tranquillity reigns. When it doesn't work—when a Lobstervillian entangles a Menemshan, or vice versa—one fisherman has to open his bail while the other reels the mess up and untangles it. Generally, it's a polite transaction. *No harm. Don't sweat it. Happens to everyone.*

Sometimes, of course, it's not. One year a fly fisherman on the Lobsterville jetty had an albie on and a Menemsha spin fisherman cast over his line and (the fly fisherman believed) started yanking. As they went back and forth, a boat steamed out of the inlet and cut the line. Pissed beyond belief, the Lobsterville fly fisherman got into his pickup truck and drove the twenty minutes around Menemsha Pond to the other side. He strutted onto the rocks, fly rod in hand, and cast over the offender's line. Things devolved from there. Choice words were exchanged and the fly line slashed, but no fists flew. Afterward, the fly fisherman apologized. People marveled that he had managed to stay so angry for the entire trip from Lobsterville to Menemsha. "You can get two warring tribal villages over there," said Nelson Sigelman, the managing editor and fishing columnist for *The Martha's Vineyard Times*. "Fishermen have been warring since they first learned how to make a bone hook. Why would this be different?"

As the jetty fills up this morning, a guy named Tony Jackson gives me an object lesson in what can go wrong. Standing out on the farthest rock, he draws his rod back over his shoulder, the treble hook of his lure dangling among the circle of fishermen, and then sweeps it toward the sea. There's a whipping sound and then his rod stops. He looks behind him and sees that he has hooked the sleeve of another angler's T-shirt. The snagged fisherman, who wears a camouflage hat and has the build of an ironworker, doesn't even flinch. He looks down at his arm and then at Tony. Somebody unhooks the lure and they go back to work. But with his carelessness, Tony has risked a savage beating. He came within an inch of the fisherman's triceps. Hookings aren't uncommon, but they usually end with an expensive and time-consuming trip to the ER, and nobody wants that on the first day of the derby. It would have made a rough morning even more trying for Tony, a red-bearded dock builder who descends from a famous maritime family. Blood is already oozing down his legs from a trio of wounds inflicted by small bottom-feeding sharks called dogfish. He had caught three of them before dawn on the jetty. As he tried to unhook one, it thrashed and the hook dug into his shin. He slipped and fell on the rocks reeling in the other two.

Lev pulls into the channel in *Wampum* and hails his friend Geoff, who backtracks off the jetty to join him. As Geoff hops aboard a guy walks up with a cup of coffee from the Texaco. "Lev, you win the derby yet?" the man asks. Lev laughs off the remark and he and Geoff cruise out and join a small armada of boats.

A fly fisherman in a dinghy drifts in close to the rocks, and on the jetty Tony gives him a warning shout. "Got enough room, cap'n?" The man motors away.

Soon, the action slows and people start to pack up, but then more albies hit the jetty and they're compelled to stay. A school of fish breaks off the end of the L near the parking lot, and a few teenagers run down in pursuit. One unleashes an epic cast, hooks up, then finds himself tangled with four fishermen who'd cast into the same fish from the tip. He fights it while everybody else reels in his lure and bites it off. Somehow the kid lands it anyway.

After a few hours of this the jetty starts to empty. As the fishermen walk toward their trucks, a few more fish crash off the beach by the parking lot and the men sprint back to fire a few final casts. But the fish disappear again and the anglers retreat to their trucks and toss their rods inside and start circling the island.

There are 830 hours left in the derby and they don't have a moment to waste.

Any way you look at it, Vineyard fishermen are a blessed lot. Their sport calls them to some of the most spectacular real estate any-where. The island's natural splendor has launched a thousand pae-ans. From the prow of the ferries that depart the mainland from Woods Hole, you first see the green sweep of the North Shore, then the lighthouses and palatial homes of East and West Chop, then the boats and tall ships bobbing in the harbors. The ferries spit you into the bustle of Oak Bluffs or Vineyard Haven, but a few minutes' drive west the road takes you past farmland hemmed in by stone walls, scrub oak forests and meadows, rolling hills and ponds, cliffs and sweeping beaches. Everywhere, potholed dirt roads connect houses and hiking trails and beaches that are secluded in the woods. Some excellent fishing can be found in the most stunning spots: along the wild, rocky stretches of Squibnocket Beach, beneath the multicolored clay majesty of the Gay Head cliffs and before the galloping rips at Wasque Point. As one derby fisherman put it, "It is not like fishing in Flatbush."

To anglers, what matters most is that the Vineyard is a rock in the middle of a stream of migrating fish. They sling locally caught bait—or the endless variations of lures imitating it, Dannys and Deadly Dicks and Deceivers—into places that might prompt a fish to stop and hunt: coves, rocky shorelines, breaks in sandbars, inlets, jetties, points, rips, curling waves in the surf, deepwater drop-offs. The island is packed with nooks like these, and if the wind or tide is wrong at one spot it's perfect across the island. The Vineyard's numerous salt ponds serve as baitfish nurseries and, when the schools depart, stripers, bluefish, albies, bonito, and fishermen are there patrolling the exits.

The First Fish of the derby is the mighty striped bass, named for the dark markings down its sides. It is one of the most storied of swimmers, the aristocrat of the surf line, a fish that is beloved and worshipped. The bass was there at America's founding: Historians say striper filets made the menu at the first Thanksgiving. In the 1860s men of means founded clubs on the sound to fish for stripers, and though the groups disbanded when the species crashed, by the 1940s when the derby began, the bass had returned to prosperity and popularity. It was not only love of sport that sent men racing to the surf with fishing rods. Stripers were local currency across New England: greenbacks with gills. Maybe they never made anybody rich, but a Jeep full of 30- to 50-pounders paid some debts. The derby gave a different twist to the pursuit. Stripers would be leveraged into tourism dollars. "On the Vineyard, fish are fellow citizens," fishermen-authors John Cole and Brad Burns once wrote in *On the Water* magazine. "They are a staple of island life, and that goes double for striped bass."

In the 1980s the population collapsed again in the face of fishing pressure and pollution, only to skyrocket in the 1990s after fisheries regulators enforced sweeping catch restrictions. Today, they are by far the most pursued saltwater fish on the Atlantic Coast. An estimated 3 million recreational anglers caught (and usually released) more than 28 million stripers in 2006—twice as many as a decade earlier and a far cry from the 1 million stripers landed in 1982. There are two explanations for the booming popularity of the striper. The first is that for the tens of millions of people living in the Washington, D.C.–to–Boston megalopolis, the fish can be caught a short drive from home. After spawning in bays and rivers —the vast majority of them in the Chesapeake Bay—they return to the ocean and embark on epic migrations along the East Coast.

Hugging the shoreline, millions of stripers course north every spring and spread out along beaches and inside estuaries from New Jersey to Maine. At night, they can be caught right in the first wave. During the fall run they chase frantically fleeing schools of herring, silversides, and menhaden. The other reason the bass are pursued with such passion is that, on any given night, a fisherman can haul in something truly enormous. Stripers weighing 50 pounds and up are caught every year. "It is therefore possible," Cole and Burns wrote, "to stand on the beach and toss a short cast to a fish big enough to nearly tear your arms from their sockets."

The bluefish, on the other hand, is the casual angler's prey, plentiful and easy to catch. The blues arrive from the south or from offshore in the spring and usually run small. But they can top 20 pounds, and a fish that size would probably turn you into a derby champion. Get into a school of blues when you're using regular fishing line to catch bass, bonito, or albies, and the blues' razor-sharp choppers will bite off the hook every other time. Needless to say, fishermen have a complex relationship with the fish. In a letter to a fishing friend penned during an 1849 bluefishing trip to the Vineyard, statesman Daniel Webster expressed the prevailing view, then as now: "It is a common opinion that they destroy or drive off several of the other valuable finny tribes. If this be so, it will be the more patriotic in you and me to take as many of them to the land as we can." Compared to the body of gushing literature that has grown up around stripers, there is really only one true paean to this fish, Vineyard resident John Hersey's best-selling classic *Blues*.

Finally, there are the heroes of the modern derby, the false albacore and the bonito—the "funny fish" that drive men crazy. These little tunas wheel in from the Gulf Stream, the bonito in July and the albies in late summer. They are smaller, with derby-winning albies typically weighing less than 15 or 16 pounds and bonito less than 11 or 12. But they are pursued with lighter tackle or with fly rods, and that makes it thrilling when they take off on their long, reel-screaming runs. First they go out, making you fear that they will outrun your line. Then they dart back in, making you think they've broken off. Then they shoot back out again to find something to wrap the line around, like a lobster pot or a boat mooring. These are the fights that turn otherwise sensible fishermen into addicts. Shore fishermen will wait for hours—days—at jetties, inlets, and other likely feeding spots. They'll suffer storms, windburn, and relentless boredom for a shot at a five-minute fight. Boaters can chase them but even when they find fish, catching one is no simple matter. Albies in particular are mercurial, popping up in one spot only to disappear in a flash, dive deep, jet away at forty miles per hour, and crash the surface half a mile off. Bonito can be difficult to find in the first place. Some seasons, only a handful are caught from shore. An otherwise talented beach fisherman can go years without catching one.

The genius of the derby format is that fishermen have a chance to catch a winner at any hour. Stripers feed best at night, bluefish at dawn and dusk, albies and bonito all day long according to the whims of baitfish, winds, and tides. Stories abound of anglers catching big fish under all the wrong conditions—a striper on a calm beach in the middle of the afternoon, say. And yet this twenty-four-hour cycle of possibility is also the bane of serious competitors, the ones who are hunting for all four species. They understand that fish are unpredictable and that the best way to improve their odds of winning it all is to fish every available moment. As many of these extreme anglers have discovered over the years, taking such a lesson to heart has something of a destructive effect on your membership in the real world. "Do you think I'd be out here if there wasn't a derby pin in my life?" Dave Skok asked me one day during his eleventh hour of fly casting for albies, his stubbled face a sunburned reddish brown except for the raccoon-mask outline where his sunglasses usually rested. "I'd be home doing normal people things."

Later on that first day of the derby, I drive across the island to Edgartown—home to the well-heeled sea captains of whaling's golden age a century and a half ago, must-see vacation stop for lollygagging tourists today. All the essential draws are here: boutiques, art galleries, coffee shops, brew pubs, trendy restaurants, historic homes, teeming gardens, beautiful waterfront vistas. During July and August the town's narrow streets get so choked that only the foolish and desperate venture down in cars. But September brings a different crowd and, when I arrive, anglers are beginning to appear on the docks. They are a ripe bunch carrying dead fish by the tail, by the gills, in plastic bags, in coolers, cradled in old T-shirts. With so much fresh seafood in the streets, you could be fooled into thinking the place is still a commercial fishermen's port, with workboats in the harbor and a parking lot made of crushed shells and fish bones, not another five-star destination crammed with yachts and BMWs. I follow the Derbyites as they make their way to the little weathered weigh station where the tournament entries are weighed from eight to ten o'clock every morning and night. The clock is ticking toward eight p.m. now, and a festive line of anglers begins to stretch around the corner.

I'm after fishing stories—the true, the exaggerated, the outright false—and there is no better place to begin than the dockside shack, the vibrating hub of the Vineyard fishing world in the fall. The point where fact ends and fiction begins, I am aware, is open to interpretation. "Believe nothing of what you hear, and half of what you see," Lev advised me, quoting the ancient proverb. A derby veteran puts it another way, pointing to a railing at the weigh station entrance that has supported the rear ends of thousands of storytellers over the decades. "More lies told here than any place in the world."

The shack has survived the hurricanes that destroyed most of its contemporaries and stood tall in the face of a far more sweeping agent of change: the gradual transformation of the working waterfront into a resort. The grand prizes are parked beside the shack, which is plastered with sponsors' banners. By the door a glass case displays up-to-date standings and statistics as detailed as any sports-page box score. A tiny window gives passersby a view of the chalk leaderboards inside the station and a peek at the night weighmaster, a tattooed, Harley-Davidson-riding highway worker in an oilskin apron and rubber gloves who puts up with no nonsense from the contestants.

Floating along the dock beside derby headquarters is a small filet barge where, under the yellow glow of an outdoor light strung up overhead, hundreds of pounds of fish are sliced into dinner-sized cuts. Tomorrow, they will be trucked over to a senior center, where they will be bagged and handed out to the elderly as part of the competition's philanthropy program. Fish after fish thwacks onto the barge deck. Kids ogle the biggest specimens and curious tourists walking off their dinners ask questions. *What kind of fish is that? Who gets the filets? Can I have a fish carcass for my chowder pot?* A harbor seal will start visiting the dock in a few days to feed on the scraps. The aroma of a fish market loiters in the air.

During the derby fish tales buzz around the island on invisible fiber optics, from tackle shops to restaurants to gas stations. "You'll catch a fish, and by the time you make it to the weigh-in they know what you caught it on, where and how much it weighed," Geoff Codding says. Sometimes they're even right. The weigh station is where the rumors and exaggerations go to die. The chattering class hangs around the front door, nursing free coffee and swapping stories. On the Vineyard, the arrival of bluefish and bass in the spring makes for a newspaper article, and serious fishermen keep a close eye on the beaches all summer. But once the derby starts there are suddenly three thousand people taking an interest in the daily meanderings of the fish population. Tides, wind directions, and weather fronts count as talk of the town. Each statement is parsed to determine if it is a secret or a lie, inside dope or disinformation.

The gabbers watch as fishermen arrive soggy, sore, and sleep deprived. The contestants walk up the ramp, take a right inside the doorway, and follow the blue-and-white rope line separating those with fish from those without. As anglers reach the weighmaster, their entries are measured on a long table slick with slime and then hoisted onto the scale. Everyone leans in to see who dragged what out of the sea.

The fact is, it could be anybody. In the last week of the 2005 derby, a twelve-year-old girl hauled a 49.22-pound striper into the station. "I thought it was an alligator," Molly Fischer told the papers. "I was scared of it when we brought it in the boat." She had been out on a charter boat that sloppy day with her father, Albert O. Fischer III, Jaqueline Kennedy Onassis's longtime caretaker, and her friend, Caroline Kennedy's son Jack Schlossberg. The catch put Molly in first place and her picture in the Boston newspapers. A week later, when nobody had topped it, she landed on the immutable list of derby champions, shoulder to shoulder with the tournament legends.

In 2003 Andrew Scheriff of Bristol, Connecticut, came down for a weekend, started casting from a jetty off Cape Poge, and caught his first bonito—ever. "I didn't even know what it was," he said. It weighed 8.12 pounds and carried the division. Another year, tackle shop owner Cooper Gilkes talked a new customer into registering, and just like the Bonito King of Bristol this guy stumbled into a grand leader. True story. Coop's honor.

Harry Beach led the 1999 derby for a month with a 42-pound striper he caught from his kayak. He would have won the whole thing, he believes, if he'd put the fish on ice instead of leaving it on the roof of his Volkswagen bus to bake in the sun for several hours; he came in second place by about a pound.

Buck Martin took the top prize with a 54.74-pound bass that hit while he was snoozing on the beach one night in 1993. Buck, at the time a twenty-nine-year-old heating and air-conditioning contractor, had never caught a saltwater striper in his life. His more experienced friends ridiculed him that night for the thirteen-foot rod he'd bought at Wal-Mart. When nobody caught anything for a couple of hours, he curled up on the sand, passed out, and awoke to the sound of monofilament zinging off his reel. As his eyes adjusted to the full moon, he picked up the rod and started cranking. He could see the big bass finning in water so tranquil it looked like a solid pane of glass. When he dragged the fish up the beach his friends were ecstatic. Buck didn't understand the fuss. "What's the matter with you? It's a fish," he said. He thought all stripers were that big. The plaque he won reads: OCT. 1, 1993—1 A.M.—ASLEEP.

Today, a first-day record of 189 fish come through the door of the weigh station, but there are no certain winners. Winding through the station is the typically eclectic cross section of derby regulars: a tackle-shop salesman with a bluefish and bloody hands; a roofer who chanced upon a rare bonito from the shore; a celebrated Harvard Law School professor with a second-place striper; a young girl carrying a bluefish to the weigh-in for the first time; a retiree who stands more or less on one rock for the entire contest; the son of a derby champion; the daughter of a plumber; and a venture capitalist in a pastel pink sports coat carrying a 10-pound bluefish that is advancing swiftly toward petrifaction. The financier and his entourage turn heads. They glide through the shack, weigh the fish, snap pictures, and head off, chortling into the night. The regulars look at each other as if to say, *Did that really just happen?*

It did, and it does. Louisa Gould, the derby's official photographer, says between camera clicks that a guy once showed up wearing a tuxedo to weigh in his fish. Another brought a violin case into the station, waited patiently in line, then popped it open to reveal a big bonito. Still another weighed in the front half of a bonito after an unidentified marine predator swiped the back end. (He still won a daily pin.)

The derby is the anti-Bassmaster. These are not hyperactive pros in tricked-out boats wearing patches that advertise trucks and boats and outboard engine manufacturers. ESPN is not following the competitors around with cameras. Nobody's carrying on for the people back home. The tournament is more like a typical rod and gun club event, but rather than running for a weekend this one seems to last forever, with people who are just out for kicks and camaraderie fishing right next to hardcore guys who are chasing prizes and glory. It aims to be the friendliest competition on the water.

Fishing tournaments exploded after World War II, when saltwater angling as recreation spread to the masses and businessmen realized they could generate a lot more money from the sport with cars, boats, and cash at stake. They have always had their detractors among those who consider fishing a dignified pursuit and believe that killing fish for money or vanity borders on immoral. "I know plenty of decent people who fish kill tournaments," wrote Ted Williams—an influential environmental writer, not the ballplayer—in *Fly Rod and Reel* magazine in 2007, "but even they admit that these events attract, enrich and empower lowlifes and, at the same time, teach the public to kill the most and biggest." Years ago at some competitions, cleanup crews would have to truck contestants' fish to their final resting place: the local landfill. Tournament tarpon in Florida were dumped off a bridge, Williams said. Today, many contests have become catch-and-release affairs, though the Martha's Vineyard Derby is not one of them.

They remain wildly popular. The American Fisheries Society put the number of annual contests in the United States, Canada, Puerto Rico, and the U.S. Virgin Islands at some thirty-one thousand. If that number seems outlandishly high—596 contests every weekend? —consider that every fishing club, every tackle shop, and every beach town has a competition or two. Most of them target blue-water billfish and freshwater bass. Some are saltwater contests with seven-figure jackpots: a team competing in Bisbee's Black and Blue Marlin Tournament in Cabo San Lucas, Mexico, took home $3.9 million in 2006. Wayne Bisbee also organizes a contest that offers fishermen the chance to host a bikini-model photo shoot on their boat while they fish for marlin, tuna, and dorado. Slogan: "Fish. Girls. Fish. Bikinis. Fish." In Oklahoma, competitors grab catfish out of the water using only their bare hands, a technique known as "noodling." The Flukemania Smackdown—its magazine advertisements feature a flounder on a golden World Wrestling Federation–style championship belt—awards $10,000 for the heaviest flounder of the weekend. BountyFishing.com runs Internet contests: longest fish wins, and anglers send in photographs of their fish as proof. The site claims to use "digital imaging forensics" to verify the reported measurements.

The Vineyard derby is regarded as the granddaddy of striper fishing contests. At six decades and counting, it's believed to be the oldest of its kind still operating on the East Coast, and it takes place on waters that are something close to sacred for saltwater anglers. The man who came up with the idea was a Boston public relations whiz and avid sportfisherman named Nat Sperber. Though he wore thick glasses, played the cello in a classical trio and stood just five feet, four inches tall, he was also prone to getting into fistfights, his ninety-three-year-old widow, Doris, told me with a touch of pride. Nat got his start as a city reporter for a Boston newspaper. After World War II he returned from a posting in Guam and began doing PR work for Massachusetts Steamship Lines, the company that had taken over the notoriously erratic and unprofitable ferry route connecting the Vineyard to the mainland. The company was grappling with major difficulties—boat mishaps, rate increases, confusion at ticket offices, outraged islanders —when Nat conceived of his "advertising scheme" in 1946. The idea was to gin up ferry traffic after Labor Day came and the summer crowd went. In those years, parts of the Vineyard were desolate enough that the military used it for bombing and rocket exercises. Island businesses welcomed anything that would bring in mainland dollars.

The island rod and gun club put the event together, and Nat teamed up with *Boston Herald* outdoors columnist Henry Moore to get the word out to newspaper writers. The fledgling *Salt Water Sportsman,* seeing an opportunity to promote striped bass fishing and magazine sales, trumpeted the new contest as "the most colossal fishing derby ever staged on the North Atlantic."

Overheated as that early propaganda was, it brought in crowds from around the country, and as the years passed off-island fishermen and their families kept showing up. For Vineyarders, meanwhile, it grew into a treasured annual tradition. Shirley Craig is a retired schoolteacher whose father was one of the original derby organizers and whose late husband, mystery writer Philip Craig, loved to fish as much as she does. On the Vineyard, she told me, the derby is like spring, or the Fourth of July, or Christmas: you can't imagine a year passing without it. "It's a part of the calendar."

Shirley at seventy-two (she doesn't look it) still gets out every fall hoping to hammer bass and blues. Septuagenarian women, teenage girls, multimillionaires—pick your demographic: the derby turns them all into fish slayers.

The Big One

*   *   *

Fishing is not in my blood, as far as I know: No one in my family ever took it up. But during high school in North Carolina I ran cross-country, and I sometimes trained on a golf course behind a team-mate's house. At the end of one of these sessions, we stopped by a deep water hazard and my friend got to telling me about catching fish in it years ago. Something about that conversation captured my imagination. I had never considered it possible to pull a big bass out of an otherwise ordinary suburban pond. Not long after that, I bought a rod—we didn't have one resting in some dusty corner of the garage, like other families—and I drove to a nearby lake, where I paddled around in a rented aluminum rowboat searching for bass. I never caught anything more impressive than bluegill.

My first week at college in Indiana I met a serious fisherman, and in my junior year we made two pilgrimages to catch trout (and drink beer) in western Montana. After graduation, I took a job as a reporter in Philadelphia, which put me an hour's drive from the ocean. It didn't take me long to discover surfcasting. It did take some time to find fish. In those first years, the Atlantic might as well have been the Mojave. Before I learned much of anything, I got transferred to State College, Pennsylvania, to write about Penn State football for two years. I spent as much time studying trout-fly patterns as I did Joe Paterno's depth charts. I learned to distinguish the Adams from the blue-winged olive, the hare's ear from the pheasant tail. Then I returned to the Philadelphia region, landed a new reporting job, got married, and moved to the New Jersey suburbs. Living near the ocean again I decided to get serious about saltwater fishing. After two years of catching small-stream trout, I wanted fish measured in pounds, not inches. I bought myself a new Ford Ranger with four-wheel-drive and started spending weekends on the beach. One year, I stole away to Cape Cod to fish the famous beach rips. I dreamed of a life where I could leave work, eat

34

dinner, and disappear for a few hours of fishing the night tides. Then one morning three years into our marriage, my wife woke me up and handed me a blue Tiffany bag. Inside, wrapped in tissue paper, I found a positive pregnancy test.

I fished furiously that year. Many nights I would leave my job and race to Sandy Hook, just south of Manhattan in northern New Jersey. I'd throw waders over my dress clothes, grab my gear, and prospect the surf for a big striper. I knew this was my last fall run before I became another thirty-something father talking to people younger than him about the days when he fished the night tides and slept on the beach to be around for the dawn bite. I had met those miserable guys—fathers, all of them—and they reminded me of an old newsman I'd met in my first week on the job who was being shoved out the door by new bosses. He pulled me into his office by the arm and grabbed a pile of yellowing newspaper clips from the 1970s. *When you were a kid! I did good stories here! Front-page stories!*

I didn't want to become him, or them. But if I did at least I wanted a photo or two (me, wind-swept, holding a giant striped bass, dead) to show some poor frightened kid when I leaned my wizened face into his and refused to let him leave until he'd heard my story, *all* of it. I was somebody! I was impressive!

Like a Vineyarder chasing a derby fish, I became compulsive, lured by this vision of a great fish and intoxicated by Sandy Hook at night. Every time I walked out into the darkness it felt new. Some nights, huge noisy swells carved cliffs in the sand. Other times, the ocean seemed asleep, the silence interrupted only by the crash of an occasional breaker sneaking up onto the beach. Giant freighters might file past within a hundred feet on their way back to sea after unloading in the city. Charter boats might drift over dropoffs near the beach. Always, airplanes flew overhead, banking and gliding toward JFK or LaGuardia. The peaks of New York kept watch over it all. One night, alone on the Hook, I watched fireworks—cocktail umbrellas in blue and red, yellow and white—opening silently over the city in the distance.

On my first visit, fog covered the beach and waves punctuated the silence at uneven intervals. I was jumpy as I fished my way up, uncertain how far north I needed to go to find the point. Two by two, fisherman appeared, ghosts trudging out of the fog. I reached the Hook to find half a dozen men slowly reeling in plugs. (These are lures fashioned from wood or plastic and fitted with treble hooks. They look like fat, four- to nine-inch cigars painted in a rainbow of colors.) I settled in among them, feeling as if I'd joined a fraternity sharing a secret at high tide. I changed lures, changed speeds, then finally cast out and let my plug sit in the current. I gave it one tug and a striper hit. I fought it to the shore, dislodged the hook, and, as the others watched silently from their spots, tossed it back into the wash. At twenty-eight inches, the fish wouldn't have won any prizes, but I didn't see anybody else catch anything that night.

A month later, at the same spot, I stumbled on a mob of men and boys packed together at the water's edge. On the beach behind them lay a dozen big stripers and bluefish. Blitz! In the waves in front of me, acres—*acres!*—of 15- and 20-pound stripers and bluefish slashed through schools of baitfish they had chased into the shallows. I tied on a heavy white bucktail and shouldered my way in, shameless, desperate, exhausted. I had slept in my truck the night before and fished all day to earn this moment. I shoehorned a cast into the maelstrom and quickly hooked up. I threw my striper on the sand and popped it on the head a few times, reclaimed my spot, cast, lost my bucktail to a bluefish, tied on a white plug, and nailed two more stripers, then a fourth and a fifth before darkness fell and the fish vanished.

I never got a giant bass that season. But as I drove to the Vineyard on Labor Day to spend some time with these masters of the fishing universe, I figured I could hold my own. I'd landed bluefish in the Chesapeake Bay and tarpon in Florida and Atlantic salmon in Ireland. Even if I'd never caught two of the derby fish—the false albacore and the bonito—I wasn't, as the charter captains call their bumblingest clients, a Joey. I had plenty of gear. My car held three surf rods, four reels loaded with fresh line, a pair of waders, and a bag full of the plugs and sinkers and lures I had collected over the years. I had also packed some foul-weather gear for the jetties and a fly rod in case I got an urge to frustrate myself in the surf for a few minutes.

When I arrived, however, it didn't take long to realize that I was a single-A ballplayer trying to make the leap to the big leagues. I recalled something Nelson Sigelman of *The Martha's Vineyard Times* had said on the phone a few weeks earlier. "If somebody comes here from the city and says they're a fisherman, they may be a fisherman by their standards. But they're not a fisherman by Vineyard standards."

Nelson tells a story about picking up a hitchhiker a few years back when he still fished the derby to exhaustion. They got to talking about fishing.

"It must be very relaxing," his rider said.

"Not the way we do it," Nelson responded.

An islander named Bob Jacobs, who goes by his handle from his taxi-driving days, "Hawkeye," spends the late summer snorkeling in his likely fishing spots. He maps the rocks and holes hidden under the waves, places where he might find stripers during the derby. When the competition begins, he slips into a sleep cycle that removes him from the patterns of the normal world. His life is no longer dictated by day and night but by the tides. He might sleep for three hours, fish a certain spot until fatigue sets in, nap another three hours, drive to another beach, and so on. "I don't have any real concept of whether it's Tuesday or it's Wednesday, or what time it is," he explains. "Three in the morning is just a number on the clock."

Fishing is muscle memory for these people. If they were born on the Vineyard, it was imprinted in their DNA. Many started casting as soon as they could hold a rod, and hunting for stripers was a childhood rite of passage. They did homework on the jetties between fish. They drive past the surf in the course of their everyday business. The beach is their front yard, their backyard, their neighborhood park. A stretch of water worth prospecting is never far from anywhere else, which explains why every other vehicle sprouts surf rods in the fall. The Vineyard is the sort of place where you see fishing tackle tucked into the back of a Porsche.

Nelson came to the island full-time in 1988, worked on the derby committee for a few years in the 1990s, and has spent two decades covering the island and its fishing life for the *Times*. I found myself turning to him and his stories time and again to help me make sense of the phenomenon I was witnessing. Like a lot of newspapermen, he is an unapologetic cynic. But he has a soft spot for the derby, which he explained is not just about winning prizes. He's come to see it as an annual reunion of friends who happen to fish. "For many people, the derby is a state of mind that has nothing to do with the number of fish you catch. It's a mass hysteria, a sort of shared state of mind." It's a lark, an excuse to get out of the house, a vacation, a friendly competition. The derby is a chance to break away from everyday life and see things you would otherwise miss if you didn't stay up all night or wake up before dawn: schools of shooting stars, eye-popping sunrises, the convulsions of predators chasing prey on the water, conversations you can only have with friends outside in the dark at two a.m. Even for those who are not trying that hard to win, the derby is a marathon.

I'll do my best to keep up. I will turn in after midnight and set the alarm to go off well before dawn. I will pull on the same jeans I wore the day before, and the day before that. I will layer on the sweatshirts and crawl into my car in the dark, gagging at the stench of dying eels and fumbling in the trash and newspapers and discarded water bottles for my gear. I will ride along the beach and hike around boulders in the surf and wade up to my chest. I will camp out on jetties and hitch rides on boats. I will pass pickups on the road and wonder: Are they coming or going? Where've they been? Are they getting fish? Why aren't I?

I'm not trying to win it. But if good fortune strikes? Well, let's just say the derby has seen stranger things.

2

"Don't Tell Him Any Secrets!"

The island's beauty is the stuff of legend.

One morning in 1934, when Nelson Bryant was eleven years old, his father bought him a twenty-gauge shotgun. He took it out to the marsh at the head of a great salt pond near his house to look for birds. The landscape around him had changed little in the past five thousand years. He could turn in every direction and see just one house. Before long, a black duck flew by, and he took aim, pulled the trigger, and watched the bird drop to the ground. It was Christmas Day.

Nelson, who would go on to spend three decades as outdoors columnist for *The New York Times,* is not naive. He understands that progress marches forward, like it or not, on the Vineyard and everywhere else. But as with a lot of islanders of his generation he can't help feeling irritated about how the changes have imposed upon his life. He now sees six or seven houses around the scene of that first duck hunt—not a subdivision but still an intrusion. In the 1940s he could bike to the beaches of the North Shore after work and fly-fish the night tides without seeing a soul. Today he would have to ask permission to roam those same beaches—an indignity he's not about to suffer at age eighty-five.

"Let's say I had a girlfriend in high school who fell upon evil times. That's how I feel about the Vineyard," he told me with a playful grin one day in his rustic West Tisbury home, a converted goat shack crammed with books, art, and fishing artifacts. "She's been degraded."

The truth is the island has been evolving from a poor, rural, un-crowded outpost of farmers and fishermen into a lively summer re-sort since before the Civil War. The first wave began in 1835, when Methodists began flocking to a campground in an oak grove for boisterous faith revivals. In 1853 the Edgartown prayer meetings ran for one hundred straight days, and one born-again townsman ignored even his ailing wife to take part. Otherwise normal island-ers were howling "like so many coyotes," his son complained. "The whole town seems to be running mad." (Swap out eternal salvation for striped bass and it starts to sounds a lot like the derby.)

Word of the island's beauty spread, and soon a resort village had grown up near the campground. "Forty years ago, it was a barren waste, and now it is one of the more fashionable watering holes on the Atlantic Coast," the *Whaleman's Shipping List* once noted about what would later became the town of Oak Bluffs. That was written back in 1871, at the start of a decade that saw the construction of majestic new beachfront hotels, restaurants, shops, and a massive roller-skating rink with hardwood floors lit by hundreds of lanterns.

It would be many years before the well-heeled arrived en masse and the whole island became a must-see destination in the minds of Americans at large. As much as people try to pinpoint exactly when and how it happened, the truth is the revolution arrived gradually. "It's kind of like losing your hearing," said Nelson Bryant's West Tisbury neighbor Whit Manter, whose family has lived on the island for centuries. "You don't notice it until you're deaf."

On the surface, the six towns of Martha's Vineyard appear to be strangers adrift on a life raft, with little in common except for their mutual separation from the rest of the United States. One is all dunes and cliffs and giant homes, another is a closely settled harborside village with white picket fences. One has a waterfront park, an old-fashioned carousel, and a collection of gingerbread cottages. Another is farmland and scrub oak.

Packed onto its 104 square miles today is an eclectic population of more than fifteen thousand that swells to seventy-five thousand in the summer. Both numbers have risen sharply over the past four decades as more and more newcomers have discovered the island. The wealthy came for peaceful summer homes and the workmen came to build them. Writers, intellectuals, artists, and hippies came to be inspired by pastoral simplicity and isolation. Middle- and upper-class blacks came to vacation in a place known for its racial harmony. The AARP set came to retire. Film stars and celebrities came to escape their fish-bowl lives. And they are all still coming. Every day in July and August, tourists arrive by the boatload to swim at the beaches, rent mopeds, and see the famous sights. They leave their dollars and take home their Black Dog T-shirts. In all, 1.7 million people visited the island in 2007.

In the late 1940s, when the derby started, the tourist crowds and the summer people were generally regarded as a saving grace. Sure, some longtime islanders may have considered them, as one writer joked, a "lower order of beings," but they spent money, they came only during the summer, and they kept mostly to the three down-island towns, Vineyard Haven, Oak Bluffs, and Edgartown. (For you among the lower order: the western towns are *up*-island and the eastern towns are *down*-island, because as you head from west to east you descend in longitude. The Gay Head lighthouse on the western tip is at 70°49.8'. Wasque Point on the east is at 70°27.0'.) By the 1970s, however, development and tourism had grown more and more important to the island's bottom line. Fears arose. Was the island becoming another Cape Cod, with its fast-food dives and clam shacks and gaudy tourist traps? Would development spoil their ponds and their beaches, their rustic vistas and their ecosystem?

In 1977, in the midst of this identity crisis, legislators in Boston proposed to eliminate the Vineyard's representative in the capital. Islanders would instead share a district with the more populous Cape Cod, and the political math all but ensured that no Vineyarder would win election to the state House of Representatives. Needless to say, that didn't go over well. "The hell with them," a local selectman and fish market owner declared. "We'll set up another state."

Secessionists drew up a declaration of independence and designed their own flag, a white seagull in flight over a red-orange sun. State officials stopped laughing after the islands got offers to throw in with Vermont, New Hampshire, Connecticut, and, bizarrely, Hawaii. Soon, someone suggested withdrawing from the United States altogether and seeking foreign aid. An interim cabinet was appointed, a national anthem composed. A reporter from the *Vineyard Gazette* called the White House and engaged in a line of questioning that, thirty years later, reads like something out of *The Colbert Report*. A Carter administration spokesman said he doubted the White House would have a comment on the fracas, the *Gazette* reported. "Asked whether the government would attack the islands if the islands declared war on the United States, he said the nation might 'if it became a matter of national security.'" The insurrectionists eventually lost the fight, which had been conducted tongue-in-cheek anyway. But it was a very Vineyard episode. It has always been a place apart, and the independent streak still runs deep. When islanders take the ferry to the mainland they might say they're "going to America."

By the 1980s it seemed as if all of America was coming to them. The island had become the fastest-growing place in the Northeast, and a poll by the *Gazette* found overwhelming support for a year-long building moratorium. Towns—some of which had only recently put into place comprehensive zoning rules—set about trying to stem the rising tide of development. "We are witnessing the build-out of the Vineyard," the newspaper warned in 1986. The following July the paper's editorial board decried a decision to sell part of South Beach to a developer, who planned to close the island's most popular beach to the general public and sell access rights at an opening price of $25,000. "The shredding of South Beach for personal profit amounts to a declaration of war against the Vineyard—all the Vineyard. And the message of what historians will call plunder at South Beach is this: The island is for sale and nothing is safe or sacred." The state eventually stepped in to save that beach, and public and private conservation groups continued to snap up land, but in 1995 the head of one such organization told the *Gazette* that "the Vineyard in 20 years is going to feel just like any other suburb"—one of the most beautiful in America, but a suburb nonetheless, with more housing developments, more fences, more no-trespassing signs.

As a New Jerseyan, I know overdeveloped sprawl when I see it, and the Vineyard doesn't exactly qualify. Not yet. A special land-use commission has blocked some of the most objectionable development proposals, and towns strictly control building. There is still no mall and no fast-food chain—they blocked a McDonald's in 1979—and though the place is big enough to support a bus service and an airport it is small enough that it has no stoplights. Ask for a phone number and some people will give you four digits and assume you know the town exchange. "It's Mayberry out here," state fisheries biologist Greg Skomal said. People don't lock their doors and hitchhiking is still fairly common. There are intersections where any reasonable municipal government would have installed a stoplight long ago. At one, ferry traffic is dumped onto a main road connecting the busy towns of Vineyard Haven and Oak Bluffs, and drivers are never quite confident about whether to go or give way. Islanders would rather have a thousand near accidents a year than one solitary red light.

It's the sort of place that celebrates its cast of characters: the Vineyard's peculiarities are a big part of its charm. There is the fisherman-farmer who went barefoot most of the year and was famously arrested for driving a team of oxen down the street while drunk. Someone told me of a cop who had turned his windshield-wiper tank into a machine that would dispense cocktails. I met a woman who desperately wanted to buy a tugboat and turn it into a house, and a man who made a home out of a chicken coop. I heard a story about a guy randomly firing antique automatic weaponry into the woods. The newspaper had an article not long ago about a policeman gunning down a feral turkey named Tom that had attacked a delivery crew. "The Vineyard is such a weird place," said Dave Nash, who retired there several years ago. "You have people who, if you took them to the mainland, they wouldn't know how to function."

By turns Vineyarders have welcomed and wept over the island's ever growing fame. They hated that, for the longest time, the only thing a lot of people knew about their home was Ted Kennedy and Chappaquiddick. But they hailed the arrival of Jacqueline Kennedy Onassis, who bought a 375-acre beachfront property in 1978 and built a dream house. In 1974 Steven Spielberg received a hearty welcome when he papered the island with $1.5 million in Hollywood cash to shoot *Jaws* (though hosting a film crew for interminable months got old). In the 1990s they cringed when the press gave blanket coverage to the Clinton vacations, Princess Di's visit, and John F. Kennedy Jr.'s plane crash into the sea off the west end of the island. They take pride in being the kind of place where the famous can act like anybody else— window-shop, eat a quiet dinner, visit the fish market—without drawing a crowd.

"Spiritually," the legendary sports columnist Red Smith wrote in 1954, "Martha's Vineyard belongs to no state at all, being a land to itself where distinctions are drawn, courteously but firmly, between residents and foreigners." To some islanders, seasonal visitors (like Red himself) would never be true Vineyarders, and tourists would never be more than a paycheck. Days after JFK Jr.'s 1999 accident, a longtime summer resident had this to say about the Kennedy family: "They may have had a house here, but no one ever called them Vineyarders."

Who *is*, then? It's a favorite parlor game in some circles, but the truth is that the roster of true natives—with roots going back generations, to the Wampanoag tribesmen, to the founding white settlers of the 1600s, to the Portuguese whalers—grows smaller and smaller all the time, gradually replaced by the retired and the rich.

I found plenty of islanders who wondered aloud if they wouldn't be better off without so many new houses and developments, without so many more seasonal residents crowding their towns, roadways, and beaches. "Summer is *wicked*," one lifer complained. Nelson Bryant admits to driving the speed limit down the long two-lane road running across the island from Edgartown to West Tisbury and seeing how many cars pile up behind him. He'll waver a little if anybody tries to pass on the left, just to make them doubt his mental state. The ornery octogenarian once pulled into his driveway, spun around, and counted seventy-two cars flying past without interruption.

Year-rounders' larger gripe is that nouveau riche newcomers have driven up the prices for real estate to levels so astronomical that those of more modest means can barely find housing they can afford. Early derby awards give one measure of the sea change. First prize in the inaugural Martha's Vineyard Derby in 1946: $1,000. Second prize: a building lot in Gay Head (now known by the Wampanoag name Aquinnah). In 1950, a plot of land dropped to *third* prize, behind a Jeep and a TV set, but above a pair of rubber boots and an outdoor jacket. The idea of giving away land today is, of course, laughable. The median home sales price has spiked over the past decade. In 2007 it reached $700,000 and topped $1 million in the most exclusive towns. Many properties sell for much, much more. An estate on Katama Bay in Edgartown went for $25.2 million in 2006, breaking the record of $22.5 million set the month before. Today, Aquinnah is where the Kennedys live, and winning the derby does *not* win you the right to be their neighbors.

A growing number of island workers live on the Cape and commute by ferry every day. Tenants might uproot their families multiple times in a single year as owners boost the rents to cash in on the summer vacationers. Some young people who grew up on the Vineyard end up moving off-island, because unless they have family land or money they have difficulty buying their first house: they're priced out. Swelling property tax assessments can put even long-time home owners in financial straits. Many people who fall in love with the island and decide to stay year-round have to cobble together jobs to pay the bills. They may have advanced degrees, but in the Vineyard economy they work at retail shops or sell art or start landscaping businesses. "Nobody does what they're trained to do," one islander said. "You do what there is to do." They earn as much as they can during the summer and squirrel it away for the winter. There is a Brazilian underclass that by some estimates numbers in the thousands. They can be found building homes, working in kitchens, and cramming by the dozen into rental houses.

The island income gap is growing ever wider. A dinner entrée in Edgartown might run $57. For $125,000, members of a new private club in Edgartown called The Boathouse can enjoy harborside fine dining, a fleet of boats, a sprawling fitness center, tennis courts, a pool and a spa. It costs $300,000 to join one exclusive golf club. The Vineyard is covered by Plum TV, a niche channel that airs only in the most elite resort destinations, including Miami Beach, the Hamptons, Vail, and Aspen. While all this goes on, Habitat for Humanity is building affordable housing.

Of course, it goes without saying that vacationers keep the island economy afloat, and the summer-home crowd finances the construction trade and shoulders a significant portion of the tax base. In other words, they remain a saving grace. Nelson Sigelman, the *Martha's Vineyard Times* managing editor, understands why people fear the sweeping changes. But he notes that people struggled to pay the bills before the boom, too, and many workers are far better off now. Electricians, carpenters, masons, and other workmen make better money than they could on the mainland. If your livelihood depends on it, tourism and development is not a threat to your way of life—it is your way of life.

On top of all these cultural changes, residents are confronted with the daily reality that they live on a shrinking island. Erosion is swallowing up five to eleven feet of real estate annually on some parts of the Vineyard; landowners have hired crews to shove their houses back from the sea. Every clash, it seems, can be traced to a land-use disagreement: the fight over where to put inexpensive housing; the battle over high-decibel chickens; the debate over how to assign mooring slips to boaters in Menemsha.

A sense of loss hangs over the place. There is a feeling among longtime Vineyarders that the island was once a secret, known only to a lucky few. They had the place to themselves and now they don't.

Perhaps no one is more sensitive to the Vineyard's dwindling open land than its fishermen, for whom the fishing spot is sacred—a secret to be protected. It may be on someone else's beach, behind someone else's gate, at the end of someone else's driveway, but they own it as if they have been issued a deed.

As a fisherman myself I understand this. I arrived on the Vineyard expecting to see subterfuge and stealth, paranoia and mistrust.

I'm not sure I expected the threats.

When I joked around the weigh station one day that I'd come to the Vineyard to write an encyclopedia of the island's best fishing locales, a derby committeeman whose day job is assistant principal at the West Tisbury School told me that I would be burned at the stake and my ashes scattered in the harbor. On a boat the following week, a charter captain who was employing an unusual tactic turned to me and said, "Can't put this in the book. I'd have to kill you." Just asking questions made me suspect. Lev, after taking me out on the water three times, asked his wife whether she thought I was really a writer, or if I was just trying to learn all of his spots and tactics so I could return the following year and win the whole tournament. One day, I ran into a crew of regular derby anglers on a beach. "We'll have to kill him," one man said to another when I introduced myself as a writer. A woman at the water's edge saw him talking to me and screamed over her shoulder: "Don't tell him any secrets!"

Some fishermen told me there aren't secret spots anymore, and on the surface that's true. If you fish the island for any length of time, you will eventually find your way to a lot of the waters that fish frequent. Many spots are mentioned in books or magazines and in Internet articles or chat rooms. *The Martha's Vineyard Times* publishes a rundown of which techniques work best on which beaches. I used Google Earth's satellite imagery to map routes to some beaches. On the water, even the most guarded boat fishermen cannot escape the scrutiny of a watchful competitor.

On the other hand, the place is built for secrets. There are miles and miles of rutted, barely passable dirt pathways that snake through the woods. Anglers can park along some roads without trouble, but on others their trucks might be towed or vandalized or locked behind a gate. Boaters throw off the competition by going out in the dark or taking circuitous routes to their fishing grounds. A good spot might be this hole next to that rock. Fish just to the left or the right and you'll get nothing.

It's also not enough to know where a spot is. The real secret, after all, is knowing where the fish are. You have to figure out when to work a spot, and how. Pick the wrong tide, you'll get nothing. Tie on the wrong plug, you'll get nothing. And just when you think you've figured it all out, everything might change for reasons that never become entirely clear. One fisherman told me he had discovered something new about a well-known spot whose location I will not divulge for fear of summary execution. Everybody generally fishes the falling tide. But for the past two years he's been catching good stripers on the rise. Nobody has caught on to the fact that he's fishing the same beach, only at an unconventional time. "Everybody's wondering where the hell my spot is. It's right under their noses. If people knew I was catching these fish out here . . ." He just laughed and shook his head.

Who you confide in and who you don't is a major part of the derby calculus. Friends may share information about where the fish are during the regular season. But come the derby there's less talking, and more conversations occur in encrypted language only a close friend can decipher. "Everybody gets weird," fisherman Morgan Taylor said. Specific locations get code names that mean nothing outside your circle of trust: *Dreamers. Dreamland. Slammers. The Rock Pile. The G-spot.*

"You want to hear lies?" one angler told me. "Try to ask someone where he caught a fish."

Whit Manter, an exceptional derby fisherman until he all but gave up the sport for golf, recalled that when somebody would ask him a question about the fishing—any question, innocent or not—he would just walk away. His father hammered the code into young Whit: you don't spill the secrets. "I was a crusty old bastard," he acknowledges. "I was respected as a fisherman, but I don't know if I was well liked. I wasn't mean. I just wasn't polite."

Geoff Codding's unassuming demeanor is interpreted as typical fisherman's caginess during derby season. "I won't lie to anybody. People'll come up and ask me shit and I'll just stare. I would never ask anybody nothing. It's the worst thing you could do. 'Oh, where'd you catch that? Did you catch that there?' You can't really ask somebody where. That's not part of the whole thing."

Secrecy is prized at all levels of the derby hierarchy. I went to visit tournament president Ed Jerome at one point and asked if I could join him for a trip out on the water. He agreed, then added, "Of course, we'd have to blindfold you."

Over the years guys have gone to ridiculous lengths to protect their spots. They've parked their cars in one lot and hopped rides to their actual destinations in friends' trucks. They've hidden in the beach grass. They've caught a load of stripers, driven them to some other beach, and pretended to have caught them there. They've buried their fish so that when the competition walks by and asks the question—*Get anything?*—they can safely say the fishing stinks. It doesn't always work. Twice, a secretive fisherman

51

told me, his gambit unraveled just as he was assuring rivals there weren't any fish around. One time, a bass in its death throes flipped sand on the guys. Another time, an angler actually slipped on the entombed striper. When the deception works, though, nothing beats watching other fishermen walk past a magic spot on the way to someplace famous.

Fishermen don't rely on subterfuge just to gain a competitive advantage. It's also about crowd control. Tell somebody you were into stripers at Wasque and that person will tell at least one other person, who will tell at least one other person. The next thing you know, twenty anglers are camped out at your spot. One morning in 2000, Steve Morris weighed in a 41.78-pound bass to take the lead in the shore division (for good, as it turned out). That night, when he returned to the spot, all the fishermen were on the beach in their pickup trucks. "I mean, it was like a parking lot. Everybody knows where everybody fishes."

It doesn't help that access to the beaches is increasingly restricted. "Welcome to the People's Republic of Martha's Vineyard," one fisherman told me. "It's like, 'Come on down, you can use this part of the beach'"—he drew a narrow strip on a piece of paper—"'but you can't park there.'" Almost two-thirds of the Vineyard's beaches are owned by individuals and private clubs. To use these beaches you need gobs of cash or ancestors who were prescient. Memberships in one private-beach association originally sold for a few thousand dollars but in recent years have commanded staggering sums. A single share fetched $375,000. Buyers receive a deed to sixty-eight feet of beachfront, but what they really get is the right to use an entire mile of sand. The dirt road leading to the exclusive strand is gated, and the keys to the lock are like heirlooms handed down from one generation of members to the next.

During the tourist season, some owners post security guards on the beach to enforce their property rights. Steve Purcell, owner of

Larry's Tackle Shop, told me stories of near fisticuffs between overly antagonistic fishermen and overly aggressive guards. Most anglers try to avoid confrontation, he said. "I know people who do army crawls past guard shacks."

Massachusetts is one of two states that permit private ownership of beaches all the way out to the low-water mark, which effectively allows deed holders to bar the public from many stretches. The law dates to the 1640s and has survived even an attempt by a State Senate president to change it. Exceptions are carved out for those engaged in fishing, fowling, or navigation, and some beachcombers have tried to apply those loopholes liberally by carrying a fishing rod with them while they "navigate" the private beaches on foot. A few years ago, a group of rabble-rousers vowed to challenge the Vineyard's "beach apartheid," as they called it. But only a new law can stop owners from kicking people off. "They don't want you down there," fisherman Janet Messineo says. Whatever the law says about fishermen's rights, after you walk a mile (or even two or three) to your spot from your car you still might have to stop along the water to debate the mechanics of a 360-year-old law with the irate owner of a property that cost him several million dollars—or a renter who's dropping $25,000 a week to get away from riffraff like you.

Fishermen have always ignored trespassing laws that keep them from irresistible stretches of water. When landowners spotted them, they tended to look the other way. Today, they might call the cops, as one man did in 1998 when Nelson Sigelman walked across the edge of his property to get to the beach.

For Shirley Craig, the island native who came of age in the 1930s and '40s, that's a huge change. A few property owners clashed with derby competitors in the early years, but back then so much more of the beach was open to fishermen. "There were a few gated places where you had to have a key. They didn't have parking restrictions, they didn't have residency stickers, they didn't have anywhere near the number of private beaches that we have now." Lev Wlodyka said that even as recently in the 1980s, when he was a boy, landowners would not object if they saw him walk across their property to get to a beach. "Now, they freak out! It's like, 'Whoa, whoa! Sorry I stepped on your scrub oak.'"

In the early decades of the derby competitors drove campers out onto the beach and spent all day and night at the water's edge. They cooked breakfast and dinner on their tailgates. Today, it is illegal to drive on many beaches, let alone camp. Even conservation land can be off-limits to fishing and other public uses. The Cedar Tree Neck Sanctuary, for example, is a 312-acre preserve of oaks, beech groves, and rocky coastline on the North Shore. But it is owned by a private conservation group whose focus is walking trails, scenic vistas, and wildlife habitat, and at the entrance is a sign reading, "Picnicking, swimming, sunbathing, fishing & other activities of the sort are strictly prohibited since they would inevitably conflict with the purpose for which this sanctuary has been set aside." Translation: Come and enjoy but please don't *do* anything.

All the new restrictions rankle fishermen, but the fact is there is still a lot of beach open to them. The Martha's Vineyard Land Bank Commission, the Trustees of Reservations, and local and state governments have saved major stretches for public use, most notably on Chappaquiddick. During the fall and spring the beach associations and departing summer residents often leave their gates unlocked for fishermen and beachcombers.

And savvy anglers figure out how to get into otherwise restricted spots. Mark Plante, who is a plumber, gets "ins" from clients with beachfront property. Julian Pepper saved a fellow angler from drowning at the Menemsha jetty one day and won his eternal gratitude, as well as something far more valuable: permission to use his property to access a good spot. Many year-rounders watch houses in the off-season—turn the water on and off, make sure everything is ready when the owner arrives, repair what's broken—and they often get parking and fishing rights in addition to a paycheck. Smart anglers get to know these caretakers. They are neighbors, friends of friends, and colleagues. They coach the kids and sit on the same civic boards. When fishermen or hunters win permission to use private land, they are discreet about how they use it, and they deliver fish or venison as a sign of appreciation.

But things change. Erosion makes it hard to drive to old spots. An owner dies and his son doesn't want fishermen using his dock, his driveway, his beach. Properties get sold to a less tolerant owner. Many working-class anglers can't help but harbor bitterness toward, as one put it, "all those rich people who build trophy houses and put up gates to keep out us little skunks."

The Vineyard is a different place than it was when the derby began in 1946. The derby pumps millions of dollars into the economy every fall, but fishing is a smaller part of the culture. "It's a big island," said Mark Alan Lovewell, who covers fisheries for the *Gazette*. "There's a lot more going on now." The Chamber of Commerce ran the derby for years but it handed off control in 1986, and in the years since then it's thrown its weight behind other tourist draws, such as the wedding industry. Today, hundreds of couples get hitched on the island every year, and derby season, with its mild weather and sparse crowds, is the most popular time. These days, well-dressed mainlanders visiting for weekend nuptials seem to fit in better on the Vineyard than derby zombies driving around with fishing rods bristling from their pickup trucks and fish guts caked on their clothes.

It took Nelson Bryant the longest time to see what was happening to the Vineyard. After returning from World War II he attended Dartmouth. One year he didn't have enough money to get back for the fall semester. But he did own twenty acres on Deep Bottom Cove, which he had inherited from his uncle. He sold it to a friend for the price of a train ticket, about $20. He's not sure exactly how much the property would fetch today. It was on Tisbury Great Pond, which is now an exclusive part of the Vineyard, and in 2006 one estate there sold for $19 million. About a decade ago, Nelson got wind of a different sort of real estate opportunity and, naturally, he jumped at it—though his decision had more to do with fishing than finance. At Dogfish Bar, a fly-fishing mecca that Nelson's newspaper columns helped make famous, parking had become tight and the police were ticketing and towing cars. So a couple of men put together the North Shore Fishing Association and sold shares of a tiny parking lot just over the dunes from the beach. A number of fishermen, including Nelson, bought in for $15,000. They all received keys to a padlock on a cattle gate at the entrance. Not too long ago, someone offered Nelson $90,000 for his key. He had to shake his head at the absurdity of a dirt lot that's apparently worth north of $1 million.

At the end of a rutted dirt road leading to another popular fishing spot is a parking area for a few pickups. It's near a multimillion-dollar house owned by a well-known couple in TV and films. (For fear of burning the spot, I'm not naming names.) The previous resident had permitted a few anglers to park there, and when the property changed hands the new owners did nothing to stop them from continuing to do so. Now, many people have discovered the place, and they assume the parking area is open to anyone. Regulars fear they'll all be cut off. On the Vineyard, if you have a good spot you keep quiet.

One night, I got to talking about the clandestine fishing culture with Zeb Tilton's younger brother Zack, a fast-talking roofer whose ancestry goes back to the island's early settlers. The brothers are great-grandsons of a legendary schooner captain named Zebulon

Tilton. It goes without saying that Zack knows more than his share of productive spots, places his family has fished for ages and places he's found on his own. He has a simple way of keeping his secrets secret: "One part truth, two parts lies. That's my formula."

Darkness won't set in for another hour and Morgan Taylor is getting antsy.

It's still the first week of the derby and the beach is crawling with fishermen. The shore bass and bluefish divisions are wide open. The biggest striper is 22 pounds, the leading blue a mere 9. One lucky night and just about anybody could be in the lead. Morgan has a spot that has been good to him this year—very good to him—and he definitely doesn't want anybody knowing where it is.

With his short-cropped hair and button-down shirts, Morgan is the straight man in a free-spirited gang of fishermen. His friend and surfcasting partner, Julian Pepper, is an artist and photographer who works at Larry's Tackle Shop, which is located in what Julian calls the Edgartown Man Mall: it also has a liquor store and a deli. ("What else do you need?") This year, for the first time, the derby includes a two-man team competition, and Julian and Morgan, who spend the winters in Hawaii working on an offshore fishing boat, are team *Hanapa'a,* Hawaiian for "fish on." They're known to work the island's hard-to-reach spots, stretches of beach where you have to hike a mile, scamper over and around boulders, and wade out until the waves are up to your neck. Testimonies to their fights with big bass hang on a wall of the shop: treble hooks that are broken, severely bent, or otherwise mangled. These guys are among the hardest of the hardcore.

I'd met Morgan a couple of times at the tackle shop and we'd gotten to talking at the end of the Menemsha jetty earlier this afternoon. He spoke quietly and seemed to use the absolute minimum number of words possible. When it became clear the fish weren't biting, we picked our way over the rocks back to the parking lot. I asked if I could tag along to his night spot, vowing not to give it away. Morgan hemmed and hawed while he returned his albie rods to their holders, which looked like a battery of rocket launchers in the back of his black pickup. He leaned over the truck bed, visibly uncomfortable with my proposition. This was a spot Julian had showed him, he explained. Fisherman's code prohibits giving up somebody else's spot. It's the lowest form of betrayal. But I pressed the issue and he relented. Soon I was trailing him out of the Menemsha parking lot toward his next stop.

When we arrive he turns on the radio in his pickup, eats a sandwich, and fiddles with his fishing tackle. Morgan is serious about his gear. He's tested all kinds of knots to find the ones that work best with the braided line he uses. (He would tie a knot, loop it around a door knob, and yank until it broke. The surgeon's knot and the uniknot came out on top.) He changes the hooks on his plugs to the strongest variety he can buy. He spent years using inferior reels before he realized he had to get the best, the Van Staals, crafted from titanium and sealed to keep salt and sand out of the gears. They cost $600 and up but he doesn't ever have to worry about his reel failing again.

He has a strategy for throwing off potential spies tonight: head down to the beach and fish some marginal water until dark, then backtrack to his spot. Before we leave the parking lot a fisherman pulls up in a truck with out-of-state plates and begins a conversation. Or tries to, anyway. Morgan does his thing—a series of barely intelligible mumbles. I follow suit with my best crusty-islander-around-a-stranger imitation. I just look. I don't say a word.

Morgan has good reason to think people might try to tail him. In June, he caught the first striper over 50 pounds taken from a Vineyard beach in quite a while. His 52-pounder ranked among the largest bass caught from the shore in New England that year, and it

58

was definitely the biggest one he'd ever caught. A few nights later he tangled with and lost what he could only assume was a bigger fish. Julian followed it up with a 43-pounder from the same spot. Get a pair of fish like that and paranoia can set in. The Vineyard's small-town vibe can start to feel suffocating. Morgan told only a few people about the spot, and local surfcasters who think they know where he got it really don't. When they took the photo—Morgan, soaking wet in his waders, hoisting the beast with his fist under the gill plate in the classic pose—they went to a completely anonymous location, with no landmarks to give a smart fisherman any clue as to where they were. "I was extremely tight-lipped about that," Morgan told me once. "Might've even lied about it a few times."

As we walked out to the beach, I couldn't help wondering why he'd agreed to take me, a stranger and a writer, to his top-secret spot. How could he know I was a man of my word? How could he be sure I wouldn't burn him? After a minute it dawns on me that we're not going anywhere near his spot tonight. He'd told me more or less where it was and how they fish it, but now I have to assume that his descriptions were more or less untrue.

We end up fishing a better-known spot for a few hours, wading out past our waists and firing plugs into the surf. After a while Julian shows up with a few others and they manage to get a few small stripers. I am decidedly not hardcore. I'd balked at dropping a couple of hundred dollars on a waterproof top, and instead I try (unsuccessfully) to use a raincoat and a wader belt to keep myself dry. The arm on my eyeglasses breaks. My reel fails in the surf. I catch nothing. Around eleven p.m. we head back to our vehicles and the five of them are talking about packing it in for the night. But when I drive off they're still milling around as if they might hit some other spot.

The next day I run into Julian at the shop. He assures me they drove straight home after I left.

True? False?

I'll give them this, the inscrutable Team *Hanapa'a:* if counter-espionage is all about keeping your competition wondering whether you're telling the God's honest truth or straight-faced lies, they've got it down pat.

3

A Black Hole for Fish

The Swordfish Harpooner: memorial to Menemsha's past.

The day after Zeb Tilton caught his 56-pounder is brilliantly sunny, and I find Lev Wlodyka at his usual stomping ground: Menemsha Harbor. He had fished hard last night in a bid to top Zeb's bass, and he returned home in the middle of the night. His wife, Jen, sits in the driver's seat of their Tundra facing the jetty while their baby boy dozes in the backseat. Most years, Jen logs long hours alongside her husband on the boat: acting goofy, doing a "Striper Dance" to attact bass, and reeling in her share of fish. But this year she's nursing the infant every few hours. She's become a classic derby widow.

Lev is out on the jetty casting at breaking fish and telling the others about Zeb's beast. He sprays casts while he talks, too wound up to worry about crossing other anglers' lines. He can get away with it because (a) he's Lev and (b) he'll somehow extricate himself without tangling anybody else's line. He whistles "Strangers in the Night" and takes a break to gnaw on an ice cream cone from the Texaco.

A fisherman in a torn T-shirt and rolled-up cargo pants climbs up the tower barefoot and casts at a school of fish. He ignores Lev's demand that he dive in from atop the tower. Somebody cracks that he'd probably do it if anyone had beer to wager. Lev watches the schools of two-inch baitfish holding in tight formation against the rocks. "The last thing in the world I'd like to be," he says, "is a peanut bunker."

Everybody is calling the high-profile boat-bass division for Zeb. To chase a 57-pounder now, derby president Ed Jerome tells the *Gazette,* "would be foolish." Nobody disagrees. There are seven other major divisions and it doesn't take a mathematician to see that you'd have better odds winning one of those. Some fisherman logging long hours on the beach could most likely top the 5.29-pound bonito or the 11.37-pound false albacore. It would be exhausting—assuming the fates didn't deliver a winner on the first cast—but when things got boring, they could remind themselves how lucky they were to be here waiting for fish to storm the beach and not stuck in a stifling office-building cubicle somewhere.

Lev is out on the jetty because he will take a derby winner however he can get it. Consider his history: In one three-year stretch as a junior he took first place in four divisions, twice from shore, twice from boat. As an adult, he caught the top boat albie in 1999, the boat striper in 2000 and 2001, and the shore bass and the boat bonito in 2002. That four-year run is unparalleled in derby history. "I think history will rank him right up there with Dick Hathaway

and Serge de Somov," veteran fisherman Kib Bramhall said. Hathaway is the only man to have won the derby six times; de Somov, a
secretive fishing genius known on the island as the Mad Russian,
caught the biggest striper in three straight competitions, from 1963–
65, and again in 1969. What connects Lev to those luminaries,
Bramhall said, is the ability to consistently catch big fish under
competitive pressure. "When the chips are down, they win."

The name is a mouthful, but if Vineyarders can't always pronounce
it correctly (repeat after me: wuh-LAH-dick-uh), they all seem to
know the family.

Lev's mother, Betty, is known in island art circles as the painter
B. Martin Wlodyka. His father, Walter, is known everywhere as
the Skunk Man. On an island overrun with both (a) skunks, moles,
and other such creatures and (b) millionaires with $40,000 gar-
dens and trophy lawns, Walter's phone number is on speed dial.
Drive anywhere on the island and you'll encounter the pungent
stench of roadkill skunk. Then you're a mile up the road and
it fades and you move on with your life. Walter lives with that
smell all day. His pickup reeks of it, leaves a trail of it behind as
he drives, the fetid residue of thousands of snuffed-out stinkers.
He doesn't much notice it anymore and, besides, it's a nice living—nice enough to support a vacation home in Costa Rica, where
he spends a few months every winter. Recently, an informal
poll at the county courthouse placed Walter among the island's
best-known personalities—and it's not just because people have
come to rely on his particular expertise. He'll also talk your ear
off, and I mean that in the best possible way. He punctuates wild
stories and outlandish theories with an unrestrained cackle. Almost anything can make him break into laughter. This being the
Vineyard, Walter the Skunk Man is friends with the actor Dan
Aykroyd.

"Lev's a black hole for fish," Walter said one day a few months before the derby started, fixing his sink while his phone rang again and again. Breaking away from our conversation to answer one call, he explained to a potential client how he would use a smoke bomb to rid her yard of moles. The woman expressed some concern. "Well, it's your choice," he replied, pulling off his cockeyed hat and scratching his balding head. "You could end up with a dirt lawn. It'll be like the Dust Storm of 1928." He ended the call and turned his attention back to his son. "Some people are born to be doctors, some people are born to be lawyers, some are born to be businessmen. Lev was born to be a fisherman."

Lev's grandfather spent his life across the sound in Fairhaven, Massachusetts, as a lobsterman and commercial fisherman. He was a strapping six-foot-one with great strength and enormous hands. "He invented work," Walter said. When he was a child, Walter spent summers on his father's boat, banding lobsters and dealing with the bait bags. He'd keep the stone crabs and sell them to Gene's Lobster Shack for 5, 7, or 11 cents, depending on their size. At age eleven, he decided he wanted a boat of his own, and instead of handing over the money his dad had him earn it on the lobster boat. He saved up $117 for a skiff and a little three-horsepower Evinrude and he started scalloping that fall. Walter's father also built boats, and he sold his son his wooden fifty-two-foot boat the *Jen-Walt* soon after Walter returned from Vietnam in 1971. ("It's not in my file," he said about the war. "I don't want to talk about it. Covert shit.") Walter's father had rerigged the *Jen-Walt* as an inshore dragger—installing nets to sweep fish off the seafloor—and for several years Walter and Betty worked together on the sea. "I just fell in love with it," he said. They spent so much time on the boat that Lev's older sister Sascha was conceived on the water, Betty once told a newspaper reporter.

After they moved to the Vineyard, Walter captained a few seventy-foot draggers that netted yellowtail, cod, and flounder. The boats were junkers. One was prone to electrical fires. Corrosion chewed a six-inch hole in the hull of another, prompting a Mayday call to the Coast Guard off Nantucket. He had some spectacular hauls, but he quickly gave up the big vessels for his own smaller boats, the *Sea Heir* and the *Freelance*. Soon he began moving away from commercial fishing altogether and tapped into the more lucrative fields of animal control and "estate management," a grandiose term for maintaining summer houses. "I could see the end coming," he said. "Nantucket Shoals was a nursery. It was where all our fish came from. And we wiped it out."

Today's New England fishermen are like guys arriving too late to a party, when the place is trashed, the liquor bottles are empty, and the girls are long gone. It had been a great run for five centuries, ever since explorer Giovanni Caboto—to his English benefactors, John Cabot—discovered the teeming fishery in the far reaches of the Atlantic and told the world about it. (Basque and English fishermen had apparently known the place for decades but they had the good sense to keep quiet about their hot spot.) By the 1580s more than ten thousand men worked in the summer fishery off Newfoundland. The Pilgrims came to the new world to found a devout colony and to catch cod, and in some respects they failed at both. They couldn't find enough fish to keep from starving in those early years and they soon splintered into far-flung settlements. But later colonists had better luck. Soon, communities dotting the New England coast sprouted acres of spruce "flakes"—vast platforms fashioned from tree bark on which they laid out fish to dry, split and salted, before shipping them to far-off lands. In the years before the Revolutionary War, fishermen catching cod on hand-lines turned Boston into a humming engine of global trade and made the merchant class wealthy.

Naturally, the men of Martha's Vineyard and their neighbors on Nantucket took to the maritime life with zeal. "Go where you will from Nova Scotia to the Mississippi," French-American author J. Hector St. John de Crèvecoeur noted in 1782, "you will find almost everywhere some natives of these two islands employed in seafaring occupations." In the 1800s more than half of the Vineyard's teenage boys went to sea as merchant seamen, whalers and fishermen. The 1850 census counted 686 mariners, making it the most popular island occupation. They were part of the long line of seafaring New Englanders who fished every square inch of water, every channel and underwater nub from Georges Bank to the Grand Banks and beyond. They sailed to China and the Arctic. They survived booms and busts, wars and trade embargoes. Men made fortunes or got swindled or drowned in horrible gales.

The island lost hundreds of its own to the sea. Edgartown listed 130 victims in a survey covering 1767 to 1827—men felled by yellow fever, drowned after whales attacked their boats, lost at sea. One was "eaten up by an alligator." In 1824 six men died in the infamous mutiny on the *Globe,* which was led by a delusional Nantucket boat steerer with a flair for the dramatic named Samuel Comstock. ("I am the bloody man!" he crowed at the end of it all.) Whaling became a key industry in Edgartown and numerous captains called it home, among them a man who may or may not have inspired the creation of Captain Ahab in *Moby-Dick,* Valentine Pease Jr. of Edgartown. Melville set sail with the typically dictatorial captain a decade before he wrote his classic novel. He jumped ship eighteen months into the voyage. Vineyard whaleman George Fred Tilton—Zeb and Zack's great-uncle—famously walked and mushed thousands of miles down the coast of Alaska to get help for a fleet of boats trapped in the ice off Alaska in the winter of 1897–98.

All the while, islanders tapped into smaller-scale fisheries closer to home. They fished the Vineyard and Nantucket sounds for bluefish, striped bass, and mackerel, and they mined the waters of Nomans

Land—a small island three miles southwest of the Vineyard—for cod. They worked pound nets stationed just off the beach. They took eels from the ponds. A summertime shantytown sprang up across the channel from Menemsha to house watermen tending to hundreds of lobster pots; naturally, it became known as Lobsterville. Even Vineyarders who did not work in the maritime trades might fish for their own food. They would haul in herring or hake, salt them, dry the catch on their roofs, and make fishcakes for the winter months. The islanders were steeped in fishing—brined, so to speak. "Everyone on the Vineyard, from the toddling child to the oldest maiden lady, knows something about fishing, whether indulging in the pastime or not," the *Gazette* reported in 1949. Even today, islanders wade into the ponds near their homes to dig up clams and scallops for dinner. A striper filet counts as legal tender in certain establishments.

Mark Alan Lovewell, the *Gazette* fisheries writer, mourns the decline in families who earn their living from the sea. He has come to see the fisherman as something akin to sachems: men who deserve islanders' attention and respect. They are keepers of a vanishing maritime history, he said. "The old guys on the waterfront are our elders." (It took a while for him to come around to that opinion. When the *Gazette* gave him the fishing beat in the 1980s, he quickly discovered he'd landed one of the paper's most trying assignments. He'll never forget the first time he drove down to the harbor to meet and photograph fisherman. "Guys would be brutal. These guys would not talk to me. They would *moon* me. I mean, they turned around and pulled down their pants!" But as the years went by these salty characters became cherished friends.)

Today, freedom on the seas has given way to nets of government regulation. Fishermen spend as much time navigating quotas, permits, and red tape as they do piloting through tricky currents, hidden shoals, and stormy weather. Convoluted rules circumscribe their working lives, determining how many days fishermen can spend at sea, which waters they can work, which species they can keep on which days, how many fish they can sell. As it is, many fish populations have declined sharply (with the exception of the striped bass). Some islanders still run small draggers for squid, fluke, and skate. They tend traps for lobster, sea bass, and conch, a Caribbean delicacy. They dredge up scallops in the fall and winter. But the days of families making a living hunting inshore fish are over. Most commercial fishermen need second and third jobs.

Vineyard fishermen had harpooned swordfish for more than a century, but long-lining—setting out up to forty miles of hooks—decimated the population within two decades. The fisheries scientists say the species is rebounding, but they are still scarce enough that a crowd of fifty people showed up when Jonathan Mayhew and the *Quitsa Strider II* returned one September day in 2006 with a 655-pound sword. It would have been considered routine two decades earlier, but now it was a newspaper story. Jonathan's twenty-three-year-old son, Matthew, hurled the harpoon that day. At least five generations of Mayhews have struck a swordfish—but Matthew may be the last. In Menemsha, a painted swordfish graces the weathervane atop the Texaco and another one, a steel and cement sculpture, rises from the dunes near the beach. It's hard not to see these as memorials to the harbor's past. Today, the Vineyard produces fish of a different sort: striped bass forged from copper that sell for $10,000 and grace the weathervanes atop the island's trophy homes, and bluefish sewn onto golf shirts and beach bags that sell for $40 at the Menemsha Blues boutique. The year his son landed the giant sword, Jonathan Mayhew put the boat on the market. A year later, he sold the federal permits that allowed him to trawl for offshore fish, protesting that convoluted government regulations had made it increasingly difficult for Menemsha's family fishermen to earn a living at sea.

When Walter Wlodyka talks about the men who are still trying to carry on the tradition, he could just as well be talking about himself. "They aspired to be fishing their whole lives, and all of a sudden the rug was pulled out from under them. There's a whole generation of independent fishermen, people who started out their lives doing what they were happiest at, making money at it, and then all of a sudden—nothing. Regulations. Closures. This, that, and the other thing."

He stopped, as if his entire fishing life were flashing across his brain.

"Hardest thing I ever did was come ashore."

Lev—it means "lion" in Russian—was born in 1979, soon after the Wlodykas moved to the island. Before he even started school he was learning about fish and how to find them, going out on the *Sea Heir* with his parents and culling through the catch they dredged up from the seafloor. "He was a fishing fool from the time he could stand up," Walter said.

Men who make a living catching fish tend to look on sportsmen's contests with scorn. There was a time, however, when Walter counted himself among the lunatic combatants trying to win the Martha's Vineyard Derby. In 1998, he did it, with a 14.99-pound false albacore. Betty once explained her family's life during the competition this way: "There's fishing, and then there's the rest of it." As a boy, Lev would whine about getting up early to go fishing. No matter. Walter would pick him out of bed at four in the morning and lay him, still dozing, in the bow of the boat. He wouldn't wake up until they were out on the water. Walter knew the kid would be more upset if he'd been left behind. On school days, he would pick up Lev at two-thirty in the afternoon and they'd load the boat with two totes of baitfish and catch ridiculous numbers of bluefish.

They'd sell what they could, weigh the biggest at derby headquarters, and release the rest.

That's how Lev won the first junior derby he entered at the age of seven. That year, 1986, the contest ended at nine on a Sunday morning. They went out at four a.m. and calculated that they'd need to turn back by seven-fifteen to get to the weigh station in time. Naturally, Lev hooked up at precisely seven-fifteen. He landed the fish and they flew back to Menemsha, jumped in the truck, and reached the weigh station with minutes to spare. The bluefish weighed 16 pounds and won Lev a bicycle he was too small to ride. Overwhelmed, he bawled his eyes out at the awards ceremony.

By age nine Lev was getting himself out of bed. "He used to sneak out of here at three in the morning," Walter said, "and I'd get up and there'd be a note." He got his first boat, a tin skiff, at age eleven. But his parents quickly deemed it too dangerous for a boy who refused to respect its obvious limitations and upgraded it to a thirteen-foot Whaler. Lev and his friends would power the boat through boulder-strewn water around the Gay Head cliffs to fish for bass. They had no radar, just a fish finder that showed water depth. When fog socked in the island or they returned after dark, it would take them an hour and a half to get home. Two of them would sit on the bow with flashlights and watch for rocks.

After that first year Lev kept winning. He was twenty when he first won the real deal. His awards crowd Walter's house. In the basement, an entire wall is lined with prize rods. In the TV room hang plaques and pictures and a front-page profile of the Wlodykas in the *Gazette,* which had the guys on Squid Row giving Lev grief. "You're cursed!" they told him. "You're never going to catch a damned thing again!" In the dining room—under track lighting—hangs the 52-pound striper Lev caught the same week the story ran, which shut the loudmouths on Squid Row right the hell up. Lev had the derby winner there in the boat while they were working him over. If he lives to be a hundred years old, he'll never experience a moment more perfectly satisfying.

In the summers as a teenager Lev went offshore for tuna, either with a captain Walter hired to run his commercial boat, the *Freelance,* or on the *Jesse J* with Karsten Larsen, the latest in a long line of island fishermen. (The Larsens run the fish markets in Menemsha and Vineyard Haven.) Lev wasn't allowed to take the family boat himself because his father knew the teenager would stay out in nasty weather and risk sinking it. The guys would do three days, come in, sleep, and go right back out. One summer, Lev must have spent fifty days on the two boats. "No horizon was too far," Walter said. "He wanted it all."

There were years when it looked like Lev's life would veer in some other direction. In high school, he was a stand-out hockey goaltender —maybe good enough for Division I, maybe good enough to make it to the NHL. But it didn't happen. He went to New England College but left after a semester. He just wanted to live and work on the Vineyard. Why did he need a college degree? Later, he took up snowboarding and carried it to predictably maniacal heights. He had a friend whose father owned a farm in Vermont and they would climb to the top of his barn, hurtle off the roof, and sail down a hill to a jump that—if they hit it just right—would send them shooting over a set of power lines. If they hit it wrong they'd break something. Lev spent one winter up there skiing and living in another friend's unheated storage barn. He'd sleep in his ski gear, tucking himself between several cast-off mattresses for warmth. When the frigid air hit his lungs each morning, it would be so cold he would gasp. A run at the professional snowboarding circuit—sponsorships, money, free gear, girls—never quite got off the ground.

Walter had it right: Lev was born to fish. Maybe it doesn't exactly pay the bills. Jen designs and plants sweeping gardens for customers who spend thousands of dollars a year on flowers. Lev helps out with her business, does miscellaneous home-repair work, and mans a Bobcat to maintain a dirt road that passes properties he could never afford. But during the six-week summer commercial striper season and the fall derby, fishing makes him an independent man on the water. In July and August, he is after tons of fish. In September and October, he is after that one rare giant that will earn him a shot at the grand prize—and more derby glory.

One morning early in the tournament, Lev's alarm clock goes off and he's up and out of bed like any other working stiff. It's 5:30 a.m. He pulls on a hooded sweatshirt and a pair of brown Carhartt work pants and stumbles through the kitchen and out the door. In the half-light he passes a dozen fishing rods lined against the house (which is tiny), a few fish coolers (enormous), and an electric drill (battered) that he uses to take old line off his reels. I drop one of my rods into the bed of his truck and we fly down the two-lane road to Menemsha. He hits the power on the radio and turns up a classic rock station. *"It's been a long time since I rock and rolled!"* Robert Plant screams from 1971. It's the first week of the derby and there's no easing into things this morning.

Lev is preoccupied with Zeb Tilton. It's not just that he's leading the boat bass division. He's also in position to wrest away one of Lev's prized possessions: the record for heaviest grand slam in the boat division, 81.61 pounds. The grand slam champions from boat and shore are regarded as the Vineyard's best fishermen, and Zeb has tallied more than 72 pounds from his boat in the first week alone. He still needs a bluefish that weighs a little more than 9 pounds but he shouldn't have much trouble doing that. If Zeb swipes his record, Lev will spend the next year (or God knows how long) taking crap about it from his trash-talking friends.

Today's plan is no different than usual: take *Wampum* out to the hot spot he found earlier in the derby and try for big bass. But when we get to the dock the wind is howling off the water, and he has second thoughts. "I'm not going out," he says. It's not the high winds or the rough seas he's worried about. That he can handle. We'd be drifting eels over the boulders, and he can tell by looking at the harbor that the wind would push *Wampum* over the rocks a bit too fast. Our baits would zip past the fish instead of floating by at a natural pace. The all-important presentation of bait to bass would be wrong, and we'd get nothing for our early-morning suffering.

Instead, he drives over to the parking lot on the other side of the harbor. He pulls up to Karsten's truck and bums a cigarette, then stops at the beach. He looks out the windows for signs of albies off the jetty and peeks in his rearview mirror to see if the Texaco has opened: he needs coffee. Antsy as always, he pulls out his cell phone to call a friend who'd gone bass fishing last night. When he hangs up he sees the owner of the gas station arrive, and he starts the engine and drives the hundred or so feet over there. But the doors are still locked. He presses his face to the glass in vain, then jumps back in the truck, shivering, and drives back to the beach. Fish are breaking off the beach but nothing is happening on the jetty.

A friend pulls up in his pickup, parks a foot from Lev's truck, and rolls down his passenger window.

"You still second in boat bass, Lev?"

"Think so," Lev says. "First loser."

4

"Sleep When You Die"

Derby fanatics Brian Long and Brad Upp.

Dave Skok is sitting on the hood of a parked Jeep, his head buried in a fly-fishing magazine. Brice Contessa leans over his shoulder and marvels at a striking photograph of an angler whose boat looks as if it is being swallowed by rough seas. Tom Rapone is slouched against the next car over, his hands tucked into his waders, peering through his sunglasses at the water.

Killing time between fish: it's the other derby pastime.

Last year, they had a lot of days like this because nobody could find an albie or bonito for the life of him. Dave went home fishless—

skunked is the term of art—nineteen out of twenty-one days. "Last year was pretty damned depressing," he says. "Last year we thought a lot about life."

You can imagine how the derby amateurs felt if three of the professionals couldn't find fish. Dave is a fly fisherman extraordinaire. He designs and ties flies for a living; his Mushmouth became a minor hit a few years back. During the derby he is a false albacore specialist, having won the shore albie division with nearly identical fish in 2000 (12.96 pounds) and 2001 (12.97). He caught both on flies—a rare victory over the guys using regular gear—and he won the boat in 2001. "Now I'm trying to figure out what I'm going to do with the rest of my life," he told one interviewer. "All I ever wanted was to win the derby." Tom and Brice are young fly-fishing guides and the three of them hold five spots on the derby's fly-rod leaderboard this year.

They're sitting beside the Edgartown marina, which buzzes with yachts and fishing boats. The *On Time* ferries, which look like little more than floating hunks of roadway, muscle relentlessly back and forth every few minutes, lugging three cars at a time across the current rushing between Chappaquiddick and downtown Edgartown. If not for the derby, it would be a perfect day to shed all of the fishing gear and lay on the beach, or go home and fall asleep reading a good book. But as we daydream about better things to do, a school of albies bursts in front of the town's black-and-white lighthouse on the other side of the harbor.

"Oh, yeah!" Dave cries out, breaking away from the magazine. "They're hungry!"

We jump into our cars and drive onto the *On Time,* and within a couple of minutes we're winding through the town's manicured streets. We park next to a path to the water, and I open the hatchback of my car and pull out my fly rod with the same sense of looming failure that I get when I approach the first tee with golf partners.

A good fly-fishing cast, in fact, is exactly like a good golf swing: it's all in the mechanics. I wish I could tell you I have them, but I don't. Casting far enough to reach these fish in the harbor will require a technique known as a double haul. It sounds complicated, and it is. Out at the water's edge, the real fly fishermen start unleashing powerful casts, their lines unfurling perfectly and their flies dropping eighty feet out, easy. But we quickly realize that none of us will be reeling in anything here. The fish are out in the middle of the channel and they're not coming in.

Dave stops casting and, while we watch and wait in vain, he starts singing an off-key dirge. "Edgartown casters! I feel sadness for you*uuuuuu*!" It's a takeoff on a preposterous German techno song, "Amusement Park Diers," by a wacky band called Porsches on the Autobahn. (Don't ask. The point is that this is the sort of distorted crap that happens when the fishing isn't.)

Dave and I get to talking about the capriciousness of the false albacore, and why anglers have struggled to get them from the beach in recent derbies. "I don't have a theory," Dave says. "There are too many variables for me to have a legitimate theory. Albies do what they want." He can calculate wind and tides and baitfish populations and still go to the wrong spots and catch nothing for days—a whole lot of days. "Memories are selective. You tend not to remember so much about years ago. You think the fishing was epic every day. You never remember those days when you fell asleep on the beach and woke up to more nothingness."

The fish continue to crash out in the distance, and one by one, the fishermen flop down on the beach and shoot the shit. Somebody catches a tiny dogfish and it writhes in the air like a snake as Tom holds it by the tail and admires its eyes, black slashes on pale lenses, the eyes of a horror-show demon. He puts his finger in its mouth to feel its bite before returning it to the water.

After a few minutes of this, I look over at Dave. He's reclined on the sand, head resting on his bag, eyes shut.

A few days later, on a nasty, raw morning in the second weekend of the derby, I take a drive over to Lobsterville, across the inlet from Menemsha, and walk out to the jetty with a mind to doing what I couldn't that first day of the tournament. I want an albie. I'd been told that the first two weeks are the time to get a big one—a cold snap could send them packing. Yesterday, somebody caught a 13.39-pounder on the beach to take the lead. No doubt another one is swimming around today and, if I understand this crapshoot division of the derby correctly, I have as good a shot as anybody of bringing it in.

Out on the last rock, I run into Tom Rapone again. The fly fisherman is in orange foul-weather gear and layers of fleece. If I had a camera I could take a picture and sell it to a fly-fishing magazine: whitecaps marching in formation, spray exploding against the rocks, Tom casting into the wind. Unlike last week, today he is all business. Conditions are right for this spot. The seas are choppy but the water is clear, the tide is coming in, and the wind is blowing the bait up to the rocks. He's been out here for six hours, since dawn, and twenty thousand casts later (his computation) he's landed one 9-pound albie and lost two others. He's cold, tired, and ready to call it a day. The weather is deteriorating.

And then, without warning, the jetty turns on, in the predictably unpredictable way of the false albacore. The fish flash around us, chasing bait and breaking the surface of the waves in quick, concentrated bursts. Unlike a week ago on the other jetty, there are only a handful of us here to see it and I have a clear shot. We make a few casts, Tom with the fly rod, me with my spinning outfit. There's a pause, and just as quickly as the fish appeared they vanish. We watch the water, swiveling our heads in three directions.

Then they're back. "Right there, Dave," Tom says, pointing to an explosion of feeding fish in the channel and at the same moment flipping his fly out into the chaos. A second later he's on. I watch him hop to the tip and plant the bowed fly rod against his hip and bring in the fish. He tucks the rod under his armpit and works the fly out with his pliers. The fish is released—it's smaller than the other one he caught—and he is back to work, casting, casting, casting.

A few minutes later the fish materialize in the channel again. I get my lure into the melee and finally hook up. I skip from rock to rock to get out to the tip so I can fight the thing without interference. I recall a piece of advice a fisherman gave me about albies: "The biggest thing is don't panic. Just let him do his thing. And you've got to be ready for the Crazy Ivans." I hold on while it zips east, then west, then in close. Finally, I bring it up to the rocks, grab it by the tail, dislodge the hook, and look it over. It's a little bullet-shaped albie with skin as smooth as glass. Its colors look like the work of an abstract artist who painted its flanks a metallic green and chrome and then scraped it with a putty knife to give it a battle-scarred effect. On its back is a band of dark squiggles. The fish is about 8½ pounds, Tom tells me, and I could keep it—I'd be one-quarter of the way to my grand slam from shore—but I put a hand under its belly, point it toward the sea, and send it diving back in headfirst. It hits the water and shoots off in a flash and I keep hunting for something bigger.

A fisherman I'd met before the derby warned me about this moment. Catch your first albie, he said, and you may forget about everything else. The little speedsters are like crack for fishing addicts. Tom leaves and I work the jetty for a while, hoping for another, and another, and another. I make a hundred casts at fish I can't see. Then the gusts start. Thirty- and forty-mile-per-hour blasts fire pinpricks of rain at me, and it becomes a struggle to stay upright.

As quickly as it had come over me the albie spell breaks. I flee for my car without a glance back at the water, thereby breaking the professional fishermen's rule about properly exiting a jetty during the derby, which is to:

(1) take three steps;
(2) stop;
(3) look back at the water;
(4) repeat until the sea is out of sight.

You never know. The mother of all albie blitzes might erupt when you have your back turned.

I'm starting to think Menemsha has gotten a bad rap. The fishermen who told me about it before the derby began had me expecting daily fisticuffs, but all I see is a succession of peaceful days. Guys work every conceivable angle to get at albies and bonito. They line Lobsterville's rocks, work the point of the Menemsha jetty, try the channel, cast from the crook of the L, use the boat dock deep inside the channel, jump on the rusting commercial fishing boats for a closer shot. Some days, when the fish are in and anglers are everywhere, the harbor seems like an amphitheater created expressly for fishermen.

The second Sunday of the derby is one of those days. Twenty-four hours after I survive the buffeting winds on Lobsterville, the storm front has moved out to sea and left behind weather made for college-football tailgating, bright and crisp. Emboldened by my first successful tangle with the false albacore, I claim a spot out at the tip and cast with newfound confidence. Next to me stands the most relentless man in Menemsha, a crusty guy who fishes the jetty nearly every day of the derby, from dawn to dusk—unless the Patriots are playing, in which case he takes the afternoon off. Lev put it this way one morning: "If he dies, we'll have to bronze him and put him out there. That dude is *rugged*." Someone calculated that he spends 350 hours on the jetty during the derby. (Alas, the granddaddy of the jetty rats rebuffed my writerly approaches. Too many lies in fishing books.)

As the jetty fills up, a big grizzly of a man named Brad Upp strides out and makes his presence known.

Brad and his friend Brian Long—a.k.a. Gib, a.k.a. Skipper—have been fishing this spot for ages, and they are about to give me a lesson in how seriously two men can take the derby. Brad shouts greetings and shakes hands and sets up his rod and reel and starts to cast. He's wearing a long-sleeved Phillies T-shirt and cargo pants and they're straining against his midsection, which he says has been expanding lately thanks to his enormous appetite. (He's been eating two large pizzas at a sitting, say, or six thick hamburgers.) He takes in the whole harbor scene: 360 degrees of happy sights, harbor, beach, jetty, waves, distant islands, the lighthouse atop the Gay Head cliffs. "All I can say is, it's great to be here. I've been climbing the walls. When I'm feeling pretty fucked up I imagine I'm standing right here."

"Here?" one of the jaded islanders says, not quite buying it.

"Yeah," Brad says. "It works. Whenever I'm having problems, I just imagine I'm standing right here. The problems just melt away."

I'd heard about Brad and Skipper, and within minutes of introducing myself they seem to have welcomed me into their circle of trust. This being their first day of the derby, they're full of vacation energy. I quickly learn that Brad lives not far from me outside Philadelphia and works in the fire protection business. His favorite Philly cheesesteak comes from Mama's on Belmont Avenue in a suburb called Bala Cynwyd. ("They have their own blend of four cheeses. And they have their own bread. Nothing compares.") His great-

great-great-uncle fought during the Civil War, Union side, and died in the bloody assault on Sam Watkins's Company H at the Dead Angle on Kennesaw Mountain in Georgia. Brad visits the battle-field every year to hunt for war relics with a metal detector—buttons, bullets, artillery shells. He plays the guitar in a band at Civil War reenactments. Skipper is Brad's former dope dealer and current best friend. He now lives in Fort Collins, Colorado, with his wife and two sons, who will be joining him on the island next week. He runs a small chain of bagel shops named Gib's NY Bagels, and has been coming to the Derby with Brad for fifteen years now.

"It's the greatest event that ever happened," Brad says. "I don't know if I can put it into words. It's an overwhelming experience."

A few minutes later he is lifting up his Phillies shirt to show me his back. "You want a good picture to throw in the book?"

"The derby tat," Skipper remarks.

On Brad's back is a tattoo that's the size of one of those pizzas he's been wolfing down. It's a fisherman's coat of arms: an eight-pointed compass rose, crested with a fleur-de-lis, encircles a map of Martha's Vineyard. A scroll wends its way around the arms of the rose and the four derby fish swim around it. Symbols float about like circling electrons: the runic symbol for daylight, or clarity; a triskele, the ancient Celtic symbol related to reincarnation and the sun; the astrological symbol for Neptune, Roman god of the seas; an alchemist's symbol for autumn.

"It's just to show the level of dedication," Brad says. "I wasn't kidding, man. Let me tell you something right now. It's not about the fishing. It's about a whole other thing. We came out here for three days in '92 in my illegal, fake-license-plate Cadillac that broke down four times while we were here." Skipper had to leave early, he explains, and Brad slept in the car, freezing under a thin Mexican blanket. The next year, Brad scraped some money together and called his friend. "I was like, 'I'll pay for it, but we've gotta go back.'

So we came back out again. And we've evolved. Now, we stay in a residence."

He watches one of the regulars down a nip and take a swig from a Bud. "Shot and a beer!" he notes with sarcastic enthusiasm, then continues. "Me and Skipper, our axis is thrown out of kilter if we don't come here to realign, get our chi back in line for the year. If I didn't come here I'd be in Norristown State Hospital." That's the nearest asylum back home.

"He's saying all this shit," Skipper says, "but it's true. It really is. I mean, it's heavy."

Here's how heavy. When they're dead and gone they want to take up residence on their favorite fishing spot. They've left instructions for their next of kin to burn up their corpses, take their ashes to the Menemsha jetty, and let them fly out into the sound.

The story behind their intensity, it gradually comes out, is that they are recovering alcoholics and drug addicts. The derby is their New Year's Eve bender. Some people go out on December 31 and get drunk. Brad and Skipper come here every September and stay sober.

"I've tried to explain it to people," Skipper says.

"They say, 'You going on your fishing trip?'" Brad says, mock condescension in his voice.

"You going on your fishing trip?" Skipper mimics.

"It's *not* a fishing trip," Brad says.

Skipper adds, "I tell them it's like dropping acid. You can't understand it until you experience it."

The two of them had arrived the night before and headed over to Coop's Bait and Tackle to sign up for the derby, where they got a hearty greeting from Lela and Cooper Gilkes. ("We just love those guys," Coop told me later. "There is a *hahd* couple of boys, let me tell you. Those guys do some fishing.") Then they stopped at the grocery store so they could make lunch to bring to the jetty. They crashed at "the shack," the rustic little house in the woods that they rent every year. The next morning, they drove to Menemsha in Brad's giant Ford pickup, opened the tailgate, and started to set up. When they arrived, a crew of photographers and models were in the middle of a shoot on the Squid Row gas dock for a women's clothing catalog called Appleseed's. A fresh-faced beauty wearing white pants and boat shoes sat in front of a spotless boat, smiling as she reached into a beach bag.

One hundred feet and a world away, Brad and Skipper stood on the beach around an abalone shell filled with flaming sweet grass, sage, and lavender. They were marking their arrival at Menemsha with an opening ceremony. Joining them was a Vineyard postman who has become part of their derby circle, a low-key fisherman they call Woolite. They etched the cardinal directions in the sand using a knife with a handle fashioned from a deer femur. Each of them took up the shell and smudged himself with the charred herbs and said a few words. They thanked the higher powers and then dedicated the derby to someone dear. Skipper chose his aunt, who had recently passed away, and a friend back in Colorado, who would die of cancer by the end of the year. They asked that the gods of the north, south, east, and west bless the derby and their friendship. After the contents of the shell burned up, they flipped it over and buried it in the sand. Only then did they take to the jetty to fish.

Their derby obsession began a few years after they met at Franklin Pierce College in Rindge, New Hampshire. They were both into drugs. Skipper was selling and Brad was buying. First, they were mortal enemies. ("He threatened to have me killed in 1989," Brad says.) Then they became friends, and eventually they both got scared straight. Skipper's epiphany came at the tail end of a three-year stretch spent following the Grateful Dead around on tour. One day he ended up in jail on drug charges—'shrooms and pot—and he realized he was destined to be a screw-up unless he could change course. Brad hit bottom on October 27, 1989. After enduring a long, heavy talk with his father, a military veteran who went to college on the GI Bill and had no interest in paying the tuition while his son got high every day, Brad had a particularly awful night. "I was crumpled and beaten up. I was just like, 'It's got to stop.'"

The derby came into their lives a few years later. In 1991 Skipper spent the summer and fall on the island. He met a surfcaster who introduced him to the whole derby drill—fish the night tides, sleep a couple of hours, fish the dawn, and then go to work. When the derby ended Skipper left for Colorado with plans to return. Soon, though, he got the idea of opening the bagel shop. (It would take him three years to turn idea into reality.) He never moved back to the Vineyard, but he returned for the 1992 derby with Brad, who loved it and insisted they return year after year.

In 1994 they learned what the derby had come to mean to them. Skipper had just launched his new business and couldn't pull himself away. Brad took the ferry over and tried to fish solo. He ended up calling Skipper at least five times a day, and after two days of that he packed the car and left. It just wasn't the same.

Ever since, they've both made the trip, although al-Qaeda made it difficult in 2001. Flights were grounded right before Skipper was supposed to leave for New England, and his mother was terrified about him flying into Logan International Airport in Boston, from which two of the 9/11 planes had departed. But they still made it. Brad commemorated their small but glorious victory over international terrorism by having "2001" added to the scroll on his tattoo.

Every year, something crops up to threaten the trip. This year during his Vineyard escape, Brad's company was scheduled to install a major fire pump for a client. Ordinarily he would have overseen the operation, but he took a deep breath and left the job in his employees' hands. (He caught a break: delivery of the pump was delayed.) Skipper left in the middle of a year when he was taking over two bagel shops from struggling licensees, which had more or less tripled his workload. "Nothing messes with the derby," Skipper said. "I gave my staff a yee-haw rallying speech. They all know about the derby, and they were like, 'Don't worry about it. You go and do the derby.'"

So here they are, on the jetty on the third Sunday in September, in their own little nirvana.

Brad, who has musical inclinations, ordered an English squeeze box to play when the fish weren't around, but it didn't arrive in time. Instead, he brought his harmonica, and when the fishing is sluggish and he's tired of talking he pulls it out and plays sea chanteys. But mostly he talks—to me, to Skipper, to nobody. His conversational abilities are expansive, and he taps a rich vein of knowledge and opinion about religion and fishing and history. Somehow, on this Sunday atop the jetty, we get to talking about holidays. Brad makes it clear—and I'm only lightly paraphrasing— that he would rather have a fishhook jammed into his hand, be thrown down concrete steps, have his foot rolled over by a car, eat glass, be diagnosed with cancer, get his throat slit from ear to ear, or be pronounced *dead* than endure another traditional holiday. Speaking of which: what he would really like to do is teach history. But the fact is the derby falls in the first month of school, and no headmaster would let him take two weeks off to go fish on the Vineyard in September. The list of official school holidays is well established—Thanksgiving, Christmas, President's Day— and the derby is not on it.

"I love history and I love teaching and I go back and forth. Did I make a mistake? Should I be teaching history? Did I sell myself short?" he asks. "But then I think about it and I'm like, I can't miss this." Call it a personal sacrifice, a lifestyle choice. Maybe he can become a teacher after he becomes independently wealthy—say, after his regular lottery habit pays off with a massive jackpot. "I'll teach recreationally, on a volunteer basis, do little programs. Like, in February. As long as it doesn't fall on Groundhog Day, which is my high holiday."

"Come on," I say.

"It's the only holiday without an agenda," says Brad, who is all about live and let live. ("Non-Judgment Day Is Near" reads one of the bumper stickers on his pickup. "Born OK the First Time" reads another.) I ask him if he's ever gone to the wild Groundhog Day festivities every February in Punxsutawney, Pennsylvania, during which thousands of people convene on Gobbler's Knob and party all night as they await the weather prediction from the overgrown rodent.

"Every year," he says proudly. "I have a groundhog suit. Dude, I'm there."

"A groundhog suit? What's it look like?"

"It's brown and I'm fully ensconced in it."

"So you're like a mascot."

"Yeah, but it's more than that. Listen, the practice of Ground-hog Day starts with Saint Brigid with the festival lights, Candlemas. We're talking seven thousand years ago, five thousand years ago. We're predating Christianity here. The Druids and the Celts—those people all celebrated this ancient ritual. Even the early nomads in Germania would wink when they saw this creature come out. 'It's time to start marauding.'"

Brad pauses, and perhaps an image flashes across his mind—a vision of himself doing Irish jigs in central Pennsylvania wearing his custom-made groundhog suit.

"My family members think I'm a heretic, man," he adds. "But hey, what are you going to do?"

* * *

A few days later I spot Brad and Skipper walking off the rocks with their rods and a couple of empty pizza boxes. Three days into their stay they are exhausted. But they've had some excitement. One of the regulars on the Menemsha jetty spotted a mortal enemy walking onto the rocks and threatened to punch the guy in the face. The potential victim did a one-eighty and bolted down the rocks, with the regular in pursuit, and hightailed it into the Texaco to call the cops, who arrived and did their best to calm things down. (The aggressor's beef, it came out later, had nothing to do with Menemsha politics, or fishing, or even the derby, but permission to use a piece of private property for hunting. It landed on the derby's Internet message board under the heading "meat heads.")

Tonight, Brad, Skipper, and Woolite are planning to fish their favorite up-island spot and they invite me along. Skipper has some sort of lung ailment, and they need night-fishing bait, so Brad is heading to Edgartown for Robitussin and frozen mackerel.

I follow Skipper and Woolite out to their house. The big kitchen table ("where things get discussed," Skipper says) is covered with cups and fishing gear and Lucky Charms and derby papers. Rods lean in the corners. They sit me down and try again to explain what the derby does to them. Skipper favors T-shirts and white skateboarding shoes and his hairstyle is best classified as windblown. He speaks in a tranquil, measured, earnest voice. During the competition, Skipper says, "every layer of the onion is peeled down. We're basically sitting there in our tighty-whities by the end. We're sitting there with maybe a little drool coming from our lips. We're worn out. It's like the biggest therapy session anybody could go through."

To Skipper, the derby commemorates his sobriety. Anytime he feels a craving coming on, he thinks about losing his wife and kids and his business. But he also thinks about losing the derby. It is his most cherished escape, something that's helped him stay clean. One night at a restaurant in Edgartown, Brad and Skipper gave me a

glimpse of how tenuous their recovery remains. We were eating dinner and I thoughtlessly ordered a beer. Each of them picked up the
glass and put it under his nose and gave it a deep, sustained sniff. If
they took one drink, they swore to me, they wouldn't stop until they
were passed out on the sidewalk in a pile of their own vomit. There
wasn't enough beer in the world to quench their thirst. When I suggested the obvious—that the derby is their safe alternative to traditional addictions, that feeling a fish strike reproduces the high they
got from drugs and alcohol—they didn't disagree. All serious fishermen are like junkies. They'll endure the elements and stay out all
night for the chance to experience one electric moment. For anglers
and addicts it's all about the next hit.

We drive to the beach, and Brad is already there. He brought
the mackerel and butterfish but not the cough syrup. He got dis-
tracted by a conversation with Coop, who had put them on this spot
some years ago and told Brad that if I described it in any detail in
my book they would be banned from Coop's for life. (Coop insisted
later that they were just pulling my leg, but I'm still not saying where
we fished that night.) The ground rules set, we trudge over the dunes
for a few hours of fishing. We're bottom-fishing: attaching lead sinkers a couple of feet from our hooks and casting out chunks of bait,
which hover just off the seafloor. But our offerings go untouched,
and around midnight I call it quits and drive back to the house in
Vineyard Haven where I'm renting a room.

I fall asleep thinking about . . . sleep deprivation. I've fished a lot
in these early days of the derby but I'm still getting six hours of shut-
eye a night. I'm starting to feel guilty, like I'm slacking off on the job.
"Sleep's overrated," a fisherman named Morgan Child had advised
me a few days ago. "Sleep when you die." He was standing on the
deck of a friend's boat, his hands tucked inside his orange foul-weather
gear. Morgan and his friend Nick Warburton were relentless. Their
drill, as far as I could tell, was to leave the dock at four-thirty in the

morning, fish until one in the afternoon, come back for food, bait, and gas, and head back out around four to fish until well past dark. Yet Morgan always had a smile on his face. "I *like* sleep deprivation," he explained. "After a day without sleep, you just don't care."

One morning a few days later I call an angler named Dave Nash to see about getting out on the beach with him. Dave is a retired state bureaucrat who bought a house on the island a decade ago. He has a laid-back manner and a high-pitched laugh, like he's in on the joke, and although he loves to fish he's not a man I would have expected to be hardcore when I first met him. He asks me how I'm doing and I tell him I'm pacing myself, trying to not to get too exhausted.

"You need to do that for a couple of days," he says cheerfully. "You need to start to experience the hallucinations." Clearly, I've read Dave Nash all wrong.

Soon enough, as it turns out, I've made a date with derby-inflicted delirium. A few hours after I hang up with Dave I'm on a boat with an anesthesiologist trolling for albies and drifting for bass. At midnight I'm out prospecting for bass and bluefish with a retired businessman; we stay out until seven in the morning. I've barely slept when I bump into Brad and Skipper a few hours later on the Menemsha jetty. It could be exhaustion starting to gnaw at my brain, but they look different than they did the last time I saw them. Things seem to be falling apart a bit. Skipper's boys, aged ten and fourteen, have arrived for a week, and one of them is at the island hospital getting treated for a sinus infection. None of them made it out last night, and Brad's upset. Woolite is nursing a cold, and as far as he's concerned the bass fishing stinks and it's not worth working the night tides until the water gets colder. Brad doesn't want to hear it. Hell if he is going to go home and lay on the couch. He can do that all winter.

One of Brad's old friends from college—he is introduced to me only as The Rogue—is on the island and we all make plans to go eat dinner in Edgartown, then fish the beach after nightfall. But when we get downtown Brad and The Rogue are gung ho to get on the water. There's no time for a meal, which, in any case, would have the effect of a tranquilizer dart to the neck. Nobody would be able to move. Instead, we hit Al's Liquor Store for nighttime provisions: Ritz peanut butter crackers, Combos, chips, Rice Krispies treats, a six-pack of Coke bottles, and, for The Rogue, a forty-ounce beer and a bottle of Yellowtail. We caravan to the South Shore and wend down a long dirt road to a parking lot. If it were June we'd need one of those $375,000 keys, but tonight the gate is open and nobody is on the beach.

Two weeks into the derby the shore categories are still wide open—a 27.99-pound bass and a 10.73-pound bluefish lead the way, both smallish by derby standards. We know the winner is still out there, some 40- or 50-pounder willing to lunge at a piece of stinking, bloody bait swaying just off the ocean bottom. Brad is not the type to bring a lot of scientific analysis to the sport, and winning isn't the point for him. But at the same time he still checks the leaderboard every day, and winning *would* be nice. The idea seems to give him hope. Like Brad's other pursuits—searching for rare artifacts with a metal detector, playing the lottery—the derby touches some deep-seated need to gamble against long odds.

We set up our rods, slice up the fish, hook on chunks, and cast them out. Brad pulls out the radio and dials in a Philadelphia station. The Phillies are losing again, and he listens with mortal dread as the game goes along. The season appears to be slipping away. It's devastating. He can't even fish when the Phils play this poorly. He lies down on his side, holding the radio up and turning it this way and that to improve the signal. He says he feels worse than Chrissie Watkins, the girl whose body parts washed up on the beach at the start of *Jaws*. The Braves go ahead 10–6 in the ninth inning on a Chipper Jones home run, and when Phillies pinch hitter

Greg Dobbs flies out to end the game Brad switches off the radio in disgust.

The need for sleep washes over me. I pack up and leave Brad on the beach—fishless again—and get in my car. I've heard a story about a guy who was so tired he had to pull over four times to sleep on the twenty-minute drive across the island. I make it in one shot, and spend five hours in a warm bed. But then my alarm buzzes at dawn and I'm up making coffee and pulling on my stinking jeans and collecting my stuff and driving back up-island.

Morgan Taylor, the hardcore bass fisherman from Team *Hanapa'a,* is nursing a cold when we meet up in Lobsterville. It's an overcast morning, frigid with gusty winds, and Morgan is apoplectic that he cannot catch a bonito. In the days since sluggish shore fishing conditions reduced Dave Skok to warbling bad techno pop, surfcasters' fortunes have improved considerably. More than three hundred albies and two hundred bonito have been weighed in, already far more than last year, and the derby is only two weeks old. The other day, a fisherman up from North Carolina named Clark Goff Jr. joined the annals of anybody-can-win-it stories. He had never caught an albie in his life when he walked out to the Lobsterville jetty and landed a beast. He didn't know if it was big enough to keep and weigh in, so he asked somebody. "Probably," came the reply. When Clark got the fish to Edgartown it weighed 15.86 pounds and took over first place. "The only thing I could think of," Lev's buddy Geoff Codding said later, "was he was so lucky he didn't catch that fish on the Menemsha jetty. They would've been like, 'Oh no, throw it back!'"

Morgan caught his albie but he needs a bonito to complete his shore grand slam, the goal of every self-respecting derbyman. He's been targeting the funny fish for days on end, at all the right spots, and come up empty. Making matters worse, four fishermen have landed bonito standing right next to him using the same lures, equipment, and tactics. (Or is it five? He's lost count. One of them was his new *girlfriend,* for the love of God.) All he needs is one certifiable Atlantic bonito, twenty-one inches or longer, and then he can focus on night fishing for a monster striped bass. Maybe then he'll get another 50-pounder from his supersecret hot spot, which would give him a shot at first place in the shore grand slam.

His nose is clogged as we pull on waders and tuck mini tackle boxes into our pockets and tramp out to the beach. A line of fishermen stretches along the bowl that curves toward the lighthouse atop the cliffs. The word is that somebody got a huge bonito near a stick that's jammed into the sand and we start casting there. I ask Morgan if he's feeling confident. He looks at me coolly. "Confident that you're going to get a bone next to me."

The fish are here, big schools of them harassing the baitfish in the surf just in front of us. I'm anticipating a hit at any moment but I'm getting nothing. Between casts, I look over at Morgan and see him cursing, flipping off the ocean, stomping his foot. He looks like a guy who's been stung by a venomous jellyfish. I walk over and he shows me his lure. "See those teeth marks? One, two, three. Deep cuts. It was a bone. If it was an albie it would be like sandpaper." He says he watched the fish chase the lure, hit it twice, get hooked, then come off. "Stupid little green fish," he mutters. "If I get one, I'm going to have to restrain myself from ripping its head off and eating its heart."

We keep working. The fish disappear, so we climb onto the Lobsterville jetty. I try to fish the channel but somebody on the Menemsha side keeps casting over the rocks at my feet. He snares my lure once, and when it happens again I start to get genuinely angry. I want to go over there and beat the serial snagger senseless for his transgressions. Soon, the sun breaks out from behind the clouds and I'm suddenly too exhausted to do anything but drive back to Vineyard Haven, wolf down a sandwich at a deli, and crash into bed. Morgan, even with the cold, the raw nose, and the frustration, is staying all day.

As I lie in bed trying to achieve rapid-eye movement the phone rings. It's Janet Messineo, the taxidermist on sabbatical who believes the best of the derby fishermen have classic psychiatric disorders. ("The people who are really good fishermen have obsessive-compulsive behaviors right?" she told me once. "It's like we do something and we do it to *death*.") Like Morgan, she has been keeping ridiculous hours to get the bonito, and she's going on and on about it, like I'm her fish therapist. She's been trying for two weeks now and she can't get one. She'd vowed to stay upbeat this derby, to maintain a positive outlook. But her struggles have her bitter. "I hate bonito fishing. There are people who come to this island for this! All they do is stand there all day and wait for fish. I'm a bass fisherman, but I want the grand slam, so I have to do it. Don't get me wrong, I love to catch them. But the waiting? To target them all day long? I don't get it." She also can't stomach the thought that somebody spending all day soaking bait somewhere might get a big bonito and think he's a great fisherman while Janet— hardcore surfcaster, student of tides and winds, woman with countless stripers under her belt—can't get one to save her soul. "It's like, 'Oh! Slit my throat!' No bonito! You're nothing! I should forget it. I'm almost sixty years old. But I can't forget it. Here I am, the great Janet Messineo, trying to prove something. I'm insane."

Janet's sanity notwithstanding, the bonito hunt isn't keeping her from fishing for stripers every night, and we make plans to go out tonight with Ed Jerome, the derby president and her fishing partner. I never get to sleep before I meet up with Ed and Janet in a grocery store parking lot. Janet has a spot in mind that she scouted earlier in the day. We caravan over there—as it turns out, Ed was joking about the blindfold—get our gear together, cross the street, and push through a gate. But when we get to the water the current is not pulling the way Janet had expected. We make a few desultory casts, but the wind has dropped out of Janet's sails. Ed leads us over a dock and past a sign warning against trespassing—walking on the beach is kosher; walking on the seawall is not—and we try another spot but Janet is done. She's fried. At eleven, she decides she needs to sleep off this bout of derby burnout and try another night. We walk back to the cars and Janet climbs into her Blazer. The door won't shut and Ed has to spend ten minutes on the ground with a pair of pliers fixing it.

Ed is game for trying another spot on his way home. I follow him through the empty streets of Oak Bluffs and then to a bridge over an inlet to a pond. We cast eels out and I quickly get a solid strike. It's been a few days since my last good fish—long enough that I give it a tuna jerk and suffer a massive backlash on my reel. Fuming silently, I fetch a new rod and reel from my car and toss out another eel. I get another hit. It's a striper that puts up a nice fight, but when I bring it to my hand I see that it's too short to keep. The tide turns, and Ed and I go our separate ways.

It's one a.m. on Thursday morning now, and three days of fishing all four corners of the compass have netted me one short bass and a bluefish almost too tiny to mention. As I drive home I add up my hours of shut-eye since talking to Dave Nash on Monday morning. Fifteen minutes in my car at three a.m. on Tuesday, three hours later that morning, plus those five luxurious hours early Wednesday morning. I'm starting to get a heavy feeling in my skull, a familiar sensation that reminds me of pulling all-nighters in college. I'm jumpy and wobbly. I need a shower. The soles of my feet are scraped raw from the day I fished barefoot on a beach with coarse, skin-shearing sand. The pain of walking is second only to the sting that comes when I take my off socks and the skin dries and cracks. I'm a mess.

One competitor had told me between yawns (no lie) that "the human body only needs four hours of sleep." Clearly, mine doesn't work that way. My thoughts have become irrational and pessimistic, which always seems to happen when I'm running a sleep deficit: *I'm an awful angler. I'm wasting my time. This whole thing is a pointless exercise anyway.*

I sleep hard, and when I wake up in the morning I decide it's time for a break from fishing. I buy *The New York Times,* walk down to a diner, and pore through the world's news over a strong cup of coffee. Another surge in suicide bombings in Iraq. Mysteriously vanishing honeybees. Starving Somalis. Kids buying steroids online. A boater's death blamed on somersaulting sturgeon in Florida. After a few pages of this, I'm ready to check out again and get back to the derby, where, it turns out, things are about to take a stormy turn. A giant fish—and a controversy sized to fit—is about to roil the Vineyard and chase the world's many crises to the farthest reaches of my mind.

5

Leadbelly

Anglers motor out at all hours.

Like a lot of serious fishermen, Lev keeps a fishing log. His, he confesses one rainy afternoon as we talk over beers in his kitchen, is distinguished by its orange velvet cover.

This, I tell him, I have to see.

"Have you seen my fuzzy orange book around?" he yells to his wife.

"I haven't seen it in a long time," Jen says. "It's in a box somewhere."

He rifles through the bookshelves in their one-bedroom house, but he can't put his hands on it. Not that it would make any sense to me. As he tells me about the log, it becomes clear that *fuzzy* is apt in more ways than one. He writes down notes at the end of the commercial striper fishing season, and again at the end of the derby, but the descriptions are nearly cryptographic. Were some rival to break into Lev's house and swipe the log, he'd be hard-pressed to learn any of the Wlodyka family secrets. When Lev reads it, the words spark mental images that help guide him to the right spot or the right technique at the right time.

He doesn't need the log to see that the time has come to try again. The night after we talk in his kitchen, the last Friday in September —two weeks after he and Zeb hauled their giants out of the water —a 48-pound bass arrives in the weigh station and bumps Lev's fish into third place. That's a hint that a school of big stripers has moved into the sound. But other than Lev himself the only person who truly believes the five-time champ will top the 56-pounder is his partner Geoff Codding. "He'll catch something big," Geoff predicts while he and I fish for blues in the sound that same Friday. "It's just a matter of time. He'll walk in there with something that'll drop everybody's jaws. Guaranteed."

Everybody else is telling Lev he can't beat Zeb. *It's over, it's over, it's over:* that's all he's hearing.

It *ain't* over, he tells them all. "You've got a loser attitude. I'll catch a bigger one."

On Sunday, a warm, clear afternoon, he drives down to Menemsha, hops aboard *Wampum,* and gets ready to put his words to the test.

Lev and I talked a few times about his fishing strategies. Our conversations always began as sparring matches. To Lev and his friends, the worst sin a fisherman can commit is to take a spot or a tactic they shared with you and spread it around to others. He gets enraged when some stranger sees him whaling on a spot, punches it into his GPS, then tells all his friends. With one finger in one second the maritime pickpocket has taken something that Lev discovered only after hours and hours of patient searching.

I wasn't interested in secret fishing locations or techniques. I could turn to a library of how-to books and magazines for that kind of information. I wanted to know how he approached the fishing game. Talk to average anglers about fishing in general, and the derby in particular, and they will tell you that getting big fish—the trophy fish—is largely a matter of chance. In one of his well-known books on surfcasting, Cape Cod surfcaster Frank Daignault lists seven great stripers and how they were caught. The bottom line in every case: dumb luck.

Lev has spent a lifetime trying to improve his odds. "It's ninety-five percent being in the right place at the right time," he told me, "and it's five percent luck. *Knowing* you're in the right place at the right time is the real key. Having your bait all set and being ready."

During the derby, he'll key on a certain fish during a certain week. Bass one week, albies one week, bonito one week. (Bluefish are a crapshoot. Anybody can get the big one, he believes.) The bass and bonito are his specialties, and he can improve his odds by fishing on certain days. He says there are four or five nights during the derby when the conditions are ideal for striper fishing—he won't elaborate, but anglers often key on full- or new-moon nights—and on those occasions his odds of success improve perhaps tenfold. His advantage is almost as dramatic with bonito fishing. He's spent years studying patterns—weather, winds, tides, lunar cycles—and experimenting with different locations, baits, and techniques to figure out which combinations work best. The trick is taking that information and synthesizing it to determine which conditions are optimal. Those are the sorts of details he's not willing to spell out. "That stuff you've got to figure out." The other major variable is the presentation of the lure or the bait, knowing how to position your boat (or, if you're on the beach, how to position yourself) so everything looks right to the fish. "A lot is learned on the small scale. Even when there are schools of tinker mackerel at the dock, you can sit there and watch them. Just by catching tinker mackerel you can learn how to catch bonito. By catching trout you can learn how to catch just about anything."

The striper is the glory fish, but Lev and Geoff pride themselves on their mastery of bonito, the smallest and the most elusive of the derby fish. Lev won the boat bonito division in 2002, and coming into this year's contest Geoff had finished in second or third place for four years running. Lev says he would rather catch a 15-pound bonito than a 60-pound striper. (The derby record stands at 12.44 pounds. The world record came from the Azores in 1953 and weighed 18 pounds, 4 ounces.)

They credit commercial fisherman Karsten Larsen with teaching them how to fish for bonito. They say that years ago Karsten challenged the conventional wisdom when it came to bonito fishing, using different bait, trolling at higher speeds, trying different lures. "He'd set out four rods and troll wicked fast on Dogfish Bar," said Geoff, who went with Lev and Karsten on some of those offshore trips for tuna in high school. "People would think he was crazy, but that's how he would do it tuna fishing."

To their competitors, Lev and Geoff seem to have bonito fishing down to a science. Geoff is congenitally modest—after winning the grand prize Titan in 2006, he took a hair dryer and heated the derby logo until all the letters peeled off, not wanting to drive around town broadcasting his accomplishment—but he told me a story about how locked in they are when it comes to the bonito. One year, he and Lev were fishing in a fleet of boats for a series of days and just murdering the competition. Of every ten fish caught they were getting eight of them.

Lev told the same story, independently, using the same numbers.

The thing of it was, Lev said, "everybody was doing the same thing."

"Really," I said, skeptical.

He nodded.

"Using the same baits?"

"Yeah."

"So what's the difference?"

"You've gotta know how a tuna fish thinks."

"You have very specific tactics."

"Very specific," he said. "Little tiny tricks. Everybody puts in ninety-five percent. Guys who get second place put in hundred percent. You've gotta put in like, a hundred and eleven percent. That's how I always think about fishing. It's the last minuscule little things you do that separate you."

"So it's paying attention."

"Oh yeah, always paying attention. Always bettering, always trying to figure out something you didn't figure out the last time." He was quiet for a moment before he continued. "Little tiny things—like, some days, the difference between three-eighths of an ounce and a quarter of an ounce means everything. Stuff people wouldn't think about: hook sizes, the way you point your boat on the drift. Millions and millions of variables."

Catching 80 percent of the bonito in a fleet of bonito fishermen? It sounds like one of those stories that wouldn't hold up against Lev's proverb ("Believe nothing of what you hear . . ."). But then again, as Geoff told me the story, he was leading the derby with the largest boat bonito, 9.14 pounds, caught early in his first baitfishing trip for the speedsters with Lev. Another talented fisherman, Patrick Jenkinson—a grand slam winner himself—told me he anchored up alongside them and started doing basically what they were doing, fishing more or less the same spot at the same time. He got two fish all day. Every time he looked over at Lev and Geoff, they were *whaling* on bonito.

"They're so good," Patrick said. "You can count on it. They go out there and everybody's catching five-pound bonito. Their boat catches two nines. *How?* What are they doing differently? Is it technique? Is it things they've learned over the years? You go look in their truck to see what they're using, see their rods, see how they're rigged up. Do they put their weight twelve inches ahead of the bait or eight inches?" He suspects they attach hooks and leaders and lures they would never use in a million years, then leave them in their trucks to confuse the spies. "That's the kind of fishermen they are."

Lev powers up the boat and cruises out of Menemsha Harbor. To know *Wampum* is to know the Wlodykas. Walter, Lev's father, spotted the boat half buried in the sand in Vineyard Haven about a decade ago. He popped open the hatches, poked his head inside, asked around about the owner, and paid the guy a visit the same day. He bought it for $400, cash on the barrelhead, then had a couple of friends help dig it out. Lev, who was a cocky teenager at the time, took one look and issued his verdict: the thing was a piece of shit. ("I was a punk," he says by way of explanation.) A few years later, after Lev started to sell stripers, he bought it from his dad for $100 more than Walter had paid for it.

Wampum is well named: it's money. The thing has carried thousands of fish back to the Menemsha dock, and with bass selling for up to $3 a pound it has paid back the Wlodykas' investment many times over. If it looks more like a floating junkyard than a fishing boat with its specks of long-hardened fish viscera (and it does), that's how the Wlodykas like it. "Look at that boat!" Walter told me once, aglow with paternal pride. "People *laugh* at us in the summertime. There's blood all over it, scales, maggots. Lev doesn't care. He says he doesn't need to clean it, the maggots will take care of it."

It's been rebuilt at least three times, first after they dug it out and brought it home and again after the 2000 derby, which ended with Lev (a) winning with a 52.32-pound striped bass and (b) swimming half-naked through hypothermic seas off Squibnocket in the final hours of the contest. "It's not one of my prouder moments," a wiser Lev acknowledged as he told me the story. On the last night of the derby he already had the first-place bass, and his friends had vowed to go out and beat it. They were baiting him and Lev bit. If there was a bigger bass in the ocean, he was going to be the one to catch it. When he got out on the water and discovered the others had stayed in, he decided he'd rather be downtown with his friends than freezing alone in his boat. The seas were flat, and he'd spent so much time in these waters that he figured he could safely anchor, swim ashore, and hitch a ride into Edgartown to get something to eat. Looking back, even he can see the madness of parking his boat just outside the boulders and taking off. He would never do it today, and he wouldn't have done it then if he had remembered to check the marine forecast. Later that night, when he returned in a friend's boat, the seas had turned nasty. He looked everywhere but couldn't spot *Wampum.* Finally, desperate, Lev stripped down to his underwear and jumped in to look for the boat among the boulders. What scared him was not the prospect of being picked up by a wave and smashed against the rocks, or being eaten alive by one of the great whites sometimes spotted patrolling the waters off the Vineyard; he surfs, and two years later he'd catch the derby-winning striper by swimming out to a rock in a wet suit under cover of darkness (*swishing,* he and his friends call it). His only fear was being impaled by one of the treble-hooked plugs the fishermen were casting into the surf from the beach.

Leadbelly

He made it in, and at daylight, he went back to the beach and found pieces of *Wampum* washed up against the rocks. A boater spotted the main section of wreckage. Only eight inches of the bow showed above the waterline. Lev called a friend and they paddled out on surfboards. Free-diving under the boat was risky. Exposed cables waved underwater like tentacles. They could have gotten tangled nineteen feet below the boat. But down they went. They attached giant floats to the stern and unbolted the engine with wrenches, and when the boat popped up to the surface they bailed it out and had a friend tow it back. Lev rebuilt it and bought a new outboard—a $12,000 lesson he will not soon forget.

Despite all the work he's done on the boat it still looks rough around the edges. Though he has upgraded to the bigger, faster *Jenny J* for charter clients interested in comfortable appointments, Lev's heart will always be with *Wampum*. There's mojo on *Wampum*.

And he'll need every bit of it tonight as he motors out to the spot we'd fished two weeks earlier. *The* spot.

He has the place more or less to himself.

The sun goes down and the show starts. It's a beautiful thing. Lev zeroes in on the fish like he can see straight to the bottom and put *Wampum* right over them. All of the hits are coming within a tiny square. He can almost predict when he will feel the whack on his line. At some point, the fish move off a ways, and he moves with them, and then they move back. He catches a couple of 20-pound stripers. Then he gets into 30-pounders and that gets his attention. Get into thirties and there's a chance that fifties and sixties are down there. He catches a fish in the 40-pound class and releases it.

Then he hooks a striper that comes right to the boat and swims past like the shark cruising past the *Orca* in *Jaws*.

The fish seems groggy (unlike the 35-pounder Lev hooked a few minutes earlier, which fought more like a 50-pounder and had him a little weak in the knees). The bass takes fifty yards of line, comes back to the boat, takes thirty more yards, and goes to the bottom and holds for two minutes. Then it comes right up and he gaffs it and pulls it into the boat. The fish is monstrous, and Lev knows immediately that if it's not a winner it's very, very close.

It's 8:45. The weigh station closes at ten o'clock. He guns it to Menemsha, docks *Wampum*, leaves the rods in the boat, deposits the cooler holding the fish into the back of his truck, and speeds east toward Edgartown, passing cars and laughing the entire way.

Word quickly spreads. Someone strolls into the weigh station with the news: a big fish is coming in.

When Lev pulls up to the shack his friend Mike Holtham walks up to say hello. Lev's third-place bonito has just been knocked off the leaderboard, and Mike wants to razz his buddy a little. But Lev doesn't say a word. His hair is mussed, the left leg of his cargo pants is soaked to the knee, and there are splotches of fish slime on his sun-bleached red sweatshirt. He looks like he engaged in a wrestling match with a sea monster on *Wampum*'s gunwale.

He walks to the back of the truck, pulls down the tailgate, and drags the cooler up the ramp to the weighmaster's table. The beast's tail is sticking out the side. A dozen spectators look on, some of whom just happened to have been wandering around the waterfront, some of whom have heard about Lev's catch. Without a word, he slaps the fish on the table.

He's all but trembling as the fish goes on the scale and the digital display on the wall ticks up and down and levels off.

It stops at 57.56.

It's the historic fish he needed—third-heaviest in derby history— and cheers break out among the weigh station staff. Some of them have known Lev forever, since he was a little kid coming in with his father. They love nothing more than seeing a hardworking fisherman get his due. Lev turns around and gives Mike a bear hug. He calls Jen and then Geoff on the weigh station phone. Someone calls Louisa Gould, the official photographer, who'd left earlier because the action at the headquarters had died down and she was freezing. She'd gone home and drawn a hot bath. While everybody waits for her to return they look over the fish.

It has a head the size of a five-gallon bucket and the build of a telephone pole. And there's this: Its belly is huge, distended and misshapen, almost like the fish with broken backs that Lev has seen in pictures.

When Louisa arrives, Lev holds up the beast by the gill plate and tail and she snaps a series of shots. Then it comes time for one last piece of business. The fish is passed to filetmaster D. J. Pothier, the last defense against blatant cheating. He cuts open any fish that takes the lead to check inside its stomach for foreign matter, a step the derby instituted more than a decade ago. It sounds ridiculous, but the difference between winning and losing can be a matter of ounces, and with thousands of dollars at stake guys have stuffed tournament fish with all kinds of things: baitfish, rocks, mercury. D. J. slices open the behemoth with a white-handled filet knife. Everybody is gathered around the filet stand—Lev and several derby staffers on the barge itself, a dozen others on the dock behind a rope line—the crowd swelling with passersby curious about all the cheering. Chris Scott, the derby official on duty, Charlie Smith, the weighmaster, and Charlie's wife, Martha, who runs the weigh station, have come out to see what a striper so enormous is eating. Martha almost expects to see a three-pound lobster inside it.

D. J. finds the stomach and cuts it and sticks his hand inside. It feels empty at first. Charlie, Chris, and Lev peer inside. Lev thinks D. J. is about to hand it back to him.

Instead he reaches all the way into the farthest recesses of the stomach, and as his hand comes out there is a clattering on the floor at his feet. It sounds exactly like change falling out of a pants pocket.

Martha thinks it's a joke at first, like that time the guy cutting open a leaderboard fish dropped a wrench out of his sleeve as he fumbled around in the stomach. It takes her a moment to see that nobody's laughing. She looks at Lev and sees his face morph from shock to horror to embarrassment before he speaks.

"*What the fuck?*"

Inside Lev's fish-of-a-lifetime, D. J. has found a fistful of lead weights.

6

Prayer to the Great Fish Gods

Steve Amaral's derby registration buttons.

"Now what are we going to do with that big fish we get tonight? We're splitting it like we do, right?"

Steve Amaral's talking about how we'll divvy up the proceeds, fifty-fifty, if we catch a derby winner. He's kidding, and he's not.

The joke is that while Zeb and Lev and all the other boating hotshots are hauling in world beaters, and the daytime crowd is celebrating the return of the albies and bonito after last year's dismal haul, Steve and the traditional nighttime beach fishermen—the surfcasters—are struggling to get anything worth taking down to the weigh station. The shore stripers and bluefish are runts so far. Some old-timers are a little vexed about the way the derby has changed. Any lucky fool can get a good night's sleep, then go out in the middle of the day and catch an albie or bonito that takes the top prize even though it's a fraction of the size of a great striper. To some guys, that doesn't seem right.

When the derby began in 1946 the surfcasters were kings. They were the legendary figures who endured long hours of suffering on the beach, got hammered by crashing waves, paid their dues for giant stripers. They had to forgo sleep and venture out at night, because that's when the big stripers came in close to shore. Back then, the men on the beach usually caught the monster bass, and they swaggered around the Vineyard like jocks. Today, the shore fishing is a shadow of the past. "You can't just say, 'I'm going out tonight and I'm going to bang some big fish,'" Steve said. "I could say that years ago but not now." Things have changed, and fisherman are hard-pressed to explain why.

The reason Steve is not entirely joking about sharing our hypothetical windfall is that he's fished in sixty derbies now, and though he's never won it himself he has been right beside men who have—three times. Ask these derby champs, and they'll tell you Steve deserves a healthy share of the credit for putting them on their fish. So he has legitimate reasons to reiterate the terms of our one-day fishing partnership in the dark on this soupy island night. The way his luck has run these past six decades, he'd take me out to his spot in his pickup, set me up with his rods and his eels, and *I'd* get the derby winner and walk away with the Boston Whaler.

These are the conditions he asks his fishing partners to accept:

(1) All expenses, including but not limited to eels and gas, will be split.

(2) If either angler catches a winner, any and all prize money will be split.

(3) Should either fisherman catch a grand leader and then choose the correct key and win the grand prize boat, the boat will be sold immediately and the proceeds split.

"If you're willing to follow these rules and regulations," he'd explained, "then you can fish with me."

As it happens, he's not asking me to fork over cash for gas and eels tonight, and I'm not planning to take half of the prize money if he lands a giant bass. A derby winner is about the only thing missing from his fishing résumé. He says he's caught eight 50-pounders in his career. Five came in a single year, 1979, among them a 56½-pounder that would have won the derby had Steve caught it two days earlier. The legendary Dick Hathaway won that year with a 55-pound fish.

He's also living with bitter memories of two surefire winners that eluded him. They are epic tales of the sort Steve is known for repeating to anybody with the stamina to listen. (As one friend put it, there are no commas in Steve's stories.) The first near-win came in 1968, the morning of the last day of the derby. Steve followed a routine. He would toss out some bait and bottom-fish for a while, and if nothing hit he would leave the rods and plug the beach. That morning, he chose a red-and-white Junior Atom, and soon enough he got into fish. *Bang!* A hit, but he missed her. Another cast. *Bang!* Another miss. What the hell is this? he wondered.

On the next cast he got another massive hit. This time he did not miss. The beach behind him curved up like a half-pipe in a skateboard rink, and the waves were crashing up on the sand and then washing back down, pulling hard against Steve's legs. Finally, he directed the fish into a wave and pulled it up the beach. The rest happened in slow motion. The wave crashed and receded and the fish started sliding, and as it did the plug fell out of its mouth. Steve had the rod in his right hand. He used his left hand to reach down and grab the fish's gill plate, but he missed and grabbed it by the tail instead. Now the fish had turned to face the ocean and was thrashing around in the wash to get free. Steve's brain—instead of ordering him to drop the rod, jump on this guaranteed derby winner, and head for the weigh-in—started cycling through a series of instinctive thought-flashes. Like, *If I drop the rod, I'll surely get sand in my reel and need to overhaul it.* Like, *If I jump on this striper, I'm going to take one of its needle-sharp fins in my waders.* And while his mind raced the fish slipped his grasp and got away.

"I released it!" he told me. "Ha-ha-hah!" It's a bitter laugh. He's replayed that one in his head too many times to count.

Then, in 2004, fishing shortly after a hurricane in pounding surf, his joints aching from a bout with Lyme disease, Steve saw his rod tip bend and limped over to it on his bum knee and set up on that fish. His mind started to race: *This is what we've been waiting for . . . I'm going to bring this one in . . . This fish is mine.*

Yet as he watched the waves, coming one after the other after the other, each crashing before the backwash of the previous wave had finished rattling back down, his brain started working again. ("I'm always thinking something can happen, because things *have* happened out there.") He analyzed the geometry of the situation. *The waves are coming from this direction. The fish is over there. I'm right here. The only way I'm going to lose this fish, the only way, is if a wave rears up and hits me directly on my bum knee.*

Twenty seconds later a wave rolled in and propelled forty-plus pounds of striped bass and God knows how much water smack into Steve's bum knee. He went down hard and dropped the rod. He got a hand on the butt but he couldn't hang on and the rod slipped out to sea. He pulled up his hood to keep out the waves and crawled up the beach, his probable derby winner swimming away with his graphite rod and reel. He and Mike snagged the rod after a few minutes of casting for it in the dark. But the striper was long gone. The guy who won the derby that year had a 42.46-pound bass.

So yes, the bottom line is that either of us could win the whole thing tonight. But at the same time it's out of our hands. Winning the derby, Steve has come to believe, is a matter for the Great Fish Gods to decide. He'll do everything he physically can, at age seventy-one, to win it. He'd love nothing more than to get on that stage and take his bows as the best damned striped bass fisherman on the Vineyard. He would deserve it, all these years he's fished, semi-retired, divorced since 1977, his two daughters grown up, not a thing to keep him from endless nights on the beach except for some plumbing and caretaking clients. The fact he hasn't won it burns the hell out of him. But if you've fished a day in your life you know it comes down to chance. *Bullshit luck,* that's his phrase for it. "The so-called superstars out there?" he asked me once. "Well, you tell me—who's caught more fish in their lifetime?"

Tonight we're standing on the south shore of the Vineyard, a sweeping expanse, sand stretching as far as you can see all the way down to Squibnocket Point, and in front of us nothing but the relentless Atlantic Ocean, big waves rolling in forever. We're taking up puny eleven-foot rods and slinging out foot-long eels. Really, who but the most faithful goes out and expects to catch a fish in this vast blank sea?

Fishing with Steve felt like fishing with a living, breathing hunk of derby history. I'd spent a lot of hours at the Martha's Vineyard Museum and the Vineyard Haven library looking through half-century-old pictures and newspaper clippings about the derby. But Steve could recount the same stories because he'd been there right from the beginning, on Sunday, September 15, 1946, when the very first contest started at noon.

The derby committee, made up of island sportsmen and business owners and backed by the ferry line, had placed a $1,000 bounty on the biggest striper caught. They spread the word far and wide. One booster sold newspaper scribes on the idea that the Vineyard was "a body of land surrounded by water and striped bass." The *Gazette* recalled the giant stripers caught off Squibnocket in the late 1800s by wealthy gentlemen-sportsmen at one of the bass clubs. They spoke of a mythic fish, nearly a hundred pounds, that had been landed in the same era. They said 40-pound stripers had swum so thick that catching one was of no moment.

The committee collected all manner of prizes: rods, reels, and fishing line, of course; a blanket; a dinghy; a car-top carrier; a pair of sunglasses; a week at an Edgartown hotel, including airfare and the use of a sailboat with a skipper; six ten-pound hams; a case of canned peas; bottles of whiskey; a wallet; shoes; and, bizarrely, three hundred pairs of chopsticks. The weather cooperated nicely, and fishermen hit the water wearing their green derby tags to compete in boat, surfcasting, bridge-fishing, fly-casting, and women's divisions. A man named Gus Amaral took his children out that first day and, if the newspaper story is to be believed, he caught the first fish weighed in at the first derby. Steve—Gus's second son—has the article in his cherished collection alongside a newspaper photo of the Amaral family slinging plugs into the surf and a photograph of Gus walking off the beach with his dog, which is carrying a bluefish in its maw.

In those days, fishermen were required to say where and how they caught their fish, so the newspapers could report that the heavyweights battled it out from boats over Devil's Bridge, the rocky shoal off the Gay Head cliffs where a long rip forms. Daniel Huntley of Buzzards Bay landed a 39-pound bass in the second week of the derby, but he finished second to Gordon Pittman, a New York City salesman who caught a 47-pounder a few days before the end. At the awards dinner in the Rod and Gun Club, sportsmen feasted on turkey and striped bass and the derby committee handed out prizes. Pittman took home the $1,000 and a free week at the Harborside Inn. Huntley won the piece of land in Gay Head.

In all, nearly a thousand fishermen showed up, and tackle shops, charter-boat operators, gas stations, and hotels saw a nice boost in business. The derby gave away more than $11,000 in cash and merchandise, which paid for pages and pages of free publicity. Stories ran in the *Boston Globe, The New York Times,* even *Time* magazine, which gave Pittman's derby victory dramatic treatment, if only for four short paragraphs.

The second year the derby offered a twenty-six-foot Steelcraft Striper cabin cruiser worth $4,200, a Plymouth coupe, and a couple of smaller bass boats. They claimed that their prize package ranked among the most valuable of any American fishing competition. Registrations came in from Canada to Cuba, from North Dakota to Florida. The owner of a massive property on Squibnocket gave contestants permission to drive across his land to get down to the beach. Eighteen hundred people registered to compete, nearly twice as many as in 1946. The *Gazette* declared Columbus Day weekend—which coincided with the end of the derby—the busiest in island history. Hotels filled beyond capacity: the Mansion House in Vineyard Haven found beds for thirty-one extra guests in nearby homes and in rooms usually occupied by their summer employees.

Vox Pop, a national radio show, came to broadcast the closing ceremonies. A packed house watched the hosts tell America about their little island and its fishing derby. The broadcasters got islanders to clown around in the *Vox Pop* way. A woman and her cousin, Dr. Clement Amaral—Steve's uncle, a dentist who went by

"Doc"—pressed a balloon between their bodies until it burst. The high school principal put on a housedress and demonstrated how to diaper a doll. A husky teenaged boy won $5 for squeezing into a pink girdle.

Quickly, the derby became a hit, an event on the social calendar, with an annual ball where they crowned a queen. Officials estimated it brought $200,000 a year into the Vineyard economy, or about $2 million in today's dollars. Many other places on the eastern seaboard had fishing contests but the Vineyard's seemed to get the best press. In those first years, PR man Nat Sperber reeled in scores of visiting writers, providing them with rooms in the elegant Mansion House, guides to take them fishing, and phones so they could hold up their end of the bargain by filing dispatches to the universe beyond the sound.

Broadway actress Katharine Cornell stumped for the contest at the big New York sport and travel exposition. One year, an island teenager presented Ted Williams with a 22-pound bass on the field before a Red Sox game at Fenway Park, and the kid invited the slugger (and top-notch fisherman) to the derby. Another year, organizers put an 11¼-pound bluefish on ice and shipped it to President Eisenhower at his vacation headquarters in Newport, Rhode Island, along with Badge No. 1 and an invitation to come down "for a whirl at derby fishing." Both the ballplayer and the general declined, but the invitations made the papers, which was the point anyway. As the first derby chairman, lawyer M. Martin Gouldey, told reporters in 1946, "Martha's Vineyard is on the map."

As time went on, the derby tapped into a mythical aura that grew up around a new generation of recreational fishermen on the East Coast after World War II. On an island with a long history in fishing, the surfcaster evolved into a shadowy figure. If these men were not quite as salty as their commercial brethren, the best of them earned folk hero status anyway. To know how to catch fish consistently—not just to chance upon them by dumb luck—was to have some rare knowledge, some special understanding of what lay hidden under the waves, and there was currency in that.

The derby gave fishermen a chance to show off, to stroll into the weigh station with a fat striper and revel in the attention. Maybe they'd take home a TV set, but it was the recognition that they craved. Fish as totem. That's what the derby came to mean to guys like Steve Amaral. When he was a teenager his father would rent a bungalow right on the beach near Tisbury Great Pond. They'd fish every day, driving in only for school and supplies. At fifteen, Steve won the junior division and brought home a Columbia bicycle with a horn and lights and big, fat wheels. He also scored a trip with the derby chieftains up to Boston, where he appeared on television in foul-weather gear handing a bass to sportscaster and ex–major league pitcher Bump Hadley (delivering dead fish to celebrities having become something of a stock trick for the promoters). Steve says he can still taste the strawberry shortcake at the hotel. Both helpings.

Even in his seventies, Steve is overcome with youthful exuberance when he gets to talking about fishing. "I'll tell you what," he said the first time I met him, his round, wrinkled mug brightening into a huge smile. "You get a big fucking fish on, mister, it's the best feeling in the world!" He favors golf shirts and jeans, sometimes with a brass fish buckle on his belt, and his accent is hard to place, not quite New England but not from any other region of the country either. For one thing, the fish he's after is a "*stripe-ed* bass." A friend is "brutha." He's been a plumber, a fireman—twenty-three years as captain of Engine Company No. 4—a fisherman, and a deer hunter, and so it came as no surprise that he has a habit of sprinkling salty language into conversations. (In that, he's most decidedly not in the minority among fishermen.)

I'm not the first angler to come calling for a ridealong with him. He once took out Secretary of State Cyrus Vance, a college buddy of one of Steve's customers. "He didn't catch nothing," Steve recalled. "But he caught a wave that knocked him on his ass." Over the decades, numerous guys have approached him about fishing together, and they've discovered that a partnership with Steve Amaral is a major commitment. Steve Morris, owner of Dick's Bait and Tackle, started fishing with him not long after winning the derby in 1983 at age twenty with a 49.96-pound striper he caught from a boat. When he speaks of their alliances, Steve Morris talks about it in a man-and-wife way. "Oh yeah," he says, "when you fish with Stevie, you *fish with Stevie*." You don't fish with anybody else, and you generally don't fish without him. Their fishing marriage lasted about two years. Steve Morris had just tied the knot for real (to one of Steve Amaral's second cousins, actually) and he had to make a choice: fishing partner or life partner? It was a kind of breakup, albeit an amicable one. "I couldn't fish as much as he wanted to fish," Steve Morris said. "I mean I could physically and everything, but just with the family . . ."

It was a common theme that ran through Steve's alliances. Bob Rose says the man just *always* wanted to fish. "He was a diehard. He never quit. He just kept going and going and going." It got to the point where Bob couldn't keep up. You can't spend *every* night on the beach, can you? But hooking up with Steve paid off for Bob. In 1968 he won the derby with a 48½-pound striper beached on the last day of the contest. Steve actually had to prod Bob into going out that night.

Steve's current teammate is a golf course superintendent, Mike Alwardt. As a teenager, Mike would sit in his truck outside Steve's house and wait for him to leave, hoping to follow him to one of his blue-chip fishing holes. His surveillance was so intense that sometimes he'd follow Steve's truck only to find himself in a convenience store parking lot, where he'd watch Steve go inside, come back out with a gallon of milk or something, and drive home. Years later they started fishing together—the "A-Team," they took to calling themselves—and it was obvious from the beginning that they were a match: supercompetitive and secretive. (The first time I met Mike, he kept his sunglasses on, even though we were in a hotel ballroom.) Mike and Steve tell of wading far off the beach to rocks and fishing until the tide made it untenable, or fighting the current to get across a pond opening and fish the other side. That sort of thing is not unusual among the younger set, but I was surprised to hear that Steve was still doing it into his fifties and sixties. "When I think of some nights I was out there, I wish I had pictures of it," he said. "People would say, 'That guy's insane.'"

A few years ago Mike became violently ill on the beach—stomach pains, vomiting, the whole thing. Steve kept asking him if he wanted to quit, and Mike kept saying no. They were on fish for the first time in a few days and no way was he leaving them. When the blitz ended, Mike went straight to the hospital. The next day he had his gallbladder removed.

They've fished together for going on two decades now. Mike's won twice, in 1995—with the second-biggest striped bass ever weighed in at the derby, 57.82 pounds—and in 2003. His son, Josh, won the junior division twice while fishing with Steve and Mike, in 1995 and 1999. "I have to give him ninety percent of the credit," Mike said of Steve. His advantage was that he had lined up permissions to fish property all over the island. He'd ask old family friends, caretakers, and especially plumbing customers with choice land. "The spots we went to just produced all the time," Mike explained. "People were dying to know where we were fishing. I fished hard and I had limited success until I hooked up with him." He paused and giggled at the memory. For a four-year stretch, he said, "we just slaughtered 'em."

At the 2003 awards ceremony Nelson Sigelman asked Mike to give up his big secret. How did he manage to win twice in a decade?

"Fish with Steve," Mike told him.

Mike ain't no dummy. And neither am I. If there were stripers to be had, I figured Steve could put us on them.

When I got to his house in Oak Bluffs at six in the evening, Steve was asleep in the recliner, the Golf Channel on the TV. Good sign. It meant he'd been out late last night, and if he'd been out late it meant he'd been on fish. When he awoke, I learned that he'd weighed in a 13.88-pound bass ("I had to get something in there") and an 8.54-pound blue that took first place for the day. He and Mike had been fishing the same spot for a few days now and he wanted to try it again. Mike couldn't go with him tonight—he planned to take his wife out to dinner—so Steve had invited me to come along.

Out in his driveway, Steve looked over my waders and my rod as I piled them into his truck. Like every fisherman I'd met up here, Steve was taking a measure of what kind of angler he'd agreed to bring along. He took a white bucket over to a rowboat marooned beside the driveway. Inside the hull, a few dozen eels quivered in a pool of water. He netted a dozen and put them into the bucket and we backed out of the driveway, a pop music station on the radio. We stopped to get ice, and before he closed the lid on the cooler he dropped in our drinks. For me, he'd brought a beer, and for himself, in a small water bottle, a drink he called the Sombrero: Arrow coffee brandy and one-percent milk.

We cruised down to Edgartown and pulled into the line for the ferry to Chappaquiddick. It was dark and misty as Steve drove on to the boat and chatted with the operator about last night. "We got a few fish over there but it was nothing big."

"Better than a poke in the eye with a sharp stick, right?" the ferry man said. As we pulled up to Chappy he added, "I'm going to make a forecast. If you guys are going on the outside, I'll probably see you about eleven. That weed is some thick in there."

"Oh, no," Steve moaned. "Jesus, don't say that."

"That big black stringy bubbly stuff."

"Almost as good as that mossy stuff." Steve restarted the truck and shifted into gear.

"Get the derby winner," the man said. "Get it over with."

Now, out on the beach, Steve gets on his knees, takes an eel from the bucket, and drops it in front of him. He uses the grit of the sand to hold it until he can hook the thing. We each cast out and return to the pickup. He sits on the bucket and I sit on the front bumper, and as we watch and wait he starts telling stories.

The Amarals are one of many Portuguese families descended from strong-backed whalers and fishermen who arrived in New England from the Azores, a series of islands about a thousand miles off the European coast. Men would sign on with American whalers visiting the islands, then jump ship when they reached New England. Steve's grandfather Clement arrived from São Miguel before the turn of the century, and Steve's father, Augustus F., was born on the island in 1903. He served as the chief of police in Oak Bluffs during the 1930s and '40s. The family car doubled as the police cruiser. Gus boxed in the semiprofessional ranks and had the bruises and black eyes to show for it, but he didn't lose much, as far as Steve knows. After World War II, Gus bought the fish market in Oak Bluffs. He taught his three sons to fish and hunt, and after school they would ride their bikes out to the ponds or the beaches and fish until dark using rods they fashioned themselves out of bamboo sticks. "We looked like Huck Finn and Tom Sawyer," Steve says.

In 1955 Steve joined the Army and was stationed about three hours away at Fort Devens, northwest of Boston. That first year, he took a leave and made it back to fish the derby. He shipped out soon thereafter and ended up in Korea guarding communications lines through the end of 1956. That forced him to miss his only derby (and let me tell you, mister, it won't happen again). He hasn't left the island much since then, and he doesn't plan to. Not long ago, a realtor showed up at his door and told him he could cash in on the demand for Vineyard real estate and sell his little place for a pile of cash. Steve looked at the man perplexed. "I said, 'Where the hell am I going to go live? Everything I do is right here.'" Where else would he be able to dig up clams, quahogs, and scallops whenever he wanted? Where else would he know the best spots to catch stripers? Where could he live the kind of outdoor life he's mastered on the Vineyard? He's hunted and fished the island for fifty straight years now, and in 2007 the derby committee inducted him into its hall of fame, a group of people who have made lasting contributions to the event. If there's something that makes him prouder, he never told me about it.

"We're here and they're not, right?" Steve says after an hour of waiting and checking the eels and pulling off the weed and recasting and waiting again. "Or we've got to wait until they get here. This may be the night they don't like eels." A few minutes pass. The guys who become great surfcasters, Steve explains, are the ones willing to go night after night. That's the only way to figure out which conditions are best. Steve might go back to a single spot several days in a row, even if the fish aren't hitting, before he'll give up and decide it's time to try someplace new. "How many nights we've stood here and wait, wait, wait?"

He gets up and checks his baits again. One of the eels is wrapped around his rig, and he spends a while cleaning up the mess and casting out again. People see Steve bringing in fish and they figure it's all action for a fisherman like him, but they don't see him on all those days when he comes home with nothing, all those nights when he's working the beach and wondering why in the hell he's out there and not home watching TV in his recliner. "Nothing's easy in this business. You don't go to the beach and they jump up on the sand."

But the payoff comes when he least expects it.

Like the night he and Mike got thirty bass in an hour, all of them in the 25-pound class, fish coming so hot and heavy that Steve started to break a sweat. They had to forget about putting out four rods and just fished a pair. They'd barely get their eels in the water and the bass would be on them. He put that night away in his memory bank, mister. Or the night back in 1975 when he got into big fish with his father and mother, Gus and Gert. A live bunker flopped up on the beach and he put it on Gert's hook and cast it out, and when the bass came and sucked in that bait, as he knew it would, he coached her on how to get it in. When that night ended, Gert had a 31-pounder, Gus had a 39, and Steve strutted into the weigh station with a 45, the derby leader for a time.

The mount of the biggest bass he ever caught glowers on the wall in his dining room. It's the 56½ he landed during an extraordinary stretch of fishing after the 1979 derby. The day before the end of the contest Steve was doing his thing: eels out, no hits, start plugging. Damned if he didn't get a 37-pounder within ten minutes. The next morning, same routine, and this time he got a 31. The derby ended but Steve kept working the spot. The night after the derby he got his first bass in the 50-pound class. "I knew it was big. He turned and went straight out with it and I says, 'Oh man, it's perfect. I couldn't ask for anything better.' I'm holding him and the drag's going and he's headed right straight out, boy. And then after he got out there I says, 'Okay, work him down the beach,' and I knew it was big, and I says to myself, I says, 'I don't care, I'll walk you down to Edgartown if I have to.' And so I just took my time with it and walked down the beach and played him till he was good and played out and waited for the right set of waves to come in. And I put that bad baby up on the beach." It weighed 53½ pounds.

The 56½ came the following night. Fellow obsessive Whit Manter was fishing nearby, and they weighed the brute on Whit's grandfather's scale. The needle settled down at 57, but the Manters knew their scale to be half a pound heavy. Over the coming days, big fish hung around feeding on sand eels, and Steve, Whit and several other hardcore fishermen hauled in bass night after night. They sold all the fish—except for Steve's trophy striper, that is—and grossed thousands of dollars in less than two weeks. Somehow, they kept the blitz a secret until it was over.

A few weeks later a friend told Steve he'd been walking up around Jacqueline Kennedy Onassis's property and he could've sworn he saw drag marks on the beach, the distinct tail marks left behind by fishermen dragging out giant stripers by the gills. He drove up-island and, sure enough, the sand eels were there, and so were the bass. Steve got one behemoth, then another, and as he pulled in the third another gang showed up.

"Jesus Christ, Steve, those are fifty-pounders!" one of the fishermen told him.

"Oh, they're close," Steve said. "I don't say they're fifty until after I weigh 'em."

He weighed 'em and the man was right. The three of them came in at a combined 155 pounds.

Tonight, however, we aren't even getting the hint of a fish on these eels, and Steve is starting to get antsy. He grabs a rod rigged for plugging and heads down the beach a bit and casts while I watch the lights atop the three baited rods. A few minutes later I see him walking back up the beach, and I can hear him cursing from a good hundred yards off. He lost a $22 plug when his line hit a loop on the reel and snapped. The good news: he's getting into fish down there—he's already caught and released a pair of bass—so I reel up the other rods, grab my plug bag, and follow him down the beach.

There are a few other regular surfcasters out here working the water. It's dark but Steve recognizes them by their trucks.

I tie on a big black plug called a Danny and whip it out into the surf. When my line comes tight and I can feel the wobble of the plug, I reel slowly and wait for the hit.

Next thing I know a little hooded figure to my left is hooked up, and as she moves my way I reel up and let her pass. She fights it to the wash, and when she's got the striper up on the beach Steve comes over and, joking, offers her a hand. (Old trick: he wants to find out what his rival caught it on.) It's Janet Messineo, and she laughs and gives him a hug when he asks for advice. Steve was one of her mentors, three decades ago, when she started bass fishing. "They're only hitting the Darter," she tells us.

I switch plugs and we get back to work, and sure enough I get a few whacks, but no hook-ups. Before long Steve is yelling again. He had a good one on and the line broke again. He reties, but pretty soon it's 11:45—time to jump in the truck and race back for the last ferry at 11:57. (Surfcasters could drive the barrier beach back to town until earlier this year, when a storm opened a new cut and made Chappaquiddick a true island. This year, they have to catch the ferry at midnight or stay overnight on the beach.)

The action, good and bad, has him in a lather. It's like someone has administered a shot of testosterone. He's been transmogrified into a spitting-mad wild man. He speeds past a guy driving slow on the rutted road out. He barks about a lollygagging pedestrian. He raves about the plugs he'd been using and rages about the braided line. He expresses shock and outrage about his line breaking not once but twice. We make the last ferry and ride through the empty streets of Edgartown.

By the time we make it back to Oak Bluffs Steve has settled down. We caught nothing to weigh-in, but there's always tomorrow, and the next day, and many days after that. Friendly, affable Steve is back, and we unwind on folding chairs in his garage over Bud Lights and Sombreros.

"Well," he asks me. "Did I pass the test for an older guy?"

One more Steve Amaral fishing story. Last one. Promise. This one is probably closest to his heart because it shows what it takes to succeed.

So it was Halloween, and Mike didn't want to fish. Steve heard that one of the salt ponds had been opened to the ocean, and that sounded far better than dealing with packs of goblins ringing his doorbell all night long. He got there just before dark, and the cut was a sliver running out, and he spotted a big striper swimming outside the opening, its maw agape. "Jesus Christ!" Steve said. He grabbed a rod and flipped an eel out in the opening and soon a striper had it and the line was flying out and he closed the bail and the bass hit with a *BANG!* and—well, you get the idea.

Steve took the fish home, laid it in his bathtub, and ran some water. The next morning he called Mike at work.

"Yeah," Steve said, "my tub's plugged up. I want you to take a look at it."

Mike came over at lunchtime and his heart sank: the bass ran 47 pounds. Steve had gotten five more, all 40-pounders. And here's the kicker. When Steve looked down the beach in both directions there wasn't a soul to be seen. A pile of giant bass and he was the only one dedicated enough to go out on Halloween and try to catch them.

All those guys who fished with him over the years? All those guys who won the derby by his side? He says they know he was the one who picked out the spots. They know he was the one who drew up the game plan.

"They know," he told me. "They know how good I am."

7

Yo-Yos in Paradise

Derby president Ed Jerome, 1983.

Within moments of the lead weights dropping out of Lev's fish the phone rings in Ed Jerome's house in Edgartown, and the derby president gets in his car and makes the five-minute drive over to the weigh station.

If a Hollywood filmmaker came to the Vineyard to cast a stereotypical hardcore island fisherman, Ed wouldn't make the short list. He drives a white Cadillac Escalade, and in all the time I spent around him I can't say I ever saw a strand of his black hair out of place. His V-neck sweaters and button-down shirts say school administrator, not fish slayer, and he did in fact spend twenty-seven years as principal at the Edgartown School. One of the highlights came in the 1990s, when President Bill Clinton turned the elementary school into the press filing center during his vacations on the island. In August 1998, while the president hunkered down on the Vineyard after admitting his affair with Monica Lewinsky, he put the finishing touches on military strikes against Osama bin Laden's terrorist training camps in Afghanistan and the Sudan. After the bombs hit, Clinton went to the school gymnasium and announced the attack to the world. Grip-and-grin shots of Bill and Ed hang on the walls of the Jerome household.

For all of Ed's polish, though, the man has a rugged side. His other car is an Isuzu Trooper, which he uses as a beach buggy, and on its hatchback is a sticker that reads, "Women Love Me, Fish Fear Me" (a friend's handiwork). In his thirties and forties, Ed was one of the Vineyard's hardcore surf fishermen. During derby season, he would go out all night every night, fishing to the point that people would find him asleep at his desk at three in the afternoon. There's a spot on Chappaquiddick that his friends refer to as "Ed's Rock." A routine day would see him fishing there deep into the morning, then greeting dawn at the Gut, a famously fishy spot where the arm of sand enclosing the Cape Poge Bay pinches the water flowing in and out. His banner derby fish hangs on the wall in his home office: a 19.84-pound bluefish that finished first among residents in 1983, back when there were separate rankings for visitors and islanders. The fish is so huge compared to its average brethren that it looks almost like a specimen from a different genus. The little office by the kitchen is where he and his wife, Maryanne, run the tournament with a computer, a fax, a printer, and a credit-card machine. His wife handles all manner of indispensable minutiae: making the rounds to the tackle shops every day to collect registrations; depositing the money in the bank; typing the entrants' information into the computer.

Ed and a group of committed volunteers salvaged the contest at a time when it looked as though it might fall apart, and the number of competitors has nearly doubled under their stewardship. In 1986 they bought the derby from the Chamber of Commerce for $1 and, with the proceeds going to an endowment and charities, won non-profit status from the IRS. Every year, the derby awards college scholarships to several local graduates planning to pursue careers in marine or environmental fields. Four students split $30,000 in 2007; over twenty years, the tournament has handed out more than $250,000 in grants.

Perhaps most important, Ed has helped give a patina of friendly civic pride to an event that suffers from some of the typical fishing tournament's warts. The derby has for decades worked to wrap itself in the sort of gauzy glow that CBS gives the Masters every April. Painter Ray Ellis produces prints of the island's most famous fishing spots each year, and people snap them up despite hefty price tags. Ed and Ray took the paintings and paired them with photos and short stories to self-publish a coffee-table book, which immediately sold a thousand copies at a crowded signing at the island ag hall. Limited editions bound in leather sold for $200. This year, the derby collaborated with Louisa Gould on a derby art show, and a small crowd gathered at her Vineyard Haven gallery for an opening the Saturday before the contest started. Taxidermist Janet Messineo's glistening stripers rested near Gyotaku fish prints by anesthesiologist-angler Steve London. (He dabs paint on a fish, then presses it against paper, creating artwork that is at once realistic and abstract.) People mingled in Bermuda shorts and short-sleeved button-downs over beer, wine and bluefish pâté. I mostly marveled at the price tags. Four figures for fish art? That's modern-day Martha's Vineyard.

The other part of Ed's job is protecting the event from that scourge of the fishing competition: cheaters. The great ongoing debate is how big the derby ought to be. If you offer huge prizes, do you risk attracting miscreants and losing sponsors? If you scale back the awards, do you risk losing competitors and running in the red? Countless hours have been spent figuring out how to strike the balance between Bassmaster and your low-rent, mom-and-pop tackle-shop derby. Though the total prize package has ballooned, and the grand-prize boat or truck can be sold for $20,000 or so (after taxes), there is no giant cash prize of the sort that has drawn crooks to other tournaments. As one committeeman grumbled about that idea: "We have enough problems as it is."

If you wanted to dream up the top ten scenarios that would give Ed Jerome and the rest of the derby brass major-league migraines, this one—lead weights tumbling out of a gigantic fish caught by a five-time winner—would definitely make the list.

At the root of the controversy is something the derby has wrestled with over the past five years, a particularly deadly fishing technique suddenly in vogue among commercial bass fishermen around the Vineyard. Inside Lev's fish were ten custom-made slugs of lead. They came in several sizes, but each sinker had the cylindrical profile of a spark plug. To a fisherman in the know, they had the instantly recognizable shape of a weight used in "yo-yoing."

The man credited with inventing the technique is a Rhode Island commercial fisherman named Dick Sevigny. Dick had retired from the Air Force in the late 1960s and taken up the waterman's life to supplement his pension. He and a compatriot often fished with live Atlantic menhaden—*Brevoortia tyrannus*—an oily baitfish that is variously known as mossbunker, bunker, or, around the Vineyard, pogy. The fish is a species of herring, blue-green on top and brassy-tinged on the sides, with distinctive spots behind the gill plate. Menhaden have traditionally been a major part of the diet of striped bass, bluefish, swordfish, cod, and many other species.

But their ranks have been depleted, and the pogy has become something of a cause célèbre among anglers. H. Bruce Franklin wrote an entire book about the lowly baitfish titled *The Most Important Fish in the Sea*. A Houston-based company named Omega Protein seines pogies by the billions and converts them for use in a surprising assortment of products: makeup, linoleum, soap, paints, chicken feed. Environmentalists argue that the industry is threatening a key member of the food chain. It's not just that pogies are an important food source for other fish. They also keep bays and river mouths healthy by feeding voraciously on phytoplankton, a natural filtering mechanism that can help prevent algae blooms, "dead zones," and fish kills.

The more immediate concern for fishermen is that the pogy fishing industry threatens a valuable bait. Pogies are effective from the "peanut" size on up to a foot or so. "Livelining" them—hooking them alive and letting them swim behind a boat or off a beach or jetty—has been a popular pogy fishing tactic for decades. Many anglers chop them up and use the chunks as bait and chum. Dead pogies are easier to handle than live ones, so around 1978 Dick and his friend began experimenting with new ways to use them. One day, they stumbled on the idea of inserting a regular, store-bought "bank sinker" into the pogy's mouth to make it drop quickly down where the stripers lay. They sealed the mouth shut with copper wire and packed the rigged baitfish in ice, flat and straight. When they attached it to a hook and dropped it in the water, the frozen bait remained stiff and looked natural for a few minutes. And they only needed a few minutes.

The men would drift over their spots, jiggling their rigs just off the bottom, and giant fish would swim out of their holding spots and attack the pogies. "The bait was harder to get than the bass," Dick says. "It was absolutely automatic." The duo tried other variations on the theme, such as stuffing a spark plug inside a live pogy's mouth and letting it swim and sink down to the bass. But using a bank sinker and a dead pogy always worked best.

For years, the men had the technique all to themselves, and they worked to keep it that way. They were incredibly secretive, carefully stowing their equipment out of sight and rigging the pogies below the gunwale. Dick still hoots at the memory of other fishermen's astonishment about their catches. "Hah! They used to come and watch us fish! Charter guys hated us so much!" No doubt he would've driven derby competitors crazy, too, if he'd ever entered. But he didn't, because he figured that as a commercial fisherman he would have had an unfair advantage. Let them have their fun. He only wanted to make a living.

A hotshot commercial fisherman named Scott Terry remembers Dick pulling up to a spot where he was catching bass on eels one day in the early 1990s. "These guys showed up and we didn't catch another fish. In the same spot where we were catching twenty-pound bass, they started pulling out two fish at a time, all thirty- and forty-pounders. They were in the oldest, most beat-up, crappy boats. Dick would just stand there with his little corncob pipe in his mouth. They'd drop that bait down and *boom!* The rod would go down. And then they'd just reel them up, calm as anything, put the little gaff in their mouth, pull them into the boat. I had never seen anything like it. I mean, it blew my mind. Because I honestly didn't think anybody could catch bass bigger than me. They just drove everybody insane. When you saw them coming, you left."

As far as its practitioners were concerned, Dick had invented the best way of consistently catching giant stripers ever devised. (His name for it, however, didn't stick. He always called it "dunking." For reasons unclear, it became more widely known as yo-yoing.) "They cannot resist a bait that doesn't swim away," said Scott, who eventually figured out how to yo-yo. "The water gets hot, the fish get lazy. They're laying in these spots resting, basically. If an opportunity presents itself they'll eat. And all of a sudden a pogy, their favorite thing in the world to eat, comes by and it looks alive but it doesn't swim away. It's amazing." Dick told me that if you dove to the bottom with a scuba tank and watched his boat drift overhead with a yo-yo rig fluttering off the bottom, you would understand. "It just looks *magnificent*. He looks better than a live one."

One year, Dick and his brother Robert and a friend named Bo Christensen made a tremendous catch while fishing around the Vineyard. Dick is seventy-seven, and his memory fails him at times, but he rattles off these numbers without hesitation in two separate conversations: 107 fish that weighed 2,348 pounds in about eight hours of fishing. "That," he said, conjuring up a spectacularly exaggerated boast, "was the best day anybody ever had anywhere." Christensen's twenty-two-foot Mako nearly sank. Time and again, the three men were hauling up fish simultaneously. They had to bail out water to stay afloat. They made it back to the dock and cleared more than $1,000 apiece that day. They went home, cleaned up, and celebrated over dinner with their wives.

No technique so effective could remain under wraps forever. Dick's friend told his friend, who told a few others, and soon a gang of Rhode Islanders were doing it. Slowly, inevitably, word leaked out to ever wider circles of fishermen. Scott Terry learned about the tactic from a tackle shop owner. Menemsha charter captain Buddy Vanderhoop traded a couple of prized spots for the secret, angering fellow islanders in the process. With Google and an Internet connection, the rest of the fishing world soon could learn about it from descriptions and diagrams that popped up on chat boards. I learned the basics over beers and burgers with a fisherman on my very first night on the island.

As the practice spread it evolved. Custom-made weights often replaced bank sinkers. Someone came up with the idea of sliding a coat hanger or something similar down the pogy's spine to keep it stiff permanently, a vast improvement over freezing it. Guys used hog rings to staple the mouths shut. Of course, there's more to yo-yoing than knowing how to rig the bait, Dick said. It takes a certain touch, a continuous shake of the rod tip as you drift over your spot. Pros might tinker with the weight and hook placement depending on the tide, wind, and current. As with every technique, the quality of the bait can be the difference between success and failure.

Despite its effectiveness, not everybody takes to it. When the Menemsha Kids started fishing the commercial bass season seriously around 1999, they didn't use pogies because the baitfish were scarce on the Vineyard and they were doing just fine with their own tactics and bait. Once they figured out their spots and honed their tactics, catching their limit of bass came easily. They could go out for a few hours on the right tide, get their fish, and go home. Then one year they started to struggle. When they saw rival fishermen whacking bass on pogies while they foundered, they realized it was time to make a change. Steve Morris, who runs Dick's Bait and Tackle, can pinpoint when it happened. The guys from Menemsha had been buying hundreds of pounds of eels from him every week. One week in July it stopped.

"What's going on?" he remembers asking one of them.

"The pogy bite's on," came the reply.

They were making regular runs in the predawn hours to net pogies. Once they turned to the usual pogy-fishing tactics it was only natural for some of them to try yo-yoing. It's not that all of them switched over entirely. Rather, some of them added it to their arsenal. Lev, for example, said he would yo-yo as a last resort, if the others were hammering bass and he couldn't make his limit some other way. Another island commercial fisherman told me he yo-yoed perhaps 15 percent of the time during the summer.

Conservation-minded fishermen, meanwhile, avoided the technique. As anglers had begun to discover, yo-yoing can have troubling consequences. When a striper hits a dangling pogy, it often knocks the baitfish free from the hook. Or, as Dick Sevigny told me, if a fish gets the bait in its mouth, "he spits it out and some other poor bastard eats it." After the flesh is digested, the hardware sometimes stays behind. One fish can conceivably eat many rigged baits.

In 2000, a fisherman sent New England's *On the Water* magazine a photograph of the contents of a 44-pound striper's stomach: more than a dozen wire skewers, sinkers, and hog rings. A columnist at the magazine set about trying to figure out how it happened (though some would later question whether all of that gear really ended up in one fish's stomach). He tracked down a tackle shop owner who explained the tactic. In his column about the photo, the writer noted, "It is a good thing you did not enter this fish in a tournament. You would certainly have been suspected of foul play." More to the point, lots of people found it repulsive to see all that hardware in a fish they loved. Even the inventor of the tactic isn't blind to the harm it may cause. "I'm sure it's doing some damage to the fish," Dick said.

Yo-yoing has become a new front in the bitter civil war between commercial and recreational fishermen over the striper. Six states have declared the bass a gamefish and outlawed its sale, and activist-minded sportsmen want the rest of the Atlantic Coast states to follow suit. Working fishermen point out that recreational anglers as a group kill far more stripers—three times as many—and say the sportsmen don't want to protect the bass but keep it for themselves. When it comes to yo-yoing, recreational fishermen have called for its ban, while its practitioners say the tactic is no more harmful than any other. Yo-yoers say the slim weights usually pass right through the fish's digestive system, though that doesn't exactly jibe with the fact that fishermen report catching bass with lead in their stomachs and wires sticking out their sides. Yo-yo sinkers fill a bucket under the cutting table where Buddy Vanderhoop filets the fish his clients catch. They line the windowsills of one island fish market.

And now they've found their way into the belly of a great derby fish.

After Ed arrives and begins asking questions, Lev categorically denies stuffing the fish. First off, he would have to be a moron to do it. "That would be like committing suicide," he says later. He has taken over the lead enough times to know that officials cut open every first-place fish. No way he would do something *that* boneheaded. Second, he says, considering how many people have been yo-yoing around the Vineyard in recent years, it's no surprise a big fish—probably twenty years old—would turn up carrying lead.

Still, by the time the weigh station reopens the next morning, people will be chattering about Lev and the big fish and how he *must* have cheated. How else would a pound and a half of lead end up inside that striper?

The situation raises two incendiary and deeply intertwined issues—cheating and conservation—that the derby committee has grappled with for decades. The derby has remained a tournament in which the fish are killed before being weighed in, even as other contests have found ways to adapt to modern sensibilities and promote catch and release. Some offshore competitions rely on time-stamped photographic evidence, and others use observers who track the number of fish caught and freed by each boat. In freshwater tournaments, bass are kept in livewells and returned to the water after being weighed. But it would be impossible for the derby to monitor three thousand fishermen over five weeks, and with major prizes at stake contestants can't be trusted to honestly report the size of the fish they release. Anglers generally do not have the equipment to keep their catch alive on the way to the scale, so it is the rare derby striper that is revived after a visit to the weighmaster. The derby has taken steps to safeguard itself against criticism. The tournament only accepts fish of a certain length and its minimum sizes are more strict than state law. It also donates five-thousand-plus pounds of fresh filets to senior citizens each year. But the conservation debate always looms in the background.

"Fishing," as the wise angler in John Hersey's *Blues* says, "is complicated." Is there morality in the sport? Is it ethical to hook a fish only for fun? Does releasing that fish absolve you of blame for the terror you inflict by hooking it, "playing it," and yanking it from its home? Or, as in bullfighting, do you give the beast dignity by killing it and eating it (or selling it) and understanding that you are a part of the terrible circle of life and death?

Competition only adds to the complexity. It has always been a central part of the fishing experience. That's the sinking feeling that washes over you when someone else gets a great fish. Talk all you want about how pleased you are for the guy who hooks a 50-pound bass, but most everybody wants bragging rights. "The biggest disease in fishing," one veteran told me, "is jealousy." That emotion is at odds with the idea that it should be a quiet sport in which man connects with nature, the idea Englishman Izaak Walton had in mind when he wrote his seminal fishing book *The Compleat Angler, or, The Contemplative Man's Recreation* in the seventeenth century.

To many fishermen, the whole concept of competitive angling seems off the mark. Legendary sports columnist Red Smith once wrote: "A surfcaster standing hip deep in foaming breakers and heaving a tin dornick toward the horizon is a pretty grim looking character at best. When he's trying to earn a $500 bond in addition to meat for the table, he looks like the wrath of Walton himself." And Red Smith actually enjoyed the derby, unlike Nelson Bryant, the *New York Times* outdoors writer who never hid his exasperation with it. "What is it about Americans," Nelson once wrote, "that they must make a competition of everything, including angling? Ideally, the competition, if there needs to be any, should be between the man and the fish." Years later, Nelson said his reasons were selfish as well as philosophical: the derby crowded his home waters during the fall run. "I liked it," he told me, "when I didn't see anybody else on the beach."

In 1984 Ted Williams, the well-known environmental journalist and fishing tournament foe, wrote a broadside in *Audubon* magazine. "I object to fishing tournaments less for what they do to fish than what they do to fishermen. They have invaded one of the last refuges of civilized man, transmuted a noble art into something it isn't and shouldn't be, and fouled our perception of wild, lovely lifeforms." He also condemned the "repulsive butchery and waste" at many contests.

Though his piece focused on other tournaments, his scathing critique appeared at the very moment Vineyarders found themselves parrying questions about their derby. By the early 1980s the striped bass population had plummeted up and down the coast. Half as many stripers came through the doors of the weigh station in 1980 as had in 1978. The *Gazette* reported, "Boat bass? Forget it. Nothing Tuesday, Wednesday or Thursday." The next year, it declared, "If it weren't for weakfish and bonito—two fish once considered, well, marginal to the real business of derby competition—the derby would be a grim affair. Bass are scarce, if not totally invisible."

John Cole, author and conscience of the striped bass fishing community, wrote years later that the *Gazette*'s reports of slim catches struck him as off-key. The newspaper seemed to be suggesting that stripers were only on vacation, taking a sabbatical, sure to return next week, next month, next year. Their fishing reports were examples of "a culture in denial," the way he saw it. In the paper's defense, just weeks after it declared the bass "scarce" in 1981, hundreds of enormous stripers assaulted the beach during the great

Columbus Day blitz. But if that seemed like a great thing at the time, it turned out to be the paroxysms of a collapsing population. Janet Messineo kept going to the same spots that had always produced fish, but she would end up writing the same bleak report over and over in her fishing log in the early 1980s. "Oh, we put unbelievable hours in. There were *no* fish. We'd go two *weeks* without even a fish. Not even a hit. It was really spooky."

In 1983 Ed Jerome told the fishermen at the derby awards banquet that the committee would make changes for the following year. Up and down the coast, sportsmen and environmentalists had begun to agitate for new restrictions, and politicians had begun to listen. Backed by Congress, regulators pressed states to cut the number of stripers caught each year. The derby had already stopped allowing fishermen to bring in as many bass as they could catch. After 1976 contestants could submit only their largest fish each day and minimum sizes were enforced. The derby haul tumbled from 4,290 fish in 1974 to 1,328 in 1978 (and the majority of those were blues). The days of dead fish piling up on the weigh station floor were over.

But killing *any* stripers had become controversial by 1984, when the committee members met to hash out their response to the declining population. They weighed a proposal to pull the fish out of the competition but ultimately voted it down, 11–9. Instead, they decided to go over and above state law, which required fishermen to throw back bass shorter than twenty-four inches. The weighmaster now would only accept stripers longer than thirty inches. Derby officials estimated that the number of bass weighed in during the contest would fall to below 150.

Still, the derby's stance on the striper seemed increasingly out of tune with prevailing opinion. Three articles that appeared in 1984 stand out. They ran in publications that were instrumental in establishing the derby thirty-eight years earlier. *Salt Water Sportsman* announced that it would not run any more stories about how to catch stripers until the population rebounded. It also published an editorial in which Hal Lyman, one of the founding fathers of salt-water fishing, criticized kill tournaments. The *Boston Herald,* meanwhile, asked how the Vineyard could continue to run a bass fishing contest under the circumstances. ("Concurrently, could there be a passenger pigeon shoot or a buffalo hunt?" the writer wondered sarcastically.)

In August things got ugly. A typed petition began to circulate under an urgent headline: REMOVE STRIPED BASS FROM THE 1984 VINEYARD DERBY! Calling the derby committee "negligent and irresponsible," the petition demanded action. "We believe it is morally wrong to continue awarding prizes and trophies for catching a magnificent fish which is in jeopardy of disappearing from our shores. On our island, numerous restaurants have taken striped bass off their menus as a conservation effort. So how can the Vineyard derby committee continue to glorify the slaughter of large striped bass, the very fish which bear the most eggs and carry perhaps the last hope for the future?" The petition drive was led by writer-environmentalist Dick Russell, who lived in a Boston-based commune known as the Fort Hill Community that had been founded in the 1960s by folk musician Mel Lyman. In 1971, the commune had been infamously disparaged in *Rolling Stone* magazine as a deranged cult tripping on LSD, but members denounced the story as a fabrication, and in the 1980s they reintroduced themselves to the world as a peaceful and prosperous collective with a successful construction business and an activist strain. The family, as they called themselves, owned property in New York and Los Angeles, a huge farm in Kansas, and a retreat on Martha's Vineyard; among its members was Jessie Benton, the daughter of famed painter and summertime islander Thomas Hart Benton. Many of them loved to fish for striped bass, and when the fish began to disappear they mobilized. By 1984 they'd already spent two years lobbying up and down the coast. In testimony before a congressional subcommittee, Russell imbued the bass with mystical qualities. "I believe that the striped bass is intrinsically linked to the spirit that created this country, and that it cannot be allowed to disappear. We need it, because this fish has a soul, and because to know the meaning of the striped bass is an experience of the soul. And in the mysterious exchange between fish and man which sheds light upon that universal lace inside us, we become more deep-connected to the meaning of life itself."

On the Vineyard the petition sparked a firestorm. Supporters and opponents nearly came to blows over the document at the annual ag fair, according to the *Gazette*. More than twelve hundred people ended up signing it, three-quarters of them from the island. Derby officials responded that they were taking steps to protect the bass already. No one wanted to see the fish go extinct, and the few caught during the derby would hardly send the striper skidding into oblivion. But critics argued that pulling the fish out would have symbolic value. "We really believed it was wrong to kill those bass for money when the whole species seemed to be on the verge of elimination," fisherman Kib Bramhall said. Some fish dealers in New England had already decided to stop buying bass. Other contests had withdrawn the fish. If the granddaddy of striped bass derbies moved to protect it, wouldn't others follow? The *Gazette* came out against the derby's position: "The striper must come out."

"It was an awakening," says Whit Manter, who, after years of catching and selling stripers, sided with the conservationists. "I was like, 'Oh my God, what have we done?'"

In the face of all of this the derby stood pat. Officials included a statement in contestants' registration brochures blaming the coastwide population decline on commercial overfishing and pollution in the Chesapeake Bay. On September 11, two days before the 1984 tournament opened, Maryland took a dramatic step: effective January 1 it would be illegal to take striped bass from state waters. The day after the derby opened, readers of the *Gazette* opened their papers to a full-page ad urging contestants to release any bass they caught: "Return them to the ocean. Give them the chance to return home." Dick Russell's group orchestrated the ad, which was signed by ten former tournament champions, several of the outdoor writers who had helped make the event famous, and many others.

During the 1984 derby only 110 stripers came to the weigh station, thanks to the new thirty-inch limit and the general decline in population. The next spring, the committee revisited the striper debate and again voted to keep it in the competition.

This time, key sponsors went for the derby's jugular. In April 1985 *Salt Water Sportsman* withdrew its backing, and the Boston Whaler company said it wanted to meet with the committee before it decided whether to follow suit. In a letter that struck the derby like a declaration of war, magazine publisher Spider Andresen —who was friendly with Russell and the family—wrote that "*Salt Water Sportsman* has been a loud voice in promoting conservation of the remaining brood stock of striped bass. For us to then turn around and back a derby that advocates the killing of these fish would be totally hypocritical." While acknowledging that only a small number of stripers would be caught, he wrote that "if every derby, tournament and fishing contest from Maine to South Carolina takes the attitude that the fish they kill are insignificant, then we have a real problem. Add all those dead fish together, and you do have a significant impact. If the dice roll up wrong, we probably have no more bass, and maybe no more derby in a few years."

The sponsors' letters surprised the committee and split its ranks. One faction believed that if they did not pull the fish sponsors would abandon them and the derby would collapse. The other side argued that the contest started as a bass contest and would wither and die without its signature fish. Some contended that striper populations went up and down in cycles, and that this was just a temporary downswing. The debate became bitterly personal. Men broke into tears. "I'm surprised," one of them told me, "a few of us didn't kill one another." To many committee members, the idea of not being allowed to catch and keep a striper as they had always done was like being told to stop breathing. "It was just a way of life," committeeman Porky Francis explained.

The *Gazette* editorial board again called for the derby to pull the bass, but the Chamber of Commerce sided with the derby and launched a broadside against the newspaper's "inflammatory and irresponsible" coverage. The embattled committee voted a second time to keep the striper in the competition, then decided to black-ball the newspaper. Their boycott was only the half of it for *Gazette* reporter Mark Alan Lovewell, who was working his first big story after leaving the production room for writing. One angry committeeman had actually threatened to beat him up.

In late May, after a full month of pressure—Andresen had been calling other sponsors and urging them to join the boycott—the committee reconvened. "That was the worst meeting of my life," said Cooper Gilkes, the tackle shop owner. "There were people who didn't want to give in. I said, 'Listen, we gotta do it, and we gotta do it now, or we're not going to have a derby.' There were guys who were really, really upset about it."

After a few hours the beaten-down committee members walked out and issued a brief statement: they would yank the bass.

"It was an either do-or-die situation, which was unfortunate," committeeman Tom Taylor told the *Gazette* after the meeting. "All the national sponsors were withdrawing. It was as if someone put a rope around the head, had a door beneath our feet and said, 'Do it or else we'll open the trap door.'"

But everything worked out in the end. Five months later, when organizers tallied up registrations, they counted 2,072, a record.

The old bass derby, it turned out, could survive even without the bass.

The derby endured and the stripers rebounded. The weigh station began accepting bass again in 1993. But the reverberations of the bitter brawl continue to be felt more than two decades later. The committee is now understandably sensitive about anything that might harm its image as a conservation-minded event. If organizers cannot turn the derby into a catch-and-release tournament, at least they can oppose overfishing and what they consider to be unsportsmanlike tactics. For instance, it upsets some conservation-minded fishermen that the derby promotes the killing of false albacore. Albie meat is so vile that almost no one will eat it. Shirley Craig has concocted a recipe that she swears is quite tasty—marinate overnight in lemon juice, olive oil, salt, oregano, minced garlic, and pepper, then grill—but she hasn't converted many fishermen. Instead, the carcasses end up at the filet barge, where they are cut in half and given to lobstermen for bait. The committee has sought to placate the critics by limiting each fisherman to three albies per derby.

In 2001, when committee members first learned about yo-yoing, they concluded that lugging around a belly full of lead did some harm to stripers, and they quickly banned the technique. But the tactic had become so widespread outside the derby—primarily among the commercial bass fishermen—that it threatened to complicate the committee's effort to separate cheaters from honest contestants. When the filetmaster cut open a fish taking over first place and found a significant amount of foreign matter in the stomach, the contestant was disqualified as a cheater of the lowest order, a fish stuffer, an outlaw who couldn't think of a more elegant way to game the system. Yo-yoing opened a gaping blind spot in that policy, as Lev's fish demonstrated.

What was to stop some character of low morals from stuffing a bass with lead and claiming the striper swallowed pogies rigged for yo-yoing? Or, conversely, what was to protect an innocent fisherman from catching a fish full of weights and being accused of cheating? Before the derby started I had posed that exact question to a longtime derby official. He told me that they could probably not invalidate a fish containing yo-yo weights. But the committee would ask a lot of questions and keep a close eye on the contestant in the future.

If all fishermen are liars, as the saying goes, it's tempting to see all fishing tournaments as a little crooked—and some of them as a lot crooked. Ray Scott, the huckster who invented the wildly successful Bassmaster tournaments, knew that to get television to broadcast fishing like football or basketball, cheating would have to be eliminated. Most events, Scott contended, are won by the guy who has the biggest fish in his freezer. "Those derbies are all alike, nothing more than little old Chamber of Commerce promotions where everybody pitches two dollars into a hat, then finds out who's the smartest at cheating without getting caught."

Many fishermen feel that way. Read the newspapers and you can understand why. A typical case: In 1985 a pipefitter weighed in a stringer of bass he had caught before a Louisiana competition and saved in an underwater bucket attached to a cypress branch. Fellow fishermen spotted the bucket, marked the fish by breaking the second dorsal fin on each of them, and called the district attorney. On tournament day, the con artist weighed in his fish and won a boat, an expensive rig, and $100 cash. Game wardens swept in and arrested him and he got two years' hard labor after pleading guilty to theft. (He had a prior criminal record.) The case prompted the state of Louisiana to make it a felony to cheat in a fishing contest. There is probably a story or two like this from every last event.

Fishermen have reportedly stuffed fish with newspapers, ice, and, in at least one case, a heavy rubber hose. Some tournaments have hired biologists and purchased special meters to check fish for freshness, hoping to combat anglers weighing in fish they bought from fish markets or caught long before the contest. One catch-and-release tournament director told *Boating* magazine of a fishing crew that hired a prostitute to keep their official observer busy while they radioed in bogus catches.

But it would be hard to top the lurid scandal involving a gang of men who won more than $350,000 by scamming freshwater bass tournaments in the early 1980s. The ringleader purchased big bass in Florida and gave them to at least four accomplices, who weighed them in as tournament fish in Texas. Organizers suspected they were cheating—some of them hadn't even bothered to fish to help sell the scam—but the men stuck by their stories and passed polygraph tests with the help of some alcohol and Valium. One of the bogus fish won a $105,000 first prize in a 1983 tournament on Texas's Lake O' the Pines. The case drew national attention after the body of one of the alleged cheaters, winner of $50,000 in a Labor Day contest, turned up dead in a lake near Dallas the day he was to testify before a grand jury. He had taken a shotgun blast to the head, and though his family suspected foul play—retribution for cooperating with investigators—the authorities ruled his death a suicide. Four men in the ring pleaded guilty in 1984 and went to prison.

No one has ever been incarcerated for defrauding the Martha's Vineyard Derby, but the specter of cheating has always loomed over it. In fact, the long knives were out for the first big fish the contest produced, a 39-pound striper caught by Dan Huntley in 1946. Reported the *Gazette:* "The Huntley fish occasioned some discussion, and questions were raised as to the proofs required for fish taken in such a manner." Right there at the start, people were apparently calling bullshit. The derby chairman vouched for the fish only after conducting a thorough round of interviews about where and when Huntley's boat had been spotted. He also put contestants on notice that the committee would investigate the circumstances of every top fish from then on. Even in its early years the derby reserved the right to cut open a fish or mark a fish that had been weighed. Boaters from off-island were required to check in at a Vineyard port for inspection before going out on a derby fishing trip.

At the same time, the derby's public stance has always been that 99 percent of the fishermen are on the up-and-up. For every cheater, there are many more men like Daniel Manter, who came upon an enormous striped bass dead on the beach one year. The fish, which might have run 65 pounds, had choked on a giant fluke. A lesser man would have claimed to have caught the thing and taken his bows as the derby's new bass record holder. This man took the giant home for dinner. The bass may have been a glutton but not old Daniel Manter.

Organizers have never had the ability to strictly enforce the rules on their own. (Not that they didn't try. Longtime weigh-station official Helen Scarborough said fishermen were told that a metal detector was hidden under the scale at the weigh station.) Instead, the derby's integrity has always depended on a somewhat shaky commodity: the honesty of fishermen. "The rules are few but we trust adequate, providing that each and every contestant lives up to the term of Sportsman," the 1953 rules declared. "If this is done, the Committee feels that every contestant will have a fair and equal chance at all prizes. Go with it; and may the best man, woman and juvenile win."

Not everybody could live up to that ideal. Kib Bramhall remembers bringing a 49-pound bass to headquarters in the 1970s only to be topped that very day by one weighing 51 pounds. "This fish was brought in with menhaden falling out of its gills," Kib recalls. Witnesses reported seeing the man who caught it brazenly stuffing baitfish into the striper on the dock at Menemsha. Rules and honor be damned, he was going to win the derby. Both the fish and the man were disqualified.

A 1975 incident shook the derby so profoundly that the committee entertained a proposal that it shut down for a year to study the problems and rehabilitate the event. A fisherman brought in an 18-pound bluefish that the derby first accepted, then recalled to the weigh station at a photographer's request. The fisherman had gone home and gutted the fish by the time they summoned him, and when the derby weighed the fish a second time, it had lost more than six pounds. Officials asked three experts—a fishmonger, a marine scientist, and the publisher of *Salt Water Sportsman*—about the disparity, and they declared the weight loss "extremely unlikely but not impossible," in the *Gazette*'s words. The fish stood, but the derby reiterated that it reserved the right to cut fish open if officials suspected foul play. "There are many stuffed fish infractions in any contest," rules committee chairman Richard Steigelman said. "It's a hard thing to control, because once the fish is gone you never know. This way, if there's a question, you just cut it open and you'll know the answer."

The committee went a step further. In 1976, fish pins, sweatshirts, and hats replaced the weekly monetary awards and plaques replaced grand-prize checks. Daily winners still took home cash and the top finishers got a shot at an eight-day trip to the Bahamas, but working-class fishermen griped about the changes. The money had helped subsidize the cost of bait and fuel, they argued, and given fishermen something to shoot for. But things had to change, derby organizer Dan Hull told the newspaper. "The money itself began to be a habit, and people in the last several years began to fish for money instead of fishing for competitive sportsmanship. It seemed to us time to put the emphasis back on the competition instead of the payoffs and place it on daily prizes instead of the big payoffs."

Curtailing the cash, they hoped, would curb the cheating. Yet over the years the event and the prizes continued to grow, and accusations of fishermen gaming the system continued apace. I heard of parents who caught a big fish and had their child weigh it in so they could get on the junior leaderboard. One angler suspected that a grand leader stuffed his big bonito with tinker mackerel. People are sure that bigger boat fish have been weighed as shore fish, and fish caught on spinning tackle have been weighed as fish caught on fly rod. Guys had been accused of weighing in the same fish on consecutive days, aiming to win the daily money twice (the tail is clipped to combat this now).

Of course, the Vineyard is a tight-knit island with no small number of personal and professional rivalries. Distilling allegations might require breaking down a series of convoluted interconnections. This fisherman married that fisherman's ex-wife. This one had a dispute with that one's father over a rental arrangement that went sour. This fisherman once owned a workboat with that guy's mother, and they had a falling out over the financial particulars of the arrangement. When a fisherman is accused of cheating—and it seems to happen every few years—the islanders' knotty relationships seem to end up factoring into the affair.

Ed Jerome assumes that much of what passes for proof of cheating among fishermen is just hearsay. But when someone files a formal grievance and other witnesses or evidence back up the story, the derby lowers the boom. Protecting the integrity of the derby is all-important. The committee had a banner year in 1998. First, a fisherman from Oak Bluffs brought in a bass that weighed more than 57 pounds. But he'd stuffed one or two pounds of frozen bait inside. Perhaps he didn't think they'd cut the thing open. Perhaps he didn't think at all. Even without the extra weight his fish would have taken the lead by about three pounds. He initially blamed an anonymous associate of stuffing the fish, then he blamed his habit of snorting heroin. "I disgraced the fish," he told Nelson Sigelman. "I disgraced myself."

Then, a few minutes before the last weigh-in was to end, a Connecticut fisherman turned up with a cooler full of bluefish. The committeemen there recognized him. He'd shown up earlier with another mess of fish. Upon questioning, he said he'd caught the fish in bounds, then brought them to Connecticut to weigh them in at another tournament before bringing them down to the Vineyard. That's illegal under derby rules, so he'd withdrawn the fish and declared it an innocent mistake. This time he had an 18-pound bluefish that took over first place, and he insisted he'd followed the rules. The derby brass doubted his story and launched an investigation with less than fifteen hours to go before the awards banquet. They interviewed a taxi driver who said he had picked up the man by the steamship dock, strongly suggesting that he had caught the fish somewhere else and taken the ferry over to the Vineyard. Technically, the rules prohibit competitors from transporting a fish out of bounds before bringing it to derby headquarters. Officials interviewed the fisherman at length and he said he'd caught the bluefish off the Gay Head cliffs in a center console and that friends had dropped him off at the dock. But the committeemen couldn't find anybody who had seen him or the boat he described on the water. An hour before the banquet they reinterviewed the man, this time with an environmental police sergeant present, and poked holes in his story. Still, they didn't have him dead to rights, Ed told me, not enough to disqualify the fish. So Ed pulled the man out into the parking lot and explained that if he chose to go in and accept his prizes the committee would keep investigating, and he could face larceny charges.

"I was bluffing," Ed says now. But the man withdrew his fish and left.

In the derby, no one is entirely above suspicion. Remember the feel-good story of 2005, twelve-year-old Molly Fischer and her 49.22-pound striper? They searched that fish, too, for foreign matter. The derby committee reserves the right to subject a possible winner to a polygraph, though they've never had to do it. (In other tournaments, lie detectors are routinely used.) Instead, the committee does something that sounds a lot like hazing. The perp enters a room and sits in a chair in the middle of a circle of pissed-off fishermen. They hammer the suspect with questions about the fish, probing for weaknesses, trying to break him down. They might suggest that he faces more than mere embarrassment: not only can he be kicked out of the tournament, he can also be charged with a crime. They might threaten to call the cops.

Make no mistake. You do *not* want to be suspected of cheating in the derby. A colonoscopy might be more comfortable.

Nobody needs to tell this to Lev. He knows. He's witnessed the whole drill play out on others: the accusations, the circle of interrogation, the lingering suspicions. He knows he's about to live his derby nightmare.

In the days and weeks before Lev caught the controversial fish, he and his friend Geoff Codding had both talked to me about feeling like they were under a microscope because they had won, or nearly won, so many times. People watched them to see where they were fishing and what bait they were using and how many fish they were catching. "There are *always* people watching you on this island. There are people watching us right now," Lev told me once as we sat in his pickup checking out the Menemsha jetty. It was six in the morning, and the parking lot was almost totally empty, but Lev wasn't laughing.

Geoff and I, out on his boat that Friday morning two days before Lev caught his giant striper, had gotten to talking about derby controversies. "The few people who've gotten kicked out have been the people who've won it a bunch of times, so me and Lev always talk about being extra careful about everything."

Two weeks earlier Lev had mentioned a fisherman who was using both eels and yo-yo rigs. If he caught a big striper on an eel, he planned to weigh it in the derby. If he got it yo-yoing he'd only weigh it in another competition—*On the Water* magazine's Striper Cup—in which yo-yoing was still legal. Even if Lev was inclined to walk that line, which he wasn't, he knew enough to see that he'd just be inviting a major controversy. He understood how the island worked: "People would say I've been cheating the whole time."

That's exactly the indictment he faces. There will be a permanent cloud over this one-in-a-million fish, the second-biggest bass Lev has ever caught, the biggest he has ever weighed in during the derby, and the eighth-largest anyone has caught in tournament history, even if you don't count the lead weights.

Lev faces the possibility that his records—the five victories, the grand slam mark—will be called into question. He faces the prospect of ending up like another Vineyard fishing legend who won time and again only to have his derby career end in controversy and disrepute. With Ed Jerome picking over those ten yo-yo sinkers, it doesn't seem at all out of the question that Lev could suffer the same fate as Dick Hathaway.

In 1997, after Dick had caught a bass grand leader for the fourth time at seventy years old, the local newspaper had hailed him as the greatest of the derby greats.

All that changed two years later after one fateful night of fishing.

8

Of Fish and Fists

Six-time champ Dick Hathaway, 1970.

It was the first night of the 1999 derby. Tisbury Great Pond was open to the Atlantic, and the best surfcasters knew what to do with a piece of information like that. Out there in the surf lashing away at the ocean were the fishermen who had taken the biggest striped bass from shore in the derby three of the previous four years: Steve Amaral's partner Mike Alwardt (1995), Mark Plante (1996), and Dick Hathaway (1997). Heavyweights, all of them.

At a heavyweight spot, too. On Columbus Day in 1981 this stretch of South Beach hosted just about the single greatest day of striped bass fishing any Vineyarder alive has ever seen. Enormous stripers blitzed the beach all day, 40- and 50-pounders, fish that could bend a treble hook straight. Even in that era before cell phones the news of the giant blitz struck Martha's Vineyard like a tidal wave, its undertow dragging fishermen away from their daily work and down to the surf line. Men caught a dozen bass so big that just one of the fish would have made their season. One caught a 50-pound bass that didn't even make the derby leaderboard. The first angler to race to the fish market in Menemsha got a good price, about $2 a pound; soon, the glut of stripers meant everybody else had to take 50 cents or ferry the bass up to the Cape. Some trucks were so loaded down with bass they sunk to their axles in the sand.

The opening at Tisbury Great Pond is a classic surfcaster's spot. The pond is a tear-shaped saltwater pool fed by springs and creeks that trickle through ancient farmland where islanders have pastured their animals for centuries. On the maps, the creeks feeding Tisbury and its twin, Edgartown Great Pond, look like the fingers of two hands clawing at the island's midsection. A mile-long barrier beach hems in the pond at the southern end. What makes Tisbury such a tremendous fishing spot is that it is opened a few times a year to let herring in and out, to adjust the salinity of its water for shellfish, and to keep houses on the pond from flooding. In the old days, it was done with a team of oxen and a plow, or with men and shovels. Today all it takes is a guy with an excavator. The machine digs away at the beach until the pond breaks through and flushes out to the sea, a conveyer belt of food that draws fish from miles around. It's a natural chum line, and for bass, bluefish, and the fishermen who chase them the opening is an event.

These days, though, getting there is difficult. The beach leading to the opening is generally closed to trucks because it's unsafe or because birds are nesting. Even if it is open, you would need connections with nearby property owners to gain access to the beach.

You could try to make a long drive from a public entrance, but you'd probably be stopped by erosion or another pond opening along your route. If you know what you're doing you can take a canoe across the pond. But what most fishermen do is park a mile off and hike in with their gear. The fact that guys are willing to do that is an indication of how good the fishing can be when the conditions are right. One fisherman I spoke with called it sacred ground.

Anyway, in 1999, all of them made the trip out there, one way or another, propelled by the promise of derby glory.

As the night wore on, Mark Plante and his fishing partner Ally Moore kept an eye on Dick Hathaway and his buddy Peter Jackson. They were apparently watching in the way that every fisherman on any beach looks at the guys around him to see who's catching bass. What they saw jolted them. State law and derby rules allowed each fisherman to take just one striper per day. It was dark out there, but there was a moon in the sky, and Mark and Ally would say later that they could see the two men as clear as day: they were hauling in bass and they didn't seem to be tossing them back.

"He was a hard man," says Tom Teller, employing the kind of praise a serious fisherman doesn't deliver lightly. "Fishing with him, you didn't get much sleep. You either fished or you went home." Tom, former district court clerk in Edgartown, met Dick as a teenager, and later as neighbors they spent a lot of nights on the beach. "He always seemed to catch the big fish. You'd always wonder. Why does the big fish always bite his hook?" (Dick's answer: He always kept his line in the water. That, and he was lucky.) One night they went out and each caught three fish using the exact same tactics. Tom's biggest striper weighed maybe 20 pounds. Dick's *smallest* came in at 25 pounds. Another time, Dick took a group of friends fishing and they caught sixteen fish. He got fourteen of them. Tom says, "I never caught more fish than him."

Look at Dick's résumé and it's hard to imagine anybody ever did. It's the stuff of folk heroes. There are the six derby-winning fish—four bass and two bluefish—landed in four different decades, including a 60-pound, 2-ounce bass he caught on a live eel on Chappaquiddick in 1978, which still stands as the biggest ever caught during the contest. He also caught the top striper by an islander one year. Dick was literally *the* poster boy. In a lot of fish grip-and-grin shots from the 1960s he's the guy pictured on the giant backdrop. He has the trophies from all the years he won the R. J. Schaefer Salt Water Fishing Contest, a coastwide, season-long tournament, and the heaviest total tonnage in the Martha's Vineyard Derby—or at least he did until he sold all but a handful to a friend who collects that sort of paraphernalia. Dick said he once did a tally of his 50-pound stripers and counted fourteen.

"He's just phenomenal," said fisherman-artist Kib Bramhall, whose photographs of Dick made the cover of *Salt Water Sportsman* three times. "He's got a sixth sense about where to fish and how to fish. I would never bet against him in any fishing contest."

Who else can say he got a bluefish from a helicopter? (I know, it sounds like an obvious whopper, but Dick showed me a newspaper clipping about the feat, which gives it more credence than most Vineyard fish stories.) One year a friend bought a two-seater and he was doing some flying to earn a pilot's license. The aviator and the fisherman got to talking, one thing led to another, and Dick ended up in the passenger seat of a helicopter hovering thirty-five feet over the water off Wasque Point. He would drop a popper into a school of fish, get a bluefish on tight, and try to reel it up. But the line kept snapping. He ordered his buddy to land the chopper on the beach, where he rigged up with 80-pound-test line. Back in the air Dick hooked a blue, fought it for a bit, told the pilot to put the bird on the beach again, then jumped out and dragged the fish in. (Try to pull *that* stunt today, you snot-nosed whippersnappers.)

Dick didn't start fishing until he was a teenager working with the Grant Brothers, a construction firm on the Vineyard. His boss, Ralph "Red" Grant, loved to fish, and he told the story of Dick's first fishing trip in Robert Post's cult classic *Reading the Water,* an oral history of Vineyard surfcasters assembled in the 1980s. One day Dick walked up to Red and said, "How about you guys taking me fishing tonight?" So Red took the kid out to Chappaquiddick. Dick had walked down the beach from the rest of them when his first fish hit the plug, an Atom. Dick told me he couldn't figure out how to get the conventional reel started—he'd never used one before—and nobody was close enough to help him, so he leaned the rod up against some tree roots and started hand-lining. He got the thing close to the shore and didn't know what to do, so he jumped on it. Red swore that Dick's first striper tipped the scales at 35 pounds. He recalls Dick hugging the beast.

In time, Red watched Dick grow into a relentless all-night kind of fisherman. One day, he arrived at Edgartown Great Pond to find Tom and Dick fishing. Red fished for a while, then walked behind Dick and watched for a stretch, then went back to his spot and fished a little more. Red came and went a few more times and finally opened his mouth. "Christ," he asked Dick. "Are you *rooted* there?"

When he was younger Dick would go out every night. He'd get off at five from his job paving roads or digging foundations or cesspools, pack something to eat, and head out to Squibnocket or South Beach or wherever. During the derby he would either use all his vacation time to fish every day or fish outside working hours. "We fished as late as we could," Tom told me. "I remember one morning we were chewing NoDoz trying to stay awake to fish." Dick had little patience for those who couldn't keep up. He would reel up or cut the lines of his weak buddies who thought they could bait up, cast out, retire to their trucks to sleep, and count on Dick to wake them up when a fish hit.

It got to the point that Dick became one of the guys people followed. "Everybody tried to trail him all the time because they always said he was half-fish anyway," the late derby veteran Bob Boren said in an interview for the Martha's Vineyard Museum. Tom remembers hearing word of Dick's whereabouts crackle over CB radios. Once, riding with Dick, Tom watched him lose a tail by speeding away and making a screeching turn onto a side road. The cat-and-mouse games fueled more than one dispute.

Once, finding a group of guys camped out on a beach where he'd been hammering fish the day before, Dick drove up and planted his line of rods directly in front of them. Another time, Tom saw him handle the situation differently. "He drove up to the guy and said, 'Why don't you find your own spots, you son of a bitch?'" He drove off, mad as hell. An hour later he came back and pulled up with a 40-pound striper on the tailgate of his truck. "There's fish all over this place!" Dick shouted at the guy. "Why don't you find your own fish!" Tom wouldn't have believed it if he hadn't seen it with his own eyes.

Naturally, Dick grew into a controversial figure. As the *Times* put it a few years ago, he is "considered a scoundrel by some, a friend by others, a good fisherman by most."

To his buddies he's fiercely loyal and generous to a fault. His friend Pete Bradshaw tells of Dick giving him antique fishing lures and asking for nothing in return. He has befriended fishermen on the beach, taken them out to his spots, and had them over to the house for dinner. One year, when a young boy had his tackle box stolen, Dick got him a new one, filled it with fishing gear, autographed the top, and won some good press.

To his critics he's hotheaded, a stubborn know-it-all, a guy who will do anything to win. "He was brutal," said Whit Manter, a contemporary.

Even his allies tell stories of his short-tempered abrasiveness. Islander Donny Benefit, who fished with the man for many years and remains a staunch supporter, remembers one devilish tactic Dick used when fighting a big striper in a crowd on the beach. Fishermen usually reel in their lines and get out of the way when another man is battling a good fish. This time, with Dick walking down the beach to keep up with the bass, a few fishermen didn't move. So, Donny says, Dick casually grabbed their lines, severed them with the tip of his cigarette, and continued on down the beach. Kib Bramhall remembers that in 1981, after Kib came in with a 42.14-pound striped bass—which is still a derby record on a fly rod—Dick ran into the guy who'd been bumped to second place, a man Dick didn't much like. "Dick went in and just batted him on the shoulder and said, 'You're beat, you asshole!'" Kib still laughs at the memory.

Dick will tell you himself that he got into his share of fights. He boxed in smokers, unsanctioned fights held on the island. But he made his reputation in the barrooms. Somebody would say something, Dick explained, and he'd put up his fists without a second thought. Eventually, the cops would arrive and drag the combatants to jail for a couple of hours until they sobered up. He said he won more than he lost. "He didn't take no shit," Pete Bradshaw told me in his English accent. "He were a wild man. He had good hands, did Dick."

He made the newspapers as much for his fast fists, it seems, as for his fishing prowess. A 1962 story was typical. Dick and some other men were shucking scallops at Eldridge's Fish Market in Edgartown. They got into an argument over the volume of the radio and one guy pointed his scallop knife at Dick. Later, on the witness stand, Dick explained what happened next.

"I hit him in the jaw once," he said.

"That's all?" the prosecutor asked.

"I might have swung again," Dick replied.

The other man ended up with a broken jaw. Dick ended up with a $50 fine.

His last documented scrap came in 1995. A shellfish constable checked to see whether the scallops Dick had harvested were of legal size and apparently found a number that were borderline. "He hit me twice," the shellfish constable told the Edgartown selectman when it came up in a public meeting. "He punched me in the arm. This guy has been a bully for God knows how long. Somebody has to stand up to him." The police report stated that Dick threatened to "get a baseball bat and beat his face in." Dick told the selectmen that the warden had singled him out for the inspection and he denied hitting him.

Dick is hardly the only island fisherman to get in a few fistfights—not by a long shot. But his reputation as a renegade made people willing to believe the rumors about that giant striper of his, the 60-pound, 2-ounce derby record breaker. He brought it in one October morning in 1978 as soon as the weigh station opened, signed his slip, stood for a picture, and quickly left, according to a newspaper account of the day. People found it odd that he didn't stick around to bask in the glory of his accomplishment. The *Gazette* called it "modesty foreign to most fishermen." Dick told me he sold the bass on the spot to some fishermen from New Jersey who had followed him off the beach to the weigh station.

What was with that bass, people asked, that a guy as ambitious as Dick Hathaway would steal away without taking his bows? When I asked around, many longtime fishermen said they were told that something unusual happened in the weighmaster's station that morning and, somehow, a 50-pounder was recorded as a 60. One guy called it the "Phantom Sixty." The story is that only one derby official was there at the time, Helen Scarborough. In those days, they used a 20-pound scale, and with big fish the weighmaster had to count the number of times the dial went around the face. Some say she misread the scale. Some say she was busy setting up the headquarters and left it to Dick to figure out the weight. Some say she had bad eyesight. In any case, once Dick walked out it was too late to double-check the weight. The fish was gone.

Of course, nobody can prove Dick's fish wasn't really a 60, but the story of the supposed shenanigans circulates in the fishing community as fact. At some point, somebody extrapolated a rough measurement of the fish by comparing it to the shingles of the building in the background of that lone photograph and estimated its weight based on a historical striped bass length-to-poundage chart. Although that strongly suggested it would not have weighed 60 pounds, the evidence was inconclusive at best. A mason named Tim White came in second place with a 56-pound bass that year. When I called him up three decades later, he said he didn't want to discuss Dick's fish. "It's over," he said. "It's history now." But White never fished the derby again.

As far as Dick is concerned the speculation is garbage. He caught a giant striped bass, they weighed it, they ran the picture in the newspaper, and that was that. So what if he got out of there before anybody could take a look at it? It was a Wednesday morning. He had to work. "This is all a big joke," he told me.

Ed Jerome was not involved in the 1978 incident—he arrived on the island the next year—and declined to weigh in on the matter. Many officials of that era have died. The chairwoman at the time, Ruth Meyer, whose father, Larry, used to fish with Dick, said she didn't recall the debate. I've been told that Helen Scarborough is the only other person in the weigh station that morning who is still alive. When I spoke to her, she said the story is false. Her husband, Henry, was working as weighmaster that year, and he read the scale correctly. "I was there," she insisted. "It was *not* read wrong." But she acknowledged the controversy over the bass. People didn't get a look at it, she said, and that gave it a stigma. Some people suggested it had been stuffed. What's the truth?

"Only he and God knows," she said. Her opinion, for what it's worth: the 60 really was a 60.

But there are those who say that if some misfortune befell Dick, well, he had it coming, didn't he? Isn't that what happens when you think the rules don't apply to you anymore, if they ever did? Who would be surprised to see Dick's karma circle back and kick him in the pants?

Then again, if somebody accused Dick of cheating, what would the derby do? Toss him out, the legend, the myth, the six-time champ?

For years, plumber Mark Plante had been the hardest of the hardcore fishermen during the derby. He's a man's man, tough, athletic, and competitive. He has a gap-toothed grin and wears a simple ring in his left earlobe. He grew up across the sound in Bourne and as a kid fished the Cape Cod Canal. Back then, so much bait coursed through the big ditch that a school of feeding bass would send squid fleeing to the rocks. Their decaying carcasses looked like a high-water mark on the walls of the canal. Today, Mark's an all-around sportsman: bow hunter, angler, first-rate skeet shooter. In 2007 he hit one hundred straight targets over at the rod and gun club on Sengekontacket Pond. He holds the derby grand slam record from shore, 77.5 pounds. The basement of his house (the "Man Cave") could pass for a tackle shop. He built a vast workbench with drawers for his supplies and a notched backboard where dozens of identical lures hang, organized by size, hooks sharpened and ready for action. I counted thirty-one rods on an overhead rack, fresh line on the reels. I didn't check but I would not have been surprised to see his instructional videos lined up in alphabetical order. *Intense* isn't a big enough word for how Mark does it.

"He'll walk out onto the jetty and reel in like nine-thousand albacore," Dave Skok told me. "It's a show. He'll take no shit from small albacore."

"He catches them by sheer willpower," Chris Windram chimed in.

"Hell, yeah, and every once in a while he'll cast. If you have an albacore on the leaderboard and *that* guy comes out to the jetty, your boots are shaking." Dave speaks from experience, two-time winner that he is.

Mark's unrelenting attitude came from going out with his father growing up. They fished to help pay the bills. Mark has never had a trophy striper mounted. There's a picture in his house of Mark when he was thirteen holding a 45-pound bass he caught. After they took the picture the big striper went to market. "Didn't grow up with a whole lot," Mark explained. "I was raised doing it differently than some people. As opposed to being fun, it was more of a job. Get out there, get the fish."

He moved to the island to make a living on the construction boom. It didn't take long for him to get into the derby. He was ambitious from the start. Sure, he enjoyed the camaraderie and good times, but he was also in it to win. The way Mark figured, he could outwork just about anybody, and he stood to win a $30,000 boat. So why *not* take it seriously and try to win it all? In his younger days, Mark told me, he wasn't above tying on a sinker and firing it over the bow of a boater who got too close.

"He's just a maniac competitor," said Johnny Hoy, island fisherman and rhythm-and-blues band leader. The first year he fished the derby his wife, Valerie, was pregnant and Mark was leading the Triple Crown—the grand slam of its era, when bass were off-limits

161

and fishermen could only weigh in bluefish, albies, and bonito. "Hold off, hold off!" he told her. And she did. He went to the ceremony, collected his awards, returned home, and crashed. Two hours later his wife woke him. Time to go to the hospital. That was his derby baby.

In 1996 he won it with a 47.37-pound bass he caught in the first ten minutes of the competition. The next year, Dick came out of derby retirement to win with a 50.75-pounder—a major achievement for a seventy-year-old man. In 1998 Dick got a 42-pounder, a pound and a half shy of making him a repeat winner for the second time. Mark's 38 finished in third place.

Though they occupied the same real estate on the derby's chalk leaderboards every fall, they didn't know each other personally. In 1999 that would change.

On the first night of the derby Mark and his fishing partner, Ally Moore, got to the pond opening early and waited for the derby to officially begin at 12:01 a.m. They hung around and chatted with Dick and his partner, Peter Jackson. Mark said he had never met Dick before that night, but Peter was an uncle of Mark's wife, and Ally had had cordial conversations with Dick on the beach over the years.

Soon, midnight arrived, and they all baited up and started fishing. They were thirty to fifty yards apart, Mark and Ally said (Dick says they were farther off) and everybody was getting fish. As they watched Dick and Peter, they started to get suspicious. When the men unhooked their fish, Mark told the *Times,* "there was more walking up to the vehicle than down to the water." Mike Alwardt told me he remembers much the same thing: "Everybody was getting small fish and throwing them back, throwing them back. They were getting small fish and throwing them in the truck." When Dick and Peter started packing up, their truck lights on, Mark and Ally

162

said they watched through binoculars as the men pulled a number of fish out of the sand and into the Jeep alongside two other fish. Mark said he walked down the beach and confronted them. He told Dick and Peter that he'd seen it all. In other words, if they knew what was best for them, they shouldn't weigh in those fish. Dick says this conversation never happened.

Mark said he returned to his truck and talked it over with Ally. They weren't sure what to do. Should they let it slide? Wait and see if they weighed in a fish? They figured they'd made their point. And as the men knew, he and Ally were both on the derby committee. Dick and Peter would be crazy to take a fish to Edgartown after that.

But a few hours later, there they were at the weigh station. A *Gazette* photographer snapped a quick picture: Dick in a ball cap and striped shirt, holding up the bass by its gill plate like the old pro he was. It weighed 28 pounds. Day One of the derby and Dick Hathaway was back in first place again.

The one-bass-per-day law arrived when the striper population crashed in the 1980s, and the derby required fishermen to follow state conservation laws. As a competitive matter, the rule forced an angler to decide whether to keep a big fish or throw it back and try to get something larger.

The fact is, like most derby rules, enforcement had never been better than spotty. Guys generally don't want to accuse other fishermen of cheating and get dragged into a mudfest.

"A lot of people wouldn't want to be the guy to tell on Dick Hathaway," Mike Alwardt said.

I asked him why.

"Retribution," he answered.

Mark said he agonized over the decision because it would mean tangling with a true Vineyard legend, a man revered as much as he was reviled. And Dick's partner Peter was family. But there was a boat on the line. Cheating to win was akin to grand larceny, wasn't it?

Ally backed him up, and that same morning they went to talk to Ed Jerome at the school. They formally lodged their complaint and the derby's jury of peers convened. The committee brought in Dick and Peter and hammered them with questions about the night. The men stuck to their stories, and some in the room seemed willing to accept their defense. The interviews ended and the group deliberated for several hours before taking a vote.

To the charge of breaking derby rules by keeping more than one fish per day, the committee found the men guilty.

The sentence: banishment for ten years.

Word spread quickly, even though the committee does not publicize cheating violations and generally refuses to talk about them in public. When the news hit the papers, Dick did what he did in the old days. He came out swinging. "We put two bass in that Cherokee," he told the *Gazette*. "I raised my right hand to God. I will take a polygraph test." Dick told an entirely different story than Mark and Ally. He said that early on the night in question he had run into Mark on the beach. Mark was cutting a fence on the beach that led to the pond opening and Dick told him to stop. A Massachusetts conservation group, the Trustees of Reservations, owned the fence and part of the beachfront. Fishermen generally drove between the surf and the fence to get down to the opening. "If you cut that fence down," Dick said he told Mark, "you'll ruin it for everyone." He said Mark stopped cutting, got back in the truck, and drove around the fence to the opening. Dick and Peter followed.

The truth, Dick said, was obvious: Mark concocted the cheating charges because he was upset that Dick had barked at him for trying to cut the fence. Dick filed countercharges against Mark and demanded that *he* be thrown out for a decade. But Mark denied it, and derby officials concluded that Dick's narrative didn't add up. A Trustees of Reservations official went out and checked the fence and reported that it had not been vandalized. Besides, Steve Amaral had permission to take the fence down entirely during the derby if it interfered with the fishermen.

"Lie after lie," Dick snorted, still denying everything eight years later. "It was so crooked."

There are those who have never quite understood how Mark and Ally saw *anything* in the dark that night.

In some circles, talk spread that the binoculars Mark and Ally used were a very expensive pair with night-vision capability, and to the conspiratorially minded on the island that prompted rampant speculation. Had they been spying on Dick? Did the derby committee want Dick out of the tournament? Nonsense, contest officials said. "Unless I'm totally oblivious to stuff," Mark told me, "there is never talk at committee meetings about, 'Okay, this guy has just gone on long enough. We've got to take him out.' It just goes to show you how people think the worst." As a member of the committee, his job includes being observant. In this case, he happened upon the incident and did what he thought was right—nothing more, nothing less. "If I was ever in the lead in the derby and then saw Peter Jackson and Dick Hathaway bump me off the board," Mark said, "I might as well not fish the derby for striped bass again."

For the record, Mark told me the binoculars were standard issue. He said you'd be surprised how much light they pull in from the moon on the beach at night. (I would add that to puzzle over a fisherman using binoculars is to feign naïveté. Every serious fisherman knows that intelligence is the road to the grand prizes, and that includes finding out what other fishermen are up to. Fresh bait and fresh intelligence—that's what gets you a shot at the boat or the truck. Unless you want to be another guy who casts until your arm falls off and waits for old Bullshit Luck to smile on you.)

Even so, some people couldn't shake the feeling that the derby brass had railroaded Dick on flimsy hearsay evidence.

Scott Terry felt that way about his own run-in with the committee in 1992. In the 1980s he had emerged as a fishing star. Before the competition one year, he caught a 66-pound striper from a boat that is among the biggest ever caught in Vineyard waters. He caught a 17.41-pound bluefish in the 1988 derby and an 18.5-pound bluefish and a 9.27-pound bonito in the 1991 contest—all of them grand leaders. He won the grand-prize Whaler in 1991. The following year his derby career hit the rocks.

Buddy Vanderhoop, the Menemsha charter boat captain who traded Vineyard fishing spots for the yo-yoing secret, took center stage in the Scott Terry incident. He admits that he always hated Scott, who had a rival charter operation, fished commercially, and, in true Vineyard fashion, moonlighted as a painter of landscapes. Buddy didn't like his personality, or his Mohawk haircut for that matter.

Scott rubbed lots of people the wrong way. He admits he wasn't the kind of guy to go quietly about his business. He had a tendency to let others know when he caught big fish. "Back then," Scott explained, "part of the reason that people who consider themselves upright pillars of the community didn't like me was because when people would follow me to one of my spots I would let them know I didn't like it. I would yell and scream and swear at them and throw beer cans in their boat." Once, he infamously dropped a couple of M-80s off his stern to scare away the fish and discourage a rival who was following his drift over a spot. "I did have a reputation for being a wild man," he admits. "If another boat came and got close it was war." (Today he says he's eased up: no more shouting, no more firecrackers.)

Of Fish and Fists

"I can't stand that freak," Buddy says. But in the same breath he insists he had no reason to lie about what he saw that October day in 1992.

During the last week of the derby, Buddy says, he was bluefishing with his daughter off Nomans Land, a former navy bombing range off the southwest end of the Vineyard, when he saw a boat steaming up from miles off shore. Buddy said he saw Scott and his friend Glenn Pachico and a bunch of wet burlap bags lying on the deck, presumably covering a mess of big fish. Buddy thought he'd caught them red-handed. Clearly, they'd come from out of bounds, and he figured they'd probably been fishing out of bounds. That night, Buddy and his daughter went to Edgartown to weigh in a little bluefish she'd caught. Scott and Glenn had already been there to weigh in fish, and Glenn's 17-pound bluefish had taken over the lead. Indignant, Buddy told the gang at the weigh station that he'd seen them come in from out of bounds.

He filed a formal grievance, and Scott and Glenn got dragged before the committee and pounded with questions. Buddy, as an outspoken Scott Terry detractor with a reputation for having a loose idea of what constitutes a fact, was not the most credible witness. In fact, many considered him the single least credible witness on the Vineyard. ("It's kind of like your divorced wife leveling charges against you," Scott told me.) But soon enough, the committee said they had corroboration from others and found the men guilty. They pulled their fish off the board and prohibited them from fishing the derby for 10 years. "This has gotten so out of proportion," Scott protested to a *Gazette* reporter. "I fish hard and I fish every day. And I was fishing in an odd place that day. But I was not fishing out of bounds."

He fought the decision and lost, but seven years later, Scott was in a good position to comment on the Hathaway scandal. Appearing anew in the *Gazette*'s op-ed pages, he questioned the legitimacy of committeemen who participate in the derby and also sit in judgment of fellow competitors. Scott wrote: "I'm not trying to imply that the Derby committee is conspiring to eliminate the best fishermen from the competition, although that sort of does seem to be the result." He said he knew Mark Plante as "an honest person who I believe would do what he thought was right." But he said a fisherman should not be thrown out solely on the testimony of another fisherman.

When I asked Scott whether he thought his success had something to do with what happened to him, he said, "You know the way people's egos are on the Vineyard about fishing. Everyone wants to be thought of as the best fisherman, and there gets to be a lot of competition, and competition turns into jealousy." At the same time, he says, "I think there's a lot of honest people on the derby committee. I believe they thought I was fishing out of bounds. But I also believe I was given no chance to defend myself. I still believe there was nothing that could be considered evidence."

Ed Jerome declined to talk about the incidents involving Dick and Scott. He is generally loath to talk about the particulars of any cheating case. He is a keeper of the derby tradition and guardian of the contest's integrity. No good can come from publicly airing disputes over bad conduct. "We just want to continue to operate a good healthy tournament," he said. "Once you start getting into 'he said, she said,' you've lost the whole idea of what the tournament's about." Ed will say only that, when an incident is reported, the derby committee gives both sides a chance to speak, and the members deliberate gravely before voting to toss someone out. "It's a pretty tough thing," he said soberly. "This is one family out here. We're not out to hurt anybody."

Mark is reluctant to talk about Hathaway anymore. Everybody is. He's old news, yesterday's hero, a guy whose place in history is sealed. If he fishes after the ten years are up or he doesn't, people say, who cares? Mark still bristles about the bruising battle. He says he took no joy in being the guy to turn state's witness. "It was a situation that sucked, dude," he told me. If he had to do it over again, he would have called the environmental police and let them deal with it. (That's why he keeps the officer's number programmed into his cell phone now.) Supporters gave him credit for sticking his neck out and blowing the whistle on a couple of apparent cheaters. Ally, for his part, is glad they had the guts to do it. But others considered Mark and Ally little more than rats. Turning in a great fisherman like Dick Hathaway is, as far as Donny Benefit is concerned, "the worst thing you could do." On an island where people take their birthrights seriously, some of Dick's allies thought that a transplant didn't have the *right* to take on a lifelong Vineyarder.

Ally said he went back out to the opening alone several times later that year, and on more than one occasion a truck pulled up behind him while he fished in the surf. The driver shined his headlights into the water for several minutes before moving down the beach to a different spot. Was it a friend of Dick's delivering a message? Ally never found out but it scared him enough that he reported it to the police.

It didn't help Mark's mental state that amid all the controversy he and his wife were struggling to find a house on the island. They'd been saving up but still didn't have quite enough. So they bounced from rental to rental. Mark started going to town meetings and agitating for action on affordable housing, an explosive issue in Vineyard politics. It was a bit controversial for a relatively recent arrival—a *washashore,* as they are called—to protest that he could not find property in his price range. Mark says he wasn't looking for a handout. He was willing to work hard to make a home on the Vineyard. But the fact is, many islanders think that housing programs should first help those who grew up on the island.

Then the craziest thing happened, just when it looked like the Plante family would have to move.

In 2000, on the last night of the derby, Mark went out on Ally's boat. They circled the Vineyard, breaking one of the central tenets of fishing: don't leave fish to find fish. They had heard reports of people whaling on bonito off the south end of the island, and that's where they planned to go. On the way, they spotted albies and bonito breaking off Vineyard Haven and then off Menemsha, but they stuck to the game plan. Mark bought a lime-green lure called a Rebel at the dockside Texaco and installed stronger hooks on the way. Within two minutes of arriving at the spot Mark hooked a bonito. In less time than that, the fish stripped almost all his line off the spool. Mark called for Ally to start the boat and follow the fish. "I said, 'Ally, if you don't get that thing in gear . . .' I can hear the line whistling." It was on the brink of snapping.

Ally got the boat moving. Mark reeled in some line and brought in the fish.

A few hours later, Mark arrived at the last derby weigh-in. His 10.37-pound bonito took over the lead and he settled in for the interminable wait until ten p.m. "You should've seen him," Dave Skok said the next day. "You'd think he was giving birth or something, wondering if there was still another big fish out there."

There wasn't, and the next day Mark got on stage with a shot at the grand-prize boat. And wouldn't you know it? Ed put Mark's key in the lock and it turned with a *click*. Mark's first thought—after the fist-pumping excitement faded—was this: I can sell the boat and make the down payment on a house. But in the end he didn't have to do it. He negotiated his way into an affordable lot, built a house, and kept the boat. Somehow, someway, it all came together.

Now, almost a decade later, Mark says he's lost some of his drive. He says that sometimes his teenage daughter has to push him to get out on the water. He says he enjoys putting her on fish as much as catching them himself. But when I asked his friend Steve Morris whether Mark had mellowed he sounded a bit dubious. "Maybe," he said, "just a smidgeon."

I can imagine Dick's head nearly shooting off his shoulders when Mark won the derby. He can't get over what happened in 1999. In some ways, the allegations boggle the mind. It doesn't make any sense that Dick, with all his records and awards, would cheat to weigh in a 28-pound fish. He'd caught countless giants. Why break the rules for a relative half-pint? And if he really did do it, and Mark really did warn him on the beach, what was Dick thinking? That nobody would believe a newcomer's word over the legend's? Did he still need to get his picture in the newspaper, still need to see his name atop the leaderboard on the first day of the derby?

Dick's steadfast denials notwithstanding, even his supporters don't consider it out of the realm of possibility that he kept a few extra fish that night. "Who knows?" said Ruth Meyer, who used to own Larry's Tackle Shop. "Probably could've happened." But lots of things have happened over the years. Lots of guys supposedly bent the rules and *they* weren't always strung up. She is among those who believe people were suspicious of Dick in part because of his reputation. "There was always that whispering going on. I mean, he was a little bit of a renegade."

Donny Benefit is still outraged about the whole thing. Dick taught him—and a lot of other people—everything about how to fish the surf. How to preserve freshly caught squid (put them on cardboard, don't let them touch each other, and they'll die a natural-looking red). How to mark a spot during the day so you can find it at night (leave a Pepsi can or tie reflective plastic to the beach grass). How to avoid leaving tire tracks in the sand (put down a short plywood boardwalk, drive on it to the end, then get out and move the boards to the front of the truck and repeat until you're out of sight).

Whatever Dick did or didn't do that night in 1999, Donny said you could drive any beach on any night of the derby and find fishermen with extra stripers buried in the sand. "It's just insane what they did to him," he said. "They made a big mistake."

To some, Dick was guilty of little more than being an old man out of step with the times, a man who was unwilling to play by the new rules. When he started fishing the derby, guys would catch as many striped bass as they could load into their trucks. They weighed in the big fish, took their bows, and drove to the fish markets or restaurants and sold the rest. Everybody did it as a way of financing their obsession. (People still do it with bonito. Geoff Codding sold a mess of them in September for $2.50 a pound, earning a couple of hundred dollars to pay for his gas and bait.) But the world had changed, and the new generation of fishermen is more concerned about striped bass conservation.

"He was just catching more bass than he was allowed," Kib Bramhall said. "He wasn't trying to cheat on the derby. He just liked to give fish to people. I think it was just very poor judgment on his part. I think he probably was enough of an icon that he felt he didn't have to obey the rules, and somebody called him on it and he got caught."

Whatever the truth, Dick goes down as the derby's Shoeless Joe Jackson, or Pete Rose, or Barry Bonds. Once a star, now an outcast. Nearly a decade later, friends say he has mellowed significantly. But his bitterness about the affair is as intense as ever. I met him one afternoon at his regular morning and afternoon hangout in front of a convenience store in Edgartown. He had just been through an operation and looked frail in a T-shirt and Crocs. The only vestige of the barroom brawler was a dagger tattoo on his forearm that he got decades ago in Boston. (He also has a couple of hearts. "I used to put the girls' names in there," he joked, "and a week later I'd be taking them out.") But he told me he still goes out on his boat for his three bushels of scallops a day during the season, and he still fishes night tides.

He always felt that in 1997, when he came out of retirement, the derby regulars didn't want him back in the tournament. They didn't do anything in particular, but they didn't do anything to welcome him either. So it felt deeply satisfying to walk into the weigh station with that 50.75-pound bass and slap it on the table and win the whole damn thing again. When he was banned from the derby in 1999, he made a vow to the *Gazette*: "After ten years, I will be eighty-two years old, and I shall return." Now he says he may never fish it again. He might just keep telling the derby folks to stick it. Then again, wouldn't it be a show to fish it again? To win it at age eighty-two? To really rub their noses in it?

Actually, he's had a different dream. In Dick's fantasy, he catches a giant bass during his 10-year banishment, gives it to a friend registered in the derby, and saunters into the weigh station to watch his pal slap it onto the table.

He's been dying to do that. That, he thinks, would just about make the derby brass insane.

9

"I'll Take Ten Fricking Polygraph Tests"

Lev and Leadbelly.

The morning after Lev catches the 57-pounder, I find him on the dock in Menemsha getting ready to go bonito fishing with Geoff—and coming unglued. He can already envision the controversy that's ahead, and no matter how he looks at it he can't see how he gets out unscathed. Fair or not, he'll end up with a cloud over his head. "Half the population is going to think I cheated because I couldn't stand to see Zebby win," he says.

He pulls open the glass door on the Menemsha Texaco to get a pack of cigarettes, a lighter, and a chocolate milk. The store is filled with regulars getting their seven a.m. coffee and gossip. The fellows know that Lev went out last night seeking a fish to top Zeb.

"How you doing?" someone asks. "You get a big one?"

"Yeah, I got a big one," Lev says. "Get this. I bring the thing down to the derby weigh-in, they gut the thing, and ten yo-yo weights fall out of its fucking stomach." The men around him are quickly struck silent. "A handful of lead! I caught the thing and I was like, 'What the fuck is wrong with this fish?' Its belly was hanging down five inches below its sphincter. They freaking cut the thing open and weights just cascade out of it."

One of the men stifles a laugh.

"I told them, 'I don't know what to tell you guys. I'll take a polygraph test. I feel like somebody took a shit on my birthday cake.' A pound and a half of lead! I was walking on air and it was like somebody just freaking clotheslined me at the ankles."

Geoff is grinning as Lev grabs his provisions and we head back outside to the boat.

"Gave those guys something to talk about for the next couple of hours," Geoff says.

"Next couple of weeks," Lev corrects.

The night before, it hadn't taken Ed long to conclude that Lev did not stuff the fish.

When he arrived, he looked over the yo-yo weights, which D.J. had tucked into a plastic bag. Then he pulled Lev aside and asked some questions. For one thing, he asked if Lev had let the fish out of his sight since he caught it. Could some saboteur have stuffed the sinkers down its gullet in an effort to smear Lev's good name? Could some buddy be pulling a practical joke? No, no, Lev said, the striper had never left his sight. Ed knew how a striper could eat pogy after rigged pogy and end up with lead in its guts. Moreover, he had no evidence that Lev caught the fish yo-yoing. Hog rings

175

found in its intestines supported Lev's assurances that he had not stuffed the fish. The gear appeared to have been inside the fish for a while. Still, Ed had little choice but to pull the fish off the leaderboard, at least for the time being. He called a committee meeting for the next day so the officials could talk things over and figure out whether to accept the fish or disqualify it.

Lev walked over to the bar across the street, where he ordered Jägermeister and tried to drum up sympathy from the Sunday night drinkers. (He picked the wrong crowd. They thought it would be a riot to create a shot, the Yo-yo, in his honor. "It would make you throw up right away," Lev said later.)

Now, as we jet out of the harbor, Geoff is trying to calm his friend down. The way he sees it, the best medicine for what ails Lev is to go out, catch a gigantic fish, carry it into the weigh station, slap it on the table, and bury the discussion. But Lev can't let go. He's recruiting everybody in the harbor into a kind of group therapy. He sees a charter captain steam out of his slip and shouts over the news about his bass. The other fisherman, not understanding that it's Lev who caught the fish, assumes the striper must have been stuffed. "Thanks for the vote of confidence!" Lev shouts. Turning to Geoff and me, he says, "See? That's going to be the general consensus right there."

For the next eight hours Lev stews and Geoff tries to talk him off the roof. Lev figures they're going to deduct the weights from the fish and he'll drop to second place. Geoff thinks they'll count the fish and the weights and Lev will take over first place.

"Personally," Geoff says, "I think they've gotta give it to you."

"They won't," Lev says. He reasons that if they start accepting fish with garbage in their bellies, they open the door to rampant cheating. Sponsors and competitors will flee and the derby will wither and die. They've got to deduct the weights.

"I think that's wrong though," Geoff insists.

"What if you caught a fifteen-pound bass with a thirty-pound rock in it?" Lev asks. "A bowling ball?" He lets out a cackle.

"I think the fact that you were willing to take a polygraph test proves your innocence."

"I'll take ten fricking polygraph tests."

They're after another leaderboard bonito today. Geoff's 9.14-pounder is still in first place, but he doesn't think it will hold up. What they want is an 11-pound bonito. They try to get into their usual fishing vibe by fiddling with bait and gear and swapping salty stories about sharks and bad storms and debating which music gets fish biting. ("Bonito like the Stones," Geoff says.) They munch on his smoked bluefish dip with Ritz crackers. Blue-collar Geoff, chewing on a piece of 25-pound-test fishing line like he's a farm boy with a piece of hay, tosses some of the juice from the dip in the water as if he's after white-collar bonito, fish with sophisticated palates—"Edgartown bonito," he jokes.

"The tide's moving that way. They'll come back with alligator friggin' shirts on."

"And a pair of reds?" Lev adds.

"Yeah," Geoff says, "Nantucket Reds." Those are the salmon-colored pants favored by the country-club set on the island.

Lev keeps coming around to that bass, though, and his demeanor shifts from anger to frustration to resignation to silliness and back. He's thinking out loud, and there's nothing his friend can say to put him at ease. "Catch the fish, and it's full of lead weights. What are the odds of that? . . . It's like *that's* why its gut was like that. It's not normal. Its belly was hanging down. It looked like a basketball in its gut. . . . I could catch a bigger one. A fifty-eight, a sixty-four. Something like that. Lay it on the table. There's definitely a sixty. If I lived there for the next two weeks, I'd get a bigger one."

"Might not be too good for the marriage," Geoff interjects.

Lev forgot his cell phone so he bums Geoff's to get updates and sympathy. His father Walter, a former derby committeeman, offers to help. He calls back later to report that the committee will weigh three options: (1) accept the fish with the weights; (2) count the fish but deduct the weights; or (3) disqualify the fish. Lev reaches the conclusion that there's no way the committee can go with the first choice and tie its own hands in the fight against cheaters. He assumes they'll pick the second option, and he'll end up in second place behind Zeb. If that happens, at least he'll have a shot at retaking his grand slam record. (As Lev feared, Zeb had caught the bluefish he needed to complete his grand slam and had amassed a record-shattering 84.69 pounds.) But if they go with option three, Lev doesn't know what he'd do. Actually, no—he knows *exactly* what he'd do. He'd quit fishing the tournament. "Then I'd go catch derby winners and nail 'em to the door when it's closed. With a note." Another cackle.

They fish all morning but all they catch is a dogfish and a skate. The tide changes, and a few hours later Geoff finally hooks a bonito. He's patient, holding his ground and letting the fish tire at the end of the line before he brings it to the boat. Lev nets it and they're disappointed—it's only an 8-pounder. Geoff thought it felt bigger out there in the current. It's a beautiful fish anyway: green racing lines along its sides, the skin like battered steel.

Geoff gets another one and so does Lev, but they're out of sorts. They're suffering through long droughts between fish. They're confused about what's happening. Over the past week and a half, they've caught progressively fewer bonito: 25, 12, 8, 5, and 3. "Oh, what a weird day," Geoff says. "The fish are just sensing the strange vibes on the line."

Lev wants to call it quits but Geoff needles him, reminding him about what awaits back on land. "When we hit the dock you have to face the music. 'That Wlodyka kid, no-good fucking cheater.'"

Lev sits on the stern watching the water. He doesn't say anything.

"I think it's going to work out," Geoff tells him, serious now. "I think you're golden. Be positive."

Lev changes his mind about going back in. "I just want to sit here and suffer," he says. "Probably the best place there is." But soon it's time to leave. They gather up the trash, stow away the gear, and motor toward shore. Nobody says anything as Lev steers between the twin jetties, which are uncharacteristically empty—not even the relentless man of Menemsha is standing watch. Lev putters up to the wharf and hops out to sell his lone bonito to the fish market. Then he eases the *Jenny J* across the harbor to his slip. As Lev docks the boat his father Walter drives up and asks about the fishing. "Slow," Lev says. "Wicked slow. We fished for like eight hours." Then he slips in some black humor, saying, "We're going to get some lead weights, fill up the bonito."

Walter unleashes one of his high-octave laughs and speeds off. The dock stinks of dead skunk as Lev loads up Geoff's Titan, rides home, and awaits the committee's judgment.

Inside the restaurant of the Edgartown Yacht Club, the fishermen on the derby committee are huddled in conversation. Some of them are wearing their official blue vests. Others rest their elbows on the black-and-white checkered tablecloths. They convened at seven and have been talking for an hour when derby headquarters opens at eight just down the dock. Some of the spectators who saw the weights drop out of the fish last night stop into the shack and ask what's been decided. Nothing yet, they're told.

Not many fishermen are coming into the weigh station early this Monday night. During the downtime, a woman sitting next to the scale pulls up the official derby Web site on her computer, and the staffers crowd around and read the chat room page about the controversial fish. Fishermen have already posted more than a dozen comments that are written with Internet chatters' usual loose regard for grammar and spelling.

"So begins the debate," one had written. "Should that bass be allowed or not?"

One fisherman thinks it should, because some of the gear ended up in the small intestine. "It would be different if it were somewhere else like in the stomach but it was not. Plus, you are talking about Lev, he is a fishing God in these parts and would never do something like that intentionally. If you need to reduce the weight of the fish by the few oz's of the weight[s], so be it, but to tell you the truth, i think those weights were part of the fish and should be included."

Another commentator notes that it was not just a few ounces of lead but a pound and a half. "This [is] going to be a very difficult decision for the derby committee. Clearly, it is not the fault of the fisherman, but is it fair to allow a fish to be weighed in with several pounds of lead inside it? On the other hand, is it fair to disallow or deduct from a fish something that it did in fact eat?" A little while later, the writer added, "Glad I'm not on the derby committee!"

Over at the yacht club, most of the people probably wish they could say the same thing. The committee is made up of thirty-one volunteers, a mix of veterans who've been involved for more than fifteen years and a crop of newcomers. They are teachers and contractors. There is a postmaster, a doctor, a yacht club manager, and a FedEx driver. They take their work seriously, and there is no shortage of egos. Like any committee it has its internecine politics. They meet behind closed doors and try to keep their deliberations and disagreements private. "What happens in Vegas stays in Vegas," thirty-one-year committeeman Porky Francis told me. Nights like these are the downside of being on the panel. It puts a damper on the derby spirit. The last thing anyone wants to do is spend hours debating when they could be out fishing.

Nobody on the committee suspects that Lev tampered with the fish in a bid to top Zeb, whatever some conspiracy theorists believe. But they have to consider the reputation of the derby and the sort of precedent they're setting in dealing with the loaded 57. And there are complicating factors. Lev isn't the first fisherman to arrive in Edgartown with a leadbellied fish. Two weeks earlier, fisherman Glenn Pachico brought in a 13.69-pound bluefish that took over the lead. The committeeman cut open the fish and two lead weights dropped out ("Plink, plink," as one witness described it to me) onto the filet table. Derby officials on the scene gathered around, had a short discussion—and decided to allow the fish. The gear looked like it had been in there for a long time. It didn't appear that Glenn had been yo-yoing. And the catch had bumped his own son, Mitchell, out of first place. They kept the incident quiet—so quiet that Ed and the top derby brass didn't even hear about it at first.

The circumstances were different when Lev lugged his fish into the weigh station last night. A more senior committeeman was presiding over the operation, and a 57-pound bass was obviously a much bigger deal than a 13-pound blue. This was front-page news. Lev had caught one of the biggest derby stripers of all time to overtake a giant first-place fish, and he had done it at a moment when everyone said it could not be done. Even if the committeeman had been inclined to deal with the situation discreetly, this one couldn't be kept quiet. About a dozen witnesses were present to see everything.

People on the committee aren't happy to discover that they didn't learn about Glenn's lead-filled bluefish until after Lev's striper came in. (The news raises some eyebrows: he was the fisherman thrown out of the derby for ten years with Scott Terry back in 1992.) The debate over what to do now is complicated. On the one hand, there is the longstanding policy of disqualifying fish that contain foreign material and the more recent rule barring yo-yoing. Some argue that the fish ate the rigged pogy, so the lead weights should count. But

181

to accept the fish as is would undercut the derby's anti-cheating and pro-conservation efforts. Others believe the committee should take a hard line and disqualify the fish, sticking to its simple, unambiguous policy. Although officials know the Wlodykas well and are fairly certain Lev wouldn't stuff a fish, how would they handle the situation if it involved a competitor they didn't know? They need a ruling that takes the fisherman out of the equation. Still others argue that yo-yoing is an increasingly common tactic, and more fishermen will be catching fish carrying weights, and it seems unfair to penalize them for something they cannot control. Couldn't they just subtract the weights? Yes, others said, but where to stop? Hooks? Swivels? Do you have to cut open every fish, weigh every piece of foreign material?

The committee members go around and around, and then they take a vote and break up. It's shortly after nine.

"That was torturous," says committee member Janet Messineo, who's wearing her jeans and hooded sweatshirt and derby hat, preparing for a night surf trip. Others just shake their heads. Two continue the debate outside. Everyone refuses to discuss their decision until Ed can issue an official statement.

Then Lev drives up. After we returned to the dock this afternoon, Lev had gone home to his wife Jen. He planned to take her bass fishing, but they didn't make it out, and instead they drove down to the weigh station to drop off something. Ed pulls him aside in the dark of the parking lot and delivers the news: the committee has voted to disqualify the fish.

Lev, predictably, loses it. A gaggle of committee members forms around Ed and Lev. Tourists and fishermen watch agape from the dock and the doorway of the weigh station. "I put thousands of hours into this!" Lev shouts. "I put my heart and soul into this. This is bullshit! To D.Q. a hardworking fisherman—I'm outraged! Personally outraged."

Ed and the others, their voices even, try to talk him down. They tell him they aren't disqualifying him, they aren't even accusing him of cheating, they're just throwing out the fish. Lev asks about how to appeal, demands they review their decision, offers to take a lie detector test. He argues that whatever they say, he'll always carry a stigma, he'll always be the guy whose lead-filled bass was disqualified. He says he understands they had a tough decision to make but they just went too far. Things get worse when he asks if they're disqualifying Glenn's bluefish and he's told that it's a closed matter, that they already accepted the fish and can't reopen the case. After a few minutes of this Lev has had enough. He storms off to the truck, slams the door as hard as he can, and yells for Jen. When she climbs in he roars away.

"This is horrible," committee member Steve London says. "This is really horrible. I feel bad for the kid." And he's a little worried about the coming days. He's been around the Vineyard long enough to know what's coming. Friendships will be strained. Arguments will break out. And everybody on the committee will get an earful about this decision—at work, at school, at the hospital, at the bank, in the newspapers. People will skewer them over this one.

10

I Fish, Therefore I Lie

Olga Hirshhorn and Captain Buddy Vanderhoop.

The well-known and the well-off have summered on the Vineyard for more than a century and a half now. As it happened, the fishing attracted some of the early visitors: The Squibnocket Striped Bass Fishing Club, founded in 1869, hosted the likes of President Chester Arthur, DuPont executive J. Amory Haskell, and Elihu Root, secretary of war, secretary of state, U.S. senator, and 1912 Nobel Peace Prize recipient. These recreational bass anglers of old found a clubhouse perched atop the cliffs, a piazza with a sweeping view of the Atlantic and eight spruce-plank fishing stands leading out to the farthest boulders at the edge of the roiling surf.

Most people, however, came for the Vineyard's uncomplicated charms. In 1887, Boston Brahmins settled on West Chop, where they swam and played tennis and whiled away the warm days. In 1919, lawyer and social activist Dorothy Kenyon bought a farm in Chilmark with a circle of liberal intellectuals and founded a rustic vacation camp. They built spartan quarters—no electricity, no running water—and they socialized in a giant barn; they called their enclave the Barnhouse. Over the years it would host such famous writers as Walter Lippman, Max Eastman, and Sylvia Plath. Their neighbors would include the painter Thomas Hart Benton, who built a summer house on Menemsha Pond, and ACLU founder Roger Baldwin, who took up residence at an up-island estate known as Windy Gates. In 1936, the actor James Cagney bought a farm in Chilmark from one of the Tiltons. Aviator Charles Lindbergh vacationed at an exclusive settlement known as Seven Gates Farm in the 1940s.

By the 1950s, word had spread about this celebrity hiding place, with its fashionably laid-back, plaid-shirted vibe. The Vineyard's rarified ranks began to swell with eminent writers, journalists, singers, and film stars. Diva Beverly Sills arrived in 1953, and author William Styron and his wife, Rose, a few years later. A "writer's row" sprouted in Vineyard Haven: humorist Art Buchwald, author John Hersey, and playwright Lillian Hellman were neighbors. James Taylor and Carly Simon, who visited the island as children with their families, made a home in Chilmark together after their 1972 marriage. In 1979, former Secretary of Defense Robert McNamara, a longtime seasonal resident, sold a beachfront house to John Belushi.

Soon, so many of the affluent and the illustrious discovered the place that some old-timers began to fret. "People are starting to care about what they wear," a lifelong summer resident lamented to a newspaper reporter in 1987, near the end of a two-decade stretch that saw the island population double. "The Vineyard is becoming like the Hamptons." The hippies who swam nude in the 1960s and '70s mostly assimilated or moved on. The literati were soon outnumbered by the glitterati.

Today, many islanders worry that their eclectic and open community is giving way to a growing exclusivity, and they gripe about a new breed of vacationer who buys a large house, then has it torn down to make room for a sprawling mansion. By tradition, the Vineyard has not been a place to flaunt your fortune, but some fear that's changing. This uneasiness has loomed behind the major land-use battles of recent years. Residents have fought to stop the construction of a slew of super-houses: mansions of 15,600 square feet on Oyster Pond, 9,670 square feet on Chappaquiddick, and 9,982 square feet on Edgartown Great Pond. The debates all seem to follow the same script. Opponents argue that the houses are too large, that they will spoil the beauty that attracted the newcomers in the first place. Owners scale back the Gatsbyesque dimensions marginally, and the giant houses go up just the same.

For sheer acrimony, no dispute in recent years tops the bare-knuckled five-year brawl over a golf course plan put forward by a Connecticut multimillionaire in 1999. The people of Oak Bluffs took sides and went to war. Eighteen holes would beat a crop of new mansions, supporters said, and the new jobs and tax revenues wouldn't hurt. Foes protested that the club would disrupt the natural habitat and pollute a nearby pond, but they also argued that something more fundamental was at stake. Another golf course would move the Vineyard one step closer to ordinary upscale suburbia. They lashed out at what the game itself represented: the sort of showy affluence that had mushroomed across the island.

"It violates the sense of who we are and what we want to be," said James Athearn, a farmer with deep island roots who sits on the Martha's Vineyard Commission, the powerful land-use body that deliberated over the golf course plan. Athearn speaks eloquently about the island as he knew it growing up: its swaths of unbroken woodland, its farmland unspoiled by houses, its culture of hunting and hiking and clamming. "To have that nibbled away at constantly has just been a grievance to me," he says. True, he acknowledges, the well-off did not just arrive in Bill and Hillary Clinton's wake in the 1990s. But a half-century ago, he said, "their money wasn't particularly important or apparent. They'd sit on the beach and read a book or paint a picture in the same ragged clothes we wore. It's one thing when they're the exception to the culture. When the culture shifts and becomes more about the well-heeled folks, and there's no connection to the land and local values, then you've got a dead place." As a practical matter, it doesn't help the tourism industry if the island's chief attributes—its natural splendor and small-town charm—are damaged by rampant development.

The commission rejected the golf course three times, and the fight devolved into lawsuits and threats. The developers retaliated by trying to push through a 366-house, maximum-density subdivision with affordable housing. They clear-cut trees on the property in defiance of government cease-and-desist orders. They threatened to install a rifle range and a pig farm. But in the end, the parties reached a settlement. The Martha's Vineyard Land Bank bought and preserved 190 acres of the woodlands for $18.6 million. In exchange, the developers won permission to build a subdivision on another 90 acres. The same sort of compromise has saved many of the island's largest parcels. Crews soon broke ground on a gated community of twenty-six multimillion-dollar homes with an equestrian theme, and the fight faded into the past. But the war between old ways and new money goes on.

For all of the skirmishes and the bruised feelings, the egalitarian traditions of the Vineyard endure. Islanders take pride in how people from different places, different circles, and different classes mix and mingle. A VIP throwing a cocktail party will invite his gardener or caretaker. During the derby, fishermen marvel that a tradesman living in a cheap rental can find himself on the same stretch of beach as a big shot in one of those trophy houses, and they both have the same shot at a fish. The pinnacle of that kind of class busting is the fishing charter, which can bring together people steeped in the outdoors with people who—for all their success in the corridors of power—might not be able to tie a simple fishing knot.

One afternoon, I find myself sitting on the gunwale of a thirty-foot boat cruising out of Menemsha Harbor listening to a bubbly group of friends chatter about the hours ahead: lunch of lobster rolls and blueberry pie, engaging conversation, a few hours of can't-miss fishing. The boat bristles with rods, the cooler is crammed with ice and pogies, and an iPod is hooked up to the boat's speakers. *Out across the endless sea . . . I would die in ecstasy,* Norah Jones sings in that perfect voice that makes tense muscles miraculously unwind.

This, I thought, is the way to win the derby.

Leading the trip is William "Buddy" Vanderhoop, the maverick Wampanoag Indian charter captain who turned in Scott Terry fifteen years ago this fall. The fifty-six-year-old stands at the steering wheel in his uniform: a ball cap with an embroidered swordfish, blue jeans, a belt with a big brass shark buckle, Crocs with leather uppers, and a T-shirt advertising his company, Tomahawk Charters. The back reads BASS IS OUR BUSINESS AND BUSINESS IS GOOD. His front teeth are chipped and the gold from some previous dental work shines through the gaps. A sign on his filet stand announces BEWARE OF ATTACK FISHERMAN but he's almost always mellow these days, with an easy laugh that starts slowly and builds into a rolling guffaw.

Buddy's client is Olga Hirshhorn, art collector and widow of the famous Joseph Hirshhorn, a mining prospector and the founding donor of the Smithsonian's modern art museum in Washington,

D.C. She wears a green sweater, white pants, and white canvas slip-on sneakers. Pulled over her gray bob is a fishing hat covered with buttons and pins from her many previous derbies. She's an elfin eighty-seven, but she has a way of speaking quickly and directly, like she's got business elsewhere and you'd better hurry it up, please. Here are two island celebrities from diametrically different circles, and the derby has placed them on the same boat buzzing out into the Vineyard Sound. I'm sure there must be other scenarios where the paths of Buddy Vanderhoop and Olga Hirshhorn might cross but I can't think of one.

The boat glides west, hugging the coast, and a few minutes later we're puttering off Aquinnah, which was called Gay Head until the town reverted to the Wampanoag name meaning "land under the hill" in 1998.

"Right here," Buddy says as we approach the foot of Devil's Bridge, the line of sunken boulders off the cliffs, "is the most treacherous part of the trip. The *City of Columbus* went down here, which was the largest marine tragedy until the *Titanic*." The 275-foot luxury steamship wrecked at four in the morning on January 18, 1884, and although it was not of *Titanic* proportions it was at least the worst sinking off the Vineyard in the 1800s. One hundred and three people drowned. Their bodies washed ashore for days. Islanders carried them in oxcarts to transport them to fish shacks and churches until their next of kin could claim them. Twenty-nine people were saved, some of them picked half-freezing off the masts still poking above the seas. Two Vanderhoops (John P. and Leonard) helped with the rescue, and each received a silver medal and $25 for their efforts. Furniture from the boat—a rosewood piano, parlor chairs, cabinets—ended up in island homes.

"This right here is the Camelback," Buddy says, pointing out another rock. The boulders here sit just below the surface and close

189

enough together that sensible boaters don't risk running between them. Buddy just unzips the boat's plastic windshield and sticks his head out to spot the hazards. "Nobody else goes through here except me, but I've been doing it since I was a kid."

"He usually goes a lot faster," says his wife, Lisa, a professional photographer who is along to document the outing for the women.

The women turn their attention to the famous cliffs below the lighthouse. Their crumbling face is composed of layers of sand, gravel, and clay—in red, yellow, tan, and white—with each layer representing a moment in the cliffs' ancient existence. Geologists have found fossils of sixty-foot prehistoric sharks, whales, rhinoceroses, camels, horses, and alligators, evidence of 100 million years of climate change: rising and falling seas, swamp forest giving way to savanna giving way to ice. The bones rested not far from where tour groups now disembark from air-conditioned buses to look at the lighthouse and buy T-shirts and ice cream.

Buddy tells the more charming story about the cliffs. According to native tradition, the Wampanoags are children of a benevolent giant named Moshup. Taller than the tallest tree, he created the island they call Noepe, or "land surrounded by bitter waters." Moshup would grab whales out of the ocean with his bare hands and smash them against the cliffs, then cook their flesh on a spit and eat them whole. Legend has it that Moshup taught the Vineyard natives how to fish, though archaeologists report that the natives used more than their bare hands. Thousand-year-old harpoons and eight-inch barbed spear tips suggest that early Vineyarders rowed out in dugouts to hunt down whales that strayed close to shore.

Olga marvels at the cliffs and poses for photographs with her fishing friends, summer resident Mary Virginia Palmer and island-born Shirley Craig, the seventy-two-year-old derby fanatic.

"This would probably actually be a pretty nice place to have a little bite to eat," Buddy says. "Would you like a cup of chowder to start out with?"

Olga is ecstatic. "I can't believe it. Chowder! How nice! I didn't expect that!"

Buddy hands the women green napkins—cloth, not paper—and food that comes from the restaurant perched atop the cliffs, the Aquinnah Shop, which is owned by Buddy's mother, Anne Vanderhoop Madison. Luther Madison, Buddy's stepfather and the Wampanoags' medicine man, reportedly blessed the blueberries.

On the typical Buddy Vanderhoop trip there is no talk about Moshup and the maritime disasters, no stopping for photographs, no pies. He races through Devil's Bridge and tries to get his customers on fish—fast. Arm-dead by eight a.m. That's his idea of a good fishing charter.

But this is a special trip. He donated it to a charity auction for an island social services agency. An afternoon with Buddy shared the bill with an assortment of enviable experiences: dining at the home of Ted Danson and Mary Steenburgen; kickin' it up a notch with Emeril Lagasse; sailing with Walter Cronkite aboard the *Wyntje*; taking home Bill Clinton's old golf clubs; winning your preteen daughter's undying affection by sending her to the set of *Hannah Montana*.

In summer dresses and golf shirts, the Vineyard's stars (and anybody else willing to shell out $25) sat in white garden chairs among hydrangeas and black-eyed Susans, drinking wine and throwing around four- and five-figure checks. Buddy sat a few rows behind Hollywood director Harold Ramis and Academy Award–winning actress Patricia Neal. Olga sat in front near *Clifford the Big Red Dog* creator Norman Bridwell. Clinton's used sticks went for

$19,000, dinner at the Danson house for $9,000, the *Hannah Montana* dream for $17,000.

When the auctioneer came to the trip aboard the *Tomahawk Too*, he took a moment to reflect on the legend of Buddy Vanderhoop. He told a story about being at a cocktail party with Buddy. In a home full of celebrities, the man everybody wanted to chat up was the Wampanoag fisherman. "Everybody thinks this is the greatest celebrity on the island," he gushed. "And he is." The audience chuckled politely and the bidding opened. Within seconds Olga Hirshhorn had muscled her way aboard. It cost her $5,000.

The auction moved on and Buddy excused himself for a smoke. Out on the sidewalk he ran into the very pregnant Sally Taylor, daughter of Carly Simon and James Taylor. "I had dinner with Bobby last week and your name came up," Sally's husband, Dean Bragonier, said.

"Bobby?" Buddy asked.

"Bobby Kennedy," he explained.

As the image of Robert F. Kennedy Jr. chatting about Buddy with Carly Simon's daughter's husband flashed through my head, my brain did a somersault.

It sometimes seems as though every boater on the Vineyard has a captain's license and every fourth fisherman runs a charter business. Most of them have taken out movie stars and pop personalities over the years. Some keep quiet about those trips out of respect for their clients' privacy, but Buddy plays up his proximity to the island's celebrity culture. "Guide to the Stars," his Web site trumpets. Blues singer Taj Mahal, filmmaker Spike Lee, and Rolling Stones guitar legend Keith Richards have all gone out with him. The *People* magazine photograph of Buddy and the diminutive director of *Do the Right Thing* and a 57-pound bass? Priceless. Buddy told me he's trying to get a Saturday-morning fishing show off the ground. He explained that the sort of episode he imagines would feature Keith Richards hunting for a great white shark somewhere off Australia. (The fact that great whites are a protected species in Australia is only one of many factors complicating Buddy's grand plan.)

Other charter captains roll their eyes at Buddy's routine. Ask around the Vineyard and you will hear that there is not enough salt in the ocean to take with a Buddy Vanderhoop tale. The man can't help himself. He is a storyteller of the first class, a real marvel to watch, a legend of his own making. "I am a fisherman, therefore I lie," he acknowledges, adding, "You've gotta have *some* fun." I'd been warned that if Buddy clears his throat, the next thing out of his mouth is quite likely a fabrication. Any number he utters must be significantly discounted using a mathematical conversion known as the Vanderhoop factor. A Vanderhoop 50 is a striper that weighs maybe 35 pounds—40, tops. A fellow charter boat captain tells a story about pulling up to Buddy on the water and seeing him weigh a nice fish his charter had caught. Buddy told him the bass was bottoming out his 50-pound scale, but that night at derby headquarters, according to the rival captain, it came in at around 37 or 38 pounds.

No one disputes that the man can catch fish, and big ones— real 50-pounders. "He was dipped in it when it comes to bass," said Louis Larsen Jr., who went swordfishing with Buddy in the 1970s and now runs the Net Result, a Vineyard Haven fish market. Brian Athearn gives as complete a testimonial to Buddy's mojo as there is. He sold his fishing boat and invested the $6,000 in a savings account to pay for half a dozen annual charter trips on the *Tomahawk Too*. "His mother," Brian says, "was half-striper."

The first time I talked to Buddy on the phone he said he'd won five of the past ten derbies. Those numbers sounded like nonsense, but when I pressed him for details later he came up with three winners in the past twelve years—one of them his own 53.60-pound derby winner, which he caught in 2002 when he stopped on a whim during a trip to the mainland for cheaper gas. He also took out his friend Jennifer Clarke to find the striper she needed to seal the grand slam award one year. And he got a giant bass for Athearn, who lost the grand leader's spot in the last week of the 2005 derby to twelve-year-old Molly Fischer. All in all, I considered this bragging pretty average by fishermen's standards.

Every time I considered dismissing one of his stories as bogus, I thought of the 64-pound bass hanging over the cash register at the Aquinnah Shop. Buddy caught that one. "It's not *all* myth," he said. And even if some of it is, he's got his stories down. I heard him tell them time and again and, although the statistics and dimensions were indeed elastic, the main gist didn't change. For example, the tale of Keith Richards's charter. The way Buddy tells it, they caught a bunch of fish, and when the trip ended the musician promised to see Buddy later that day. Damned if he didn't fly over Buddy's boat in a rented World War II bomber, the plane buzzing the boat while Keith waved from the gunner's turret. True? False?

The guitarist's publicist said he was unavailable to talk, but a photo of Richards is there on Buddy's Web site, sitting on the dock wearing a giant grin, a pair of Tommy Hilfiger boat shoes, and a Tomahawk Charters cap, with seven dead stripers by his side. If you believe what you read, the guy may have snorted his dead father's ashes. Okay, he denied it, but who's to say he didn't rent a Flying Fortress and scare Buddy's afternoon charter shitless?

For every Buddy story I heard, I was assured that there were a dozen more like it. Here's one I particularly enjoyed.

Buddy has an old rusty hatchet in his boat that he calls his tomahawk. He has no qualms about playing his Indian heritage to the hilt (even though his Dutch last name is a clue that his native blood is diluted by generations of intermarriage). In July and August the water around the island is thronged with boats, and the competition for prime real estate is fierce among recreational anglers, charter captains, and commercial striper fishermen. One day this summer he was forced to wave the tomahawk around and do a wild-eyed Wampanoag routine. Some jerk from Virginia squeezed his boat between Buddy's *Tomahawk Too* and the *Femme Fatale*, piloted by Jennifer Clarke, who went on to become a charter captain after winning the grand slam. (This being Martha's Vineyard, she also has a recording career and is married to TV actor and comedian Lenny Clarke.) They'd been catching fish and this guy was "jumping" them.

"No, no, no," Buddy said he told the man. "This isn't going to happen. You've gotta move."

The guy looked over at Buddy. "What're you going to do about it?"

That's when Buddy brought the corroded ax out from its spot next to the captain's seat. He's pretty sure he could put the thing in a dock post from fifty feet. No doubt he could bury it in this Reb's skull from about that distance. But he happened to have a lawyer on the boat with him and counsel advised him not to unleash the tomahawk. So instead Buddy poked a hook through an oily pogy head with the guts hanging off and cast the thing as hard as he could at the offending boat. "It probably was doing a hundred and fifty miles per hour when it hit the pilothouse of his boat." The bait bounced off, whizzed past the shirtless guy, and splattered blood and gore all over his deck. Then Buddy reared back as if he were setting the hook and missed snagging the guy by millimeters— *millimeters*, he swears.

In the end, it was probably for the best that Buddy didn't hook the dude, drag him overboard, reel him over to his boat, and beat the living crap out of him, as he had wanted to do. No two ways about it: that would've been bad for business.

It wouldn't exactly have surprised anybody, though. "I have never in my life seen anyone like Buddy," his mother, Anne, told me. "I don't think I ever will. He's just so different. Does his own thing. Always has."

As a toddler, Buddy would vanish from the Vanderhoop homestead and turn up at the one-room school down the road. At three, he disappeared with the cocker spaniel, Cecil. When it started to get dark and the dog came home alone Anne called the police. A search party combed the woods of Gay Head, still wild and mostly undeveloped in those days. Word was that the woods harbored patches of quicksand. "We thought he was dead," Anne said. But after a few hours the searchers came upon Buddy. The *Gazette* reported that "'Buddyhoop,' as he styles himself," was cold, scared, and walking in circles. His mother remembers him being entirely unperturbed and perplexed by all the fuss. "He knows practically where every berry is in Gay Head," she said, with characteristic Vanderhoopian exaggeration. "He used to take his brothers out in the morning and pick wild strawberries for their cereal before breakfast."

The Vanderhoops' fishing bona fides go back centuries. Godless savages though they may have been in the first white settlers' eyes, the indigenous people of New England did know how to reap the good Lord's bounty from the seas. The natives settled near water and trekked to the rivers and shoreline when the fish ran. Wars could be halted (or at least postponed) while combatants converged at the foot of a waterfall to spear spawning sturgeon and salmon. They set up colossal fish traps. They caught cod and stripers on hemp hand-lines. Some of the hooks were made from bone shards that were sharpened at each end, baited, and hung by a hole in the middle. Swallowed by a fish, the ingenious device turned sideways and impaled the fish from the inside. For their catch, the natives suffered depredations no modern-day angler would try, at least not while completely sober. One witness reported that they "lay their naked bodies many a cold night on the cold shoare about a fire of two or three sticks, and oft in the night search their nets." (To which I say: *hardcore!*)

The Wampanoags were celebrated whalers. In 1902 Amos Smalley harpooned a ninety-foot white sperm whale, for which he earned some minor fame when the 1956 movie version of *Moby-Dick* came out. Smalley was Buddy's great-uncle, and the whaleman gave Buddy a tooth from the whale years ago. The ivory is scrimshawed with a sailing ship chasing a whale. Buddy's great-grandfather also worked on whalers and ran fish traps along the North Shore. His father, William Vanderhoop Sr., went out on Menemsha harpoon boats—part of his job was to row a dory over to fish that had been lanced and pull the line hand over hand until they were in.

Buddy told me a story about catching his first striper at age five on the beach at Lobsterville. He grabbed the thing by the gill plate and started dragging. "It was probably a twenty-pounder," he said. (That's before applying the Vanderhoop factor, I take it.) "I had to stop every hundred feet and rest. By the time he got home he didn't have a tail left." Buddy remembers biking home from school as a sixth grader, throwing his books in his bedroom, grabbing his gear, and running down the cliffs at Gay Head to fish for stripers. When he wasn't out fishing for pay, William Sr. would take the boys out fishing for play. "What else is there to do?" Buddy said. "He didn't play golf or anything." They'd get fluke, tautog, and bass on William's twenty-two-footer, the *After U.*

"They were brought up with the fish," Anne said. "It's just what they did."

Another thing Buddy did was drugs and alcohol. The way he tells it, he got busted his senior year in high school for pot and hashish and the judge gave him a choice: the army or jail. It was the middle of the Vietnam War but the military didn't sound half bad. "I was really gung ho to go over and kill people," he admitted. Then his cousin got shot in the head and he saw guys coming back strung out on drugs, so he had second thoughts. At boot camp he asked a friend to call his mother and tell her his orders had changed, and home he went. When his mother started to get suspicious about his long leave of absence he took off on his brother's motorcycle. He witnessed the psychedelia in Woodstock and rode all the way to Florida before returning to turn himself in.

Buddy said he wanted to go to the University of Rhode Island to study marine biology, but he never made it. After doing a couple of months in a military prison he followed his father into commercial fishing. He went out on Menemsha swordfishing boats, which paid well enough, he told me, that he soon had a BMW, an Audi, a new house, and as much marijuana as he wanted. When his swordfishing career ended he went to work building houses for a while. He'd become a Gay Head selectman, and he lobbied unsuccessfully to get a marina built on the Lobsterville side of Menemsha Harbor. He harvested scallops in Menemsha Pond in the winter and seined fish from the annual run of herring in the pond that the tribe managed, as his father had done. (One year he got into a minor scrape for illegally shooting a bunch of cormorants feasting on the baitfish. Discharging a shotgun on the pond at a "species of critical concern" understandably upset many people, but Buddy remains unabashedly proud of killing the cormorants. It was beautiful, he said. Some of the birds dropped right into his brother's truck.)

Buddy admits he was a wild man for a while—"a good man at a party," one friend recalled—before he kicked the drugs and alcohol some years ago. In the late 1980s he got into fishing charters, and over the years he's discovered that guiding the rich and famous has its benefits. He said one client spent a day on the water griping about his spiteful divorce proceedings and how his ex-wife had already taken his $130,000 Mercedes SL600 (0–60 mph: 4.4 seconds). He'd *burn* his BMW 850i before he'd give it to her. "Don't burn it!" Buddy cried. "What do you want for it?" For a little cash and eight full-day charters—in all, about the cost of a new Hyundai—he obtained a red hot rod that retailed for $100,000.

Chartering is far safer than the offshore commercial fishing he did in his twenties—he decides when he goes out and when he stays in—though he's still had his close calls over the years. Once his boat hit a log and almost sank. Another time, he thought he'd have to jump overboard when a fire broke out. In 1999 he took a borrowed boat and a party of four offshore for a day of yellowfin tuna fishing and they nearly ended up shark bait after the battery died and the waves came up and the boat started to fill with water. That one required a Coast Guard rescue.

But hey, there was an upside. It gave him another good story to pass the time between fish.

When lunch is finished, Buddy maneuvers the boat into position and gets down on his knees to cut pogies into slices on top of his cooler. He casts out the lines as Lisa makes conversation. About maritime superstitions: whistling brings up the wind; to say the word *P-I-G* on a boat is to invite bad luck; same goes for bringing a banana on a fishing trip. About her lucky number 13: it's her birthday, her dog's birthday, Buddy's high school basketball uniform number, and the date they first met. About her entrepreneurial ideas: she's collecting tiny starfish and baby doll clothing and she plans to dress up the starfish in miniature bikinis and sunglasses, photograph them inside toy fishing boats and pink Cadillacs, and turn the photos into postcards. ("Martha's Vineyard," the caption would read, "Home of the Stars.")

Soon enough, the women are bringing fish on board. Shirley gets an 8-pound bluefish and starts dreaming about a daily pin. Mary Virginia gets a bass in the twenties and plans a visit to the weigh station. Olga, the octogenarian, hooks a bluefish ("Oh, he's mad!" she cries out) but it breaks the line before Buddy can gaff it.

The tide slackens and so does the fishing and the women get back to talking. Olga has a way of uncorking curveballs at Buddy. "Do they prefer the head, the middle section, or the tail?" she asks as he prepares another pogy. The women giggle. "I just want to know," Olga adds.

"Well," Buddy says, pondering, "they bite the heads better."

Olga is quiet for a moment. "If I were a fish, I wouldn't like the head," she says. "Because of those two eyes looking at me before I bit it. I wouldn't enjoy that at all."

What Olga does enjoy is spending time with people who are as interesting as she is. A Vineyard friend, Tamara Buchwald—humorist Art Buchwald's daughter-in-law—has tried in vain to get Olga to write her memoirs. "It's hard to start writing about it," Olga explains. "It's still going on."

She grew up in a working-class Ukrainian family in Greenwich, Connecticut, married her English teacher, and had three children before they separated. She ran an employment agency hiring out cooks, maids, and chauffeurs, and soon crossed paths with a man who would change her life. Joseph Hirshhorn was born in Latvia in 1899, the twelfth of thirteen children. A few years later, after his father died, his mother moved the family to Brooklyn. She worked seventy-hour weeks in a purse factory to support the family. "Poverty," Hirshhorn said later, "has a bitter taste," and he quickly found a way out. At fourteen, he went to work as an office boy on Wall Street earning $12 a week. By seventeen he'd turned $255 in savings into $168,000. At thirty, just before the 1929 crash, he took $4 million out of the stock market. Over the next three decades he made a fortune mining gold and uranium, eventually amassing a bankroll worth more than $100 million. By the 1960s he'd gone through three marriages and several of Olga's servants when he struck up a conversation with the woman who so efficiently supplied his help. Joe and Olga began dating and they became husband and wife in 1964.

Around the same time, the world discovered another side of the man: Hirshhorn the art addict. He'd begun buying pieces seriously two decades earlier, and since then he'd built one of the largest private collections of paintings and sculptures in the world. "He bought art by the armful," *The New Yorker* wrote. If he couldn't decide which of an artist's pieces to buy he'd buy them all—and fast. Witnesses described him arriving at a gallery and saying, "I'll take that, that, that, and that." Then he would march out. The homes Olga moved into in 1964 were crammed with the fruits of her husband's voraciousness. Rodin in the garden. Picasso above the mantel. Lesser works crammed into closets. He bought work by Arshile Gorky, Thomas Eakins, and Jackson Pollock, and they socialized with Picasso, Chagall, and Miró.

Two years before Joseph and Olga were married a Guggenheim Museum exhibit introduced his bounty to the world. Soon, major museums around the world were vying for the honor of adding his art to their permanent collections. President Lyndon B. Johnson invited Joseph to the White House and Lady Bird Johnson visited the Hirshhorns at their Connecticut mansion. All the presidential attention touched the patriotic immigrant in him, and in 1974 the Hirshhorn Museum and Sculpture Garden opened on the National Mall, exhibiting some of the six thousand pieces of art he had donated to the public. Upon his death in 1981, the rest of the collection—thousands of pieces more—went to the Hirshhorn.

Although Olga had begun to buy art before her husband's death (her first: squares inside of squares by Josef Albers), she suddenly found herself alone in houses with many empty walls. She amassed a large collection of her own, though she was as likely to buy art at a thrift shop as at a gallery. She has filled her three current homes—a comfortable place in Naples, Florida, a five-hundred-square-foot "Mouse House" in D.C., and the summer home in Vineyard Haven—with an eclectic mix of works. The collection at the Mouse House has been exhibited at the Naples Museum of Art and features de Koonings, a Dalí, a Georgia O'Keeffe, and six Picassos, one of which is inscribed *"Pour Olga, son ami Picasso."*

She bought her place on the Vineyard in 1989. The house was just a dour rancher and the barn out back needed work, so she put her architect to work and it was soon transformed into a bastion of open space, natural light, and art everywhere she looked. Over the doorway of her huge back porch hangs a wooden fish that must stretch eight feet. It's black with dirty yellow bars, like a negative image of a striped bass as imagined by a Pop artist. Below the fish is a thick boat rod with a gold big-game reel attached. On one of the exposed A-beams hangs a whaling oar she bought at a thrift shop for $150. Over the stairs to the basement is a painting of a giant garfish about to attack a woman in a bikini. Back inside the house, the laundry closet doubles as a bar. At parties, the wine and ice go in the washing machine. On the wall is a little door that holds a swing-down ironing board; a topless, bejeweled woman adorns the underside. In the bathroom are the Dump Dollies, a dozen nude plastic dolls she's rescued from the island junkyard, cleaned up, and placed in a little shower alcove. They grace postcards she hands out to visitors.

This is Olga. She donated a collection worth $10 million—her own art purchases, not Joe's—to the Corcoran Gallery of Art in Washington, D.C., but every summer she helps organize the Chicken Alley Art and Collectibles sale at the Thrift Shop in Vineyard Haven, where artwork can be had for a song.

I came to learn two other things about the woman. In addition to collecting art she's collecting far-flung experiences. After Joe died, she took up skiing at Crested Butte, boated the Amazon, traveled the Trans-Siberian Railway, snorkeled the Great Barrier Reef, visited the Galápagos Islands, and danced the polka in Leningrad (breaking her wrist in the process). After the derby, she tells me, she's taking a trip to Antarctica and braving the Drake Passage to walk among the penguins. Second, I learned that she isn't about to let her age slow her down. This is a woman who still drives herself from Washington to the Vineyard—a ten-hour trek—in her little Honda Prelude. The elderly at the senior centers can take their handout striper filets from the derby philanthropists. She plans to get hers the old-fashioned way.

After she started summering on the Vineyard, she gravitated toward the islands' cultural and philanthropic circles, and every August she would find herself at the charity auction where she both donated and bid on lots. In 1995 one item in particular caught her attention: a fishing trip offered by Cooper Gilkes and Nelson Sigelman. The tackle shop owner put the winning bidder on fish, and the journalist documented the excursion in his weekly "Gone Fishin'" newspaper column. The first time Olga won the auction and turned up for the trip, Nelson didn't know what to make of this seventy-something woman with three homes and a museum to her name. How could she possibly be interested in a day spent fishing? He quickly found out. "The lady," he wrote, "loves to catch fish." That first trip began on a freezing morning and lasted all day. Olga was so cold she put on a pair of Nelson's sneakers over her shoes. After eleven hours, they caught some sea bass, a small striper, and a little blue—nothing worth weighing in. She asked them to drop her off in Vineyard Haven with her sea bass. Walking through the streets of town with the fish on a stringer made of fishing line, she said, "I felt just like Tom Sawyer."

She won the trip six more times—"Olga and the Cooperettes," Nelson took to calling the art maven and her friends—and they

203

had better days. Olga got a pin for a third-place striped bass once. But as the years passed they got restless and decided to raise the stakes. They wanted a grand slam: one legal-sized bluefish, bonito, albie, and bass for each of them. In 2002 Coop took Olga and her friends out all day. They drifted for bass. They caught their bonito. They trolled for false albacore. By day's end Olga showed up at the weigh station with four fish. Derby official Chris Scott saw what she had and blanched. "I'm going to kill myself," he said. Even he, Chris Scott, son of a commercial fisherman, had never achieved that mark of derby greatness, the one-day grand slam. But when the weighmaster put Olga's albie on the table, it was a shade too short. Not to be thwarted, Olga went back out with a friend the next week and had a sizable fish on, but if she'd hooked the albie she needed for her grand slam, she never found out. The fringe of her scarf wound into the reel and the fish broke off.

In any case, Olga impressed the hell out of Coop, who knows a hard fisherman when he sees one. His respect is not easily earned. "That girl's got more drive . . ." he said, trailing off in admiration. "In her eighties!"

Olga won't be getting a derby grand slam this year. Buddy is a bass specialist, and his bait attracts bluefish, too, but he's not one to chase around the funny fish. Olga knew what to expect. She'd gone fishing with Buddy a few weeks before this trip. "I caught a thirty-seven-pound striped bass," she told me afterward in her high-pitched voice. "It was huge! Huge!"

Now the fish aren't biting and Olga is beginning to fret. Had word spread among the local stripers to look out for hooks? Is there a fish school at which the elders describe the dangers of the seas to their offspring?

"We're all going to catch more," Buddy assures her, chomping on a Padron that he's been trying in vain to smoke as he deals with bait and lines and the boat.

To pass the time Lisa and Buddy start spinning another yarn. This one is about how he almost got gored after he shot a deer from their deck. A decade earlier he had come home with the old town fire truck. He said something about turning it into a fish-delivery vehicle. Could he rig it to suck the baitfish out of the seine at the herring run, like they do on commercial fishing boats, then drive his catch to tackle shops? (Answer: no.)

Anyway, a fire truck was now parked on their property in the high grass alongside their other cars and old boats. One fall day Lisa heard gunshots outside. She opened the door, she tells the women, "and there was a big buck in our yard—"

"Seven-point buck," Buddy clarifies.

"—that he had shot kind of in my garden."

"It was eating the tomatoes."

"So he goes, 'Honey, honey, come here,' and he wanted me to go out and watch him slit its throat. I went, 'Uh, no, no thanks, I'll pass, but thanks for thinking of me.'"

She went inside and, as Buddy stepped up to deal with it, the deer revived.

"He was really pissed," Buddy says, picking up the story. "He got up and charged me and chased me around the fire truck. I had to jump up on top of the fire truck so he didn't gore me."

"The fire truck saved your life," Lisa says.

Buddy was up there for a while before the deer started to walk away. Now the Wampanoag was pissed. He got his gun and shot the deer in the back of the head. But it kept going and Buddy tracked it to his sister's house, where he came upon the animal "staring me down with his really ugly, pissed-off eyes and I said, 'Okay, I have

205

a gun, and you don't,' and I shot him between the eyes. Finally offed him. Superdeer."

Buddy goes back to work, moving about the boat slowly, eyes on the water, watching the tide and the chum and the rods. He's set the reels to free spool with a clicker engaged, so when a fish picks up the bait and swims off the reel screams. He instructs everybody to wait five seconds before flipping the switch that locks the spool and, if things go right, automatically sets the hook.

Suddenly, Olga is on. "Eeeeeeeeeya!" she squeals. "Aaah!" She fights the fish in a folding boat chair, her eyes bulging, her face contorted. It comes up and it's a bass—eating size, not derby size.

A few minutes later she's on again.

"It's a really big one!" Mary Virginia says.

"No it isn't," Olga shoots back. "I know what a really big one feels like." In the end she's right. It's a bluefish, 6½ pounds.

The fish keep coming, fast and furious. The women get tangled. Lisa brings out brie and grapes and crackers but the women are too busy with fish.

"Zzzzzzz!" screams Olga's reel.

"Nail it!" Buddy coaches.

"Ooooooo!" Olga cries as she sets the hook. "He doesn't like it! He doesn't like it!"

"It's a big one," Buddy says as the bluefish comes to the boat.

"Don't lose him!" she shrieks.

He gets it on board and Olga is ecstatic.

"Weigh it! Weigh it, weigh it!"

"Okay," Buddy says. "This one is . . . almost nine pounds."

Olga turns to Shirley. "Does it beat yours?"

"Yep," Shirley says. "It does."

Mary Virginia looks at me, her eyebrow cocked. "We are not messing around here," she says.

A minute later Olga's line is back in the water and she's on again.

"Okay, girls, get out of the waaaaaaay!" she screams as the fight ensues. "Oh, he jumped. He's *mean*!"

The next morning I meet Olga and her breakfast friends at the Tisbury deli on Main Street in Vineyard Haven. She's wearing a denim dress, a Robert Indiana–style LOVE ring, and a fresh pair of white slip-on sneakers. She'd left yesterday with bluefish gore spattered on her other sneakers. "Sheer proof," Buddy had noted, "that she killed something." She tells me that she owns four pairs of the shoes, and she's already scrubbed the blood off the pair she wore yesterday. Joining her is Tamara Buchwald, a couple who are visiting from Bolivia, and some friends from Oak Bluffs.

"Sit down!" Olga says, waving me into my seat and quickly filling me in on the weigh-in last night. They arrived at eight sharp to wait in line. Mary Virginia's bass, at 21.62 pounds, placed third for the day. Olga was hoping for a daily pin but her bluefish weighed a bit less than 9 pounds and got knocked off the list by a spate of 10- and 11-pounders. "Buddy was sure I'd win the bluefish," she says, disappointed.

No matter. She has another story to put in the bank and she regales her friends with a description of the black sea bass they'd caught. "It was a big ugly fish!" she says. "An angry fish!"

11

"There Is a Black Cloud
Over this Fish"

A thicket of fishermen.

After the committee votes to disqualify Lev's fish, Janet Messineo
goes home and cries. Derby chairman John Custer has trouble sleeping. Lev paces angrily around his house past midnight.

At the meeting, the committee had approved a new policy that
more or less codified its long-standing position on dealing with
cheaters. The derby, the rule read, "cannot accept a fish that moves
into any position on any leaderboard that contains what the Derby
committee deems significant unnatural material or matter that alters
the weight of the fish." But in this case nobody believes Lev cheated,

and the decision to disqualify his striper and not Glenn Pachico's bluefish has sparked angry protests.

The powers that be spend Tuesday defending themselves against Lev, Jen, and their band of passionate supporters. The committee members feel embattled as they field calls and offer explanations. "There was just no way we were going to walk out of that meeting last night without it being bad for somebody," Mark Plante tells me. "Everybody was like, 'What if it was me? How heartbroken would you be?' I feel bad for him. God, it's gotta suck." Some committee members are arguing that the situation is best viewed as a hard-luck case, like losing a big fish in the surf, or catching a derby winner one day late. It happens. Get over it.

All over the island people are lobbying. Tackle shop owner Steve Morris went fishing Monday night with his son and missed the committee meeting. He never expected them to disqualify the fish, and he's flabbergasted by the decision—outraged, really—and he lets one of the committee members have it. "The honest angler has no control over what his fish eats," he's telling people. Steve's the man in the middle. He's a former derby chairman and honorary committeeman, but Lev and his supporters are also loyal customers. He hadn't been feeling well as it was, and the stress is only making matters worse. He pounds aspirin and stretches out on his couch with a hot pack on his neck.

Ever since Lev spoke with his father the other morning, Walter has been revved up, and he's making calls on his son's behalf. Jennifer Clarke, Buddy Vanderhoop's friend and a fervent Lev backer, is giving committee members hour-long earfuls about how prevalent yo-yoing is and how the weights end up in fishes' bellies. She drives over to Larry's Tackle Shop and asks if she can withdraw from the derby and get a refund. (Not on your life.) She starts a list of boycotters and has it posted on the bulletin board behind the register. Between charters in Menemsha, Buddy takes a black permanent marker and draws a thick line through his derby button. Committee members talk about resigning in protest. Angry posts appear on the derby's Internet chat room. Someone with the handle "stealthmode" writes: "absolutely ridiculous, I am disgusted at the derby's decision. this is just not right. that's that." FlashyLadyBoat says: "Sorry, but my opinion is 'Bad Call.'"

Derby hall of famer Kib Bramhall e-mails a letter to the committee. He sympathizes with the difficulty of the members' deliberations but argues that they got it wrong, that they humiliated a great fisherman with their decision. "This was a legitimate catch by a master angler who did nothing wrong in the catching or weighing-in of a trophy striper. There is NO reason to punish him with this disqualification."

On Tuesday morning Lev is back at the weigh station asking how to appeal the decision, and nothing he hears is placating him. He insists that by disqualifying his fish the derby officials are suggesting he cheated—their statements about his integrity notwithstanding. In response, Lev says later, he is urged to stop fighting the ruling and instead go and catch another giant fish. He is told that, because he has won the derby so many times, he should take this bit of bad luck in stride and be the bigger man. "There is a black cloud over this fish," he says one derby official tells him. He retreats to Menemsha with Jen, where he loiters in the parking lot smoking cigarettes and raging about the unfairness of it all to anybody who comes within earshot. There are albies breaking off the jetty but he doesn't even have his rod with him.

"This whole thing is a bummer," fisherman Patrick Jenkinson said in the midst of the debate. "A fifty-seven-pounder—how do you take that away from a guy? He doesn't care about getting a key to the truck. He just wants his grand slam record back."

Later, Nelson Sigelman calls the house to interview Lev for a story that will run in Thursday's newspaper. Lev is still cycling through emotions. After the interview, Nelson tells me later that evening, he tried to give him a little advice. "I feel bad for him. I like Lev. I think he's a decent guy and a great fisherman who can be greater in some regards. I'd like to see him get beyond this. It's kind of a defining moment for him." If he handles the situation with grace, he has a chance to be seen not just as a great fisherman but also as a class act worthy of the fishing community's respect.

For now, his name is on the lips of every fisherman on every beach and every tackle shop on the island. And if I've learned anything about Lev, I know that's just about the worst thing he can imagine. He goes home, comes down with some sort of bug, and climbs into bed with his temperature spiking.

This freaking 57-pounder. He wanted it, he hunted it down, and he got it. Now it's going to be the death of him.

It soon becomes obvious that the derby committee will have to reconsider. They can't get away with overlooking Glenn Pachico's bluefish, now in second place overall. Glenn has offered to withdraw his fish in light of the controversy and the new rule, but Ed Jerome calls a second meeting two nights after the first one to reopen the debate about the entire situation. This time, the committee convenes at the rod and gun clubhouse, which is tucked at the end of a dirt road on the shores of Sengekontacket Pond.

Like a star athlete under questioning for doping, Lev has written a public statement—a letter to "fellow fishermen and others who are concerned." He's given it to Steve Morris to read aloud at the meeting. In it, Lev is by turns combative and deferential. He begins by apologizing for his hotheaded reaction two nights earlier but then complains about how the committee delivered its ruling in the dark of the weigh station parking lot. For all his anger, Lev says the debate isn't ultimately about him but about the integrity of the tournament.

The derby should establish a hard-and-fast rule and apply it across the board.

"I did not cheat," he writes, "the fish did not cheat. This old fish simply employed good technique in snagging many baits. Basically I am being punished for catching an extremely smart fish. In spite of everything, I want to thank the Derby committee for giving us the best that they are able. I understand that you all put a lot of time and energy into this event. I hope that somehow together we might find ways to continue to make the Derby better than it is. It's the amazing spirit of the Derby that we all love so much. In the end, I guess this fish and I had a lot in common—we both got something that was totally indigestible and hard to swallow."

He ends by signaling that he's not going to pack up his rods and sulk. "See you on the water."

The deliberations go around and around for some time. In the end, one argument seems to persuade people who are unhappy about the idea of counting leadbellied fish: innocent anglers would be unfairly penalized by a blanket rule throwing out any fish with material in its stomach. Would it really be good for the derby to have a child catch a giant striper—a fish of a lifetime—only to face disqualification if yo-yo weights are found inside?

They take another vote and it's a bit of a surprise. The committee reverses itself. The lobbying has worked.

A new rule is drafted. It is remarkable for its legalistic language, a far cry from the vague decrees that often pass for derby law: "If any inorganic material . . . is discovered when the fish is cut open, this material shall be examined by the Derby Committee and, if deemed to be inside the fish prior to it being caught by the angler weighing it in, the weight of such inorganic item(s) shall be deducted from the official weight of the fish." In other words, if anything other than fish food is inside when the filetmaster cuts it open, the material will be subtracted from the total weight. But the committee still reserves the right to disqualify anglers if it has reason to suspect they stuffed their catch. Any fish moving into the top three spots on the leaderboard would now be cut open—not just first-place entries.

Under the rule, 1.68 pounds are deducted from Lev's striper, dropping its official weight to 55.88 pounds—good enough for second place. Glenn's bluefish loses 0.29 pounds and remains in second in that division.

The committee also addresses the potential environmental and public health implications of the controversy. From now on, the filetmasters will open the stomach of every fish donated to the senior centers. If lead is found, the bass will be discarded and a sample of its flesh will be sent for testing to determine whether lead leached into the meat. The derby reiterates its stand against yo-yoing, and Ed resolves to apply more pressure on the Massachusetts Division of Marine Fisheries to ban the practice.

Not everybody is happy with the about-face. Though the decision seems to discourage blatant cheating—why stuff a fish if you know the weight will be deducted?—some people say that the derby has soiled its image. Old-timers have difficulty understanding how a fish with lead in its gut isn't immediately invalidated. "If that'd been anybody else, the whole fish and the guy would've been disqualified," fisherman Pete Bradshaw said. "They opened up a whole can of worms."

I stop in to see Steve Morris at the tackle shop the next day, and he's rigging up a fishing rod in the basement. Decisions take time, he says. "Sometimes decisions are made hastily. Maybe some people needed to sleep on it. And that's what happened. People slept on it. We're human. And this shows that."

Later, Nelson Sigelman explained the political dynamic of the derby in the *Times:* "In Afghanistan, tribal leaders convene what is called a *loya jirga* (literally, a 'grand assembly') to deal with important issues. On the Vineyard, the Derby convenes a committee meeting with representatives of the Menemsha clans, charter war-lords, tribal members from Oak Bluffs and Edgartown sheiks to hash out issues. Somehow it all works out."

When it's over, after days of talking about lead, people get back to talking about fish. It's like a storm has passed and cloudless days have returned. There's a lot of derby left. The day after Lev's mon-ster is reinstated three contestants appear in Edgartown with en-tries that will be tough to beat.

Chris Morris, Steve's thirteen-year-old son, brings in the biggest shore blue of the competition to date, an 11.70-pounder. It's a bi-zarre story in the derby tradition: the teenager caught the fish twice. The big bluefish got hooked once and managed to slash itself free. A few minutes later it struck again, and this time Chris brought it up the beach. As father and son looked over the fish, they discov-ered two of Chris's leaders attached to its jaw.

Dennis Gough brings in a 7.77-pound bonito he caught on the Memorial Wharf in Edgartown, taking over first place in that divi-sion. It would be his second grand leader in three years. He also caught a 16.71-pound albie in 2005.

And Zack Tilton caps a nearly fishless two-week hunt for a shore bass by catching a 40.61-pound striper, good for first place. He'd started the striper search after catching a 5.29-pound bonito on the first day, just by random luck. He was preparing to throw it back when Janet Messineo told him he should definitely weigh it. (I couldn't help but wonder if Janet—crazed by her fruitless hunt for a bonito in recent derbies—had to restrain herself from popping Zack over the head and stealing that fish.) Then he got a shore albie and started thinking about the grand slam. He won't admit it but his friends say sibling rivalry put him over the edge. Once Zeb got his 56, Zack started fishing the beach hard at night, harder than he had in years, every night for a few hours in all the old spots, sometimes swimming out to rocks in a wet suit. He quickly got a bluefish, but the striper took two weeks of casting. It's his first bass of the derby. Amazingly, Geoff Codding—who predicted Lev's big catch—correctly called *this* one ahead of time, too. "The guy to watch out for is Zachary," he told me six days before his friend weighed in his leader. "He's going to get something big. I wouldn't be surprised if you turn the computer on one morning and he's got a forty-pounder off the beach."

Zack overtakes Morgan Taylor, who assuaged his bonitoless derby by beaching a 35-pound striper a week earlier. Before you get all weepy for poor Morgan Taylor losing the lead, however, consider this: He entered the 52-pound bass he caught five months earlier in *On the Water* magazine's Striper Cup, which got him a shot at *its* grand prize Toyota Tundra. He went up to Boston over the weekend and won the thing. He also won the magazine's shore angler of the year title.

Steve Amaral comes in with a 19-pound bass from shore, Louisa Gould with a 31-pounder from a boat, Tom Rapone with a 29-pounder caught on a fly. And then into the weigh station comes Lev, recovered from the fight and the fever and carrying a little bonito he'd caught from shore. At 4.74 pounds, it's worth only fourth place on the day. The only thing that matters, though, is what it says in the spot for second place on the chalk leaderboard in the weigh station: *L. Wlodyka 55.88.* Lev needs an average bluefish—it's like a layup to him—and he'll have his grand slam record back from Zeb Tilton.

12

Till Death Do Us Part

Wyatt Jenkinson and the false albacore.

Patrick Jenkinson took his son Wyatt out on the water that day Lev caught his giant fish. It was such a bassy evening, a few days after the full moon, and in his younger days Patrick might have stayed out longer. But he needed to get the nine-year-old home. He came puttering into the harbor and noted that Lev's boat was not in its slip. He called over to one of Lev's friends on the dock. "Where's *Wampum?*"

"Bass fishing."

"Uh-oh."

Coming in and out of Menemsha, Patrick makes a habit of looking over at Lev's slip to see if the Wlodykas' boat is out. He's spent years wondering what the kid is up to, how he's doing it, what kind of bait he's using, what rocks he's drifting over, when he's fishing, when he's at home sleeping. "I've seen him going out in some of the shittiest shit," he tells me. Patrick will be heading back in and the weather will be so rough and he'll be so glad to be going home. And then he'll see *Wampum* going out, flying straight up in the air over the waves and tearing around the Gay Head cliffs, and he'll just shake his head. Sure enough, he'll think, he's going to whack 'em.

All these years of surveillance and he still hasn't cracked the Wlodyka code. "He shits horseshoes and lucky charms," Patrick says, and he includes Lev's partner Geoff Codding in that assessment. "Take any information you can get out of them and treat it like gold." Lord knows Patrick has. He has nothing but the highest respect for them.

He talked to Lev during the maelstrom over the 57 and Lev told him he'd gone out *intending* to get a 50-pounder that night. He actually said those words, "I just wanted to go out and get a 50-pounder." It made Patrick's head spin. He's been fishing for how long now? He's fished in all the right spots, used all the right techniques, studied the tides and the winds, spied on the best and the rest, and he's never gotten a 50-pound striper. And Lev is going to go ahead and call it in advance, like he's some kind of maritime Babe Ruth?

Patrick and I are marveling over all of this as we get ready to leave the dock in Menemsha a few days after Lev caught his fish. He's picked up his son from West Tisbury School and come straight down to Menemsha, where Patrick's father leases a lobster shack and keeps his work boat, the *Solitude,* tied up to the dock.

"He's fun to watch," Patrick says of Lev.

"Dad, it's like you said," Wyatt adds. "It's his derby, we're just fishing in it."

Patrick's no slouch. His rivals hold him in high regard. And yet he's never gotten up on the stage with a shot at the boat or the truck. Guys like him have spawned the maxim that the derby is at least half luck. But Patrick takes it in stride—especially this year. He has bigger things to worry about: His wife, Wendy, has brain cancer. The doctors are giving her a slim shot at surviving, and they're both desperately trying anything they can find to beat it. "Five percent make it three years," he says. "That's the life I live right now."

The Jenkinsons go back five generations on the Vineyard—further back than the Wlodykas, not quite as far back as the Tiltons. Patrick's great-grandfather Jack Jenkinson worked as mate on the coasting schooner *Alice S. Wentworth,* which was captained by Zebulon Tilton, the cross-eyed great-grandfather of this year's derby leaders. For years, Jack and his wife, Fannie, sailed with Tilton hauling freight between Maine and the island. "Aunt Fannie," as she came to be known, would live to be 101 and become something of an island legend in her own right, driving the school bus, running a diner and gas station, organizing bake sales. Patrick's father, Walter "Pat" Jenkinson, worked as a mechanic, survived a garage explosion in 1973, then went into lobstering full-time. He and his wife live in Captain Tilton's old homestead, and the red Mobil pump from his grandparents' old filling station sits out front. (Typical Vineyard: it no longer dispenses fuel but stands as a nostalgic roadside curiosity for photographers to shoot and artists to paint.)

Patrick looks like a hell-raiser with his big, thick goatee, his shaved skull, his fullback's build, his hands like slabs of steak. But he's friendly and upbeat, the sort of guy who always seems willing to overlook someone's shortcomings and focus on the positive. After graduating from Newbury College in Boston he took a job in the airline industry. The free flights sounded like a great perk until he realized he didn't get any vacation time. A year of that and he went back to the Vineyard to run the gas station his father bought in 1970, Up Island Automotive in West Tisbury. He's one of the many islanders who left, got the degree, tried mainland living, and then discovered they'd rather be back on the Vineyard. "This place is everything to me," he says.

He met Wendy a few years after he returned. She ran a catering company, and when things slowed down in the winter she made sandwiches and delivered them to workmen and businesses. Up Island Auto was on her route, and she would come in and they'd talk and talk. One day, out of the blue, Patrick walked over and gave her a kiss.

"Well," he reasoned, "I'm either going to lose the gas station for her suing me and getting it for sexual harassment, or she's going to marry me and it's going to be hers either way." So their first date came after their first kiss. Soon enough, they were on a farm in West Tisbury getting hitched. Patrick is the genius who customized his wedding vows to ensure that marriage wouldn't interfere with his tireless hunt for a derby-winning fish. "Now if she gives me any trouble about it, I says, 'Honey, do I gotta go talk to the minister here and have him bring up the paperwork?'"

She never gave him any trouble about it, even in the beginning of their marriage when fishing was his most intense passion. He had fished as a boy with his dad and he won the junior derby in 1978 and 1980. Then he got away from fishing, became a bit of a teen-aged rabble-rouser. After he quit the airline and returned to the Vineyard in the 1990s, he'd take the whole month off from the gas station and try to rack up derby pins. He won the boat grand slam one year. He got a single-day grand slam in two consecutive years and the top rod—most pins overall—four times. He racked up fourteen daily awards one year. Now Wyatt's old enough that Patrick is taking him out and letting him reel in most of the fish. He's content to help his son's derby career along. But the fire isn't entirely extinguished. Patrick still wants to catch a 50-pounder, still wants the chance to step up on the stage and feel the jittery excitement of a shot at that big prize. He tries not to get his hopes up, he says. "Then maybe some day I'll be surprised."

If ever there was a year for the Great Fish Gods to smile on the Jenkinsons, this is the one. The tumult started in June, when Wendy began having nearly nonstop headaches. A CT scan at the hospital turned up the tumors, and in the past three months she's been through two operations, six weeks of radiation and chemotherapy, and a few weeks of experimental treatment as part of a clinical trial. They've been back and forth to Boston too many times to count.

The island has come through for them in a big way. Wendy, who trained at Le Cordon Bleu, the famed culinary institute, caters parties and private dinners for some of the Vineyard's heavy hitters, and they've taken care of her in turn. Comcast honcho Brian Roberts hooked them up with a friend of his in Boston who gave them an apartment to use, free, while she got treatment. Peter Farrelly, the filmmaker who made *There's Something About Mary* and *Dumb and Dumber,* called to offer a hand. Friends and clients put together a big fund-raiser in August at the ag hall barn to help the Jenkinsons cover costs over and above their health insurance. (The family planned to donate some of the proceeds to create a fellowship in Wendy's name at the neuro-oncology department at Massachusetts General Hospital.) Actors Ted Danson and Mary Steenburgen, who are clients of Wendy's, showed up at the event with a couple of old friends staying at their Chilmark home: Bill and Hillary Clinton.

Patrick's wife and son are everything to him, and he shows it. Take a look at his derby buttons, for example. It's an insignificant thing, maybe, but fishermen pick numbers that mean something to them. One guy gets his lucky 13. A lawyer I met used part of his bank PIN. Philadelphian Brad Upp goes with 1776. Patrick buys two pins, a regular pin and a fly-fishing pin. For one, he uses 1102, his anniversary, November 2. For the other, it's 4309, Wyatt's birthday, April 3, and age, nine.

Through it all Wendy has stuck to her vow. This cancer is not going to stop the boys from fishing the derby. Patrick had taken an extended leave of absence from the gas station to help care for her, but he and Wyatt cannot miss the tournament. "The derby is one of those things that makes you feel *normal*," says Wendy's best friend, Nicole Cabot. "You can put everything aside and just be out on the water. That heals a lot of wounds." Wendy's chemotherapy treatments ended in the third week of the competition, and now Patrick and Wyatt are back on the water every afternoon after school. Patrick wants to stick close to his son through this crisis, and what better place than on *Wyknot*, six feet apart?

"Where are we going, Cap'n?" Patrick asks his son as we float through the harbor toward the channel. Wyatt thinks aloud and settles on the west end of the island. He'll try for bass today. It's the fourth week of the contest and Wyatt is doing well in the junior division. "I have a first-place albie. I had a first-place bonito but it got knocked to second. I had a first-place striped bass, but right now—am I out?"

"You're out," Patrick says.

"I'm out. And I have a mystery prize. I have a whole bunch of dailys. A lot of dailys. And a grand slam." A first-place grand slam, actually, with 53.46 pounds. But his lead is tenuous—only six-tenths of a pound—and he probably needs some bigger fish to hold on for the next week and a half.

The junior division is every bit as competitive as the adult derby. Like every youth sports league, much of the zeal is driven by parents who want to see their children excel. Father-son teams dominate. The kids can be brutal. A little girl who caught a 25-pound bass with Buddy Vanderhoop told her father she looked forward to seeing one of her rivals cry when she bounced him off the leaderboard.

When we arrive at Patrick's spot, we see one of Wyatt's rivals, William Kadison, working the same stretch of water with his father.

"He's a nice guy," Patrick says.

"He's our *archenemy*," Wyatt corrects.

Wyatt, a solidly built fourth-grader wearing black cargo shorts and black waterman's boots, brought along his geometry homework in a binder. As he ties a plug onto his line he alerts his dad to a problem. "I'm not going to get a chance to do my homework," he says.

"Why?" Patrick asks.

Wyatt holds up the lure and slips into a southern accent.

"Because that thing hunts."

"That *dawg* hunts," Patrick says with a laugh. They watch a lot of fishing shows, and they love the ones hosted by southerners who spout colorful truisms like this. Out on the water, Patrick can't help shedding his New England accent and slipping into authentic North Carolina: *You've gotta get it in the hydrillas . . . You gotta use the chartreuse, get 'em up into the hydrillas . . . Pree-sen-taytion, pree-sen-taytion, pree-sen-taytion.*

They get the lure in the water and Patrick gooses the engine while Wyatt sits on the cooler and does his worksheet on classifying quadrangles. First exercise: "A parallelogram is a quadrilateral that has two pairs of parallel sides. Draw a parallelogram." He charges through the work and before long he's got a fish on. It's been pulling line out for a while because Wyatt forgot to set the clicker, and it takes him a few minutes to crank the thing in. "That's a rat," Patrick says—a bluefish not big enough to keep.

The plug is running deep and, although they're not getting the striper they want, they are dragging up all sorts of interesting stuff. "What've you got there?" Patrick asks as Wyatt reels in another small blue. "Ah! We're fishing the bottom, so we've got a starfish, a black sea bass, and a couple of rats. Not exactly a tour de force."

As the hours pass fog settles over the water until we can't see anything beyond a few hundred yards. Patrick takes off his sunglasses and puts them on backward over his ears, as if he has eyes in the back of his head. Condensation coats every surface of the boat and coils of mist twirl across the sea like saltwater tumbleweed.

Wyatt's reel gives a scream.

"That's our big bass right there," Patrick says. "Either that or it's that boat that's right behind us."

"Is that Kadison?" Wyatt asks.

"It sure is," Patrick says.

"Flex your muscles at him," I joke.

"Errrr!" Wyatt growls and pumps his fist over at his rival. Patrick scolds both of us. "Don't give him any, Wyatt. Concentrate on fishing."

Wyatt cranks and cranks, breathing heavily. Could be a good bass, could be a good blue, could be something to boost his grand slam numbers. Patrick leans over the gunwale and issues the verdict. "It's a little blue." It's big enough that they consider driving it to Edgartown for a possible daily. Patrick hangs it by the jaw from a Boga-Grip, a fancy handheld scale. "I don't think it's that big a-tall," he says. End of discussion. He pitches it behind him without looking and it slashes into the sea and darts away. Patrick puts the boat back in gear and eyes Wyatt's reel. The line is crammed all on one side.

"Wyatt," he reminds him gently, "when you reel that in, walk the thumb back and forth, all right? You had everything on one side that time."

"It's so hard to remember when you're, like—"

"When you're sitting there posing for Mr. Kadisan?"

We fish until dark but the big bass and blues aren't biting. Wyatt is starting to think he's going to live or die with his 10.70-pound false albacore. He caught it back in the second week. "I really really hope my albie stands," he says.

"That was awesome," Patrick says. "We were casting into a bunch of breaking fish. I was just about to switch lures. I said, 'Wyatt, let me see it when you're done.' Wyatt goes, 'Oh-oo-ooo!' We fought that thing for—"

"Twenty minutes!" Wyatt shouts, getting excited again in the retelling.

"It must have been," Patrick says. He couldn't do anything to gain ground on the fish. The line just kept going out and out. "It was *eeee-eeee-eeee*!"

"It almost spooled me!" Wyatt says. "You should put this in your book. It almost took all the line off the rod!"

"I was backing down on it like in *Jaws,*" Patrick adds.

"Put that in the book!" Wyatt says.

Off the water, the cancer never leaves their thoughts. During the fourth week of the derby, Wendy and Patrick fly to Rhinebeck, New York, for something of a laying-on-of-hands by John of God, the Miracle Man of Brazil. Patrick says that the trip—by private jet—was arranged by the couple they know as "Ted and Mary": Danson and Steenburgen.

Over the past thirty years, thousands of people have made the trek to South America to seek help from John of God, whose actual name is João Teixeira de Faira. They go because they've exhausted the tra-

ditional avenues of healing, because the doctors and pills and chemotherapy and surgeries haven't worked. He says he is simply a
medium, a body through which history's great healers and theolo-
gians work, men like King Solomon, Dr. Oswaldo Cruz, Saint
Ignatius. He conducts two types of operations: invisible, during which
a patient meditates in a group while John issues healing blessings;
and visible, during which, in front of an audience, John cuts out a
tumor or scrapes a cornea with a kitchen knife or twists forceps into
a nostril, though he has no medical training and uses no anesthetic.
He might prescribe herbal remedies and ask a patient to swear off
alcohol, spices, and sex for forty days. Predictably, his methods are
controversial. "Is John of God a healer or a charlatan?" asked ABC's
Primetime. Some say he cured their ailments. Others say they found
spiritual, if not bodily, healing. John of God appeared in Rhinebeck
for several days, and Wendy and Pat went up for the last day.

Patrick is not very religious in any traditional sense, but he was
willing to give it a shot. They were among the few to get a private
audience with the healer. He placed his hands on Wendy's head and
they had a brief conversation. Then Wendy and Patrick returned to
the masses for several hours of meditation—people had their palms
to the sky and their eyes closed as they recited prayers. Down-to-
earth Patrick harbors a healthy skepticism about the whole thing.
At the same time, who is he to say it's not the answer?

"It was pretty neat," Patrick told me later. "The trouble is he
says I gotta go to Brazil five times. I said, 'Five times! How's the
peacock fishing that time of year?' But no, I'll do anything to save
my wife. I talked to people who said they went to Brazil, went down
there for a last resort. They were told they were full of tumors, they
didn't have very long—and the next thing you know they went
down there and they came back and had a CT and the tumors were
gone. You know, believe what you want to believe. But, man, I
can't argue with medicine like that. If it works, it works. I'm in a

desperate situation. I'll do anything for my wife. I told her I'd walk to the end of the earth, I'd swim to the bottom of the ocean. Going to Rhinebeck is nothing. Going to Brazil might be a little more of a struggle but I could do it. It's just another thing. Positive thinking is the biggest healer in cancer. If you go at it with a bummer attitude, you'll have a bummer outcome."

I spend another long day out on the water with Patrick, catching bonito and albies, talking about sports and politics and whatever else, listening to Howard Stern interview porn stars. As we head back I understand why Patrick and Wyatt need to get out on the boat despite the family's trials. A good afternoon of fishing is like sitting through a great movie at the theater. Everything else fades away, and you return to the real world with an altered mind-set, a clear head. "Three hours goes by in no time," he says. "I can spend whole days out here."

On the dock, we run into a guy who went out bass fishing with Lev the night before. He says they were throwing back 40-pounders. So who knows? Maybe this is the year Patrick gets his 50-pound bass, the fish that separates greenhorns from pros, the lucky from the star-crossed.

As we shake hands and prepare to go our separate ways, I tell him, "You'd deserve it this year, man, for all the shit you've been through."

Patrick is realistic. He's a family man going through a horrible crisis, and he knows the derby can't be anything more than a temporary escape, a few hours in la-la land. "I deserve whatever I get. But man-o-man, it wouldn't be a bad ending. Then again, it don't mean shit. The only thing that means shit right now is Wendy, Wendy, Wendy—to be as happy and healthy as she can be for as long as she can be. You start reading statistics that your wife has a five percent chance of making it three years and you start looking at things a different way."

13

Hardcore Derby Heartbreak

Classic derby obsessive Janet Messineo.

A short walk along the waterfront from the weigh station in Edgartown, past the seafood restaurant, the tackle shop, the ice cream stand, and the souvenir store, is Memorial Wharf. In the nineteenth century whaleships unloaded the fruits of their years-long hunts here. Today, a few commercial fishermen still use the dock, but it's more of a tourist haunt, a place where visitors can climb up to the deck on the roof to take in the sweep of the harbor: the black-and-white lighthouse, Chappaquiddick, the millions of dollars' worth of pleasure boats cruising in and out.

In September and October, however, the place is dominated by the Wharf Rats, a motley crew of manic fishermen who count the dock as home base. Here is where they start most days: gossiping and catching bait and, if conditions are right, hammering albies and bonito. The Rats are a tight-knit bunch, forged by long hours, great fish, and the occasional appearance of 180-proof homemade Anisette. As at Menemsha, it takes a certain temperament to fish the wharf. There is more than the usual banter. But ask polite questions, as the tourists do, and you're apt to get lies. ("Getting anything?" *Nooooo.* "Been here long?" *Just got down here.*) There are certain rules about who fishes where, and that has led to some altercations over territory. Boaters declining to give way when a fish is on have been met with withering profanity. There are also obstructions that interfere with successful fishing, notably the towering pilings and the *On Time* ferries that swing across the harbor every few minutes.

Longtime Rat Dennis Gough told me this story about the wharf. A New York City cop used to drive up for the derby, park his station wagon just off the wharf, and unload all his stuff—rods, umbrella, radio, cooler. One day, when nobody was getting fish on fresh bait, he put on some frozen butterfish and started getting hits. The first fish, an albie, relieved him of all his monofilament and broke free. He went back to the car, got another rod and reel, rigged up with frozen bait, and hooked another albie. This one swam around a piling and broke off. He repeated the process and snagged a *third* fish. At this point, the rest of the wharf crowd was officially surly. Before they could string him up, though, the fisherman's rod broke into three pieces and he lost the third fish. The poor bastard threw his busted rod in the trash, packed up his stuff, and left, never to return. Or so the story goes.

The best wharf story I heard involved Bob Jacobs, the fisherman known as Hawkeye. While fighting a big albie in 2004, Hawkeye's line snagged a ferry boat that was tied up to the dock. He jumped aboard and ran this way and that, trying to free the line. A crew member rushed over and tried to shoo him off the boat. Hawkeye would tell the *Times* later: "She comes running up at me, really nasty, really challenging, and she goes, 'Sir, what are you doing on our boat?' And I just said to her, 'Yeah, I have a fish on.' And then I tuned her out. And I realized later, yeah, a fish on, that explains it." As the ferry boat patrons looked on, Hawkeye pulled on a mask and snorkel and dove into the water to try to untangle the line. He failed but it made for another great story.

Nelson Sigelman interviewed the crew member later, and she called Hawkeye positively manic. "He was not of sound mind," she said. "The man was a *nut*."

I drive down to the wharf one lazy, overcast morning around seven. I'm late. The action starts at four a.m., when the hunt for baitfish and squid begins. Pros keep them in the water in laundry baskets with floats attached, but a bucket on the dock works just as well. At first light the live bait goes in the water and the waiting begins.

I find a Rat named Sherry Mele, a.k.a. "Squid Mama," daughter of former Red Sox outfielder Sam Mele, leaning up against one of the pilings on the corner of the wharf. She's wearing white sneakers and shorts, a ball cap over her short-cropped blonde hair, and a T-shirt that reads "Edgartown Wharf Rats." (She and her husband had them made up before the derby this year.) A tiny heart is tattooed on her right ankle. She's been trying for bluefish—that and a striper and she'll have her grand slam—but she can't catch one that meets the derby's twenty-two-inch minimum to save her soul. "If I get another twenty-inch bluefish I'm going to slit my throat," she says.

For now, she's at her station trying for funny fish. Next to her is Ron McKee, who's wearing a yellow fisherman's shirt with "Striper

Maine-iac" embroidered on the breast. They're casting and retrieving, casting and retrieving, and they have hope. Just yesterday, Dennis Gough got his 7.77-pound, first-place bonito right here.

A guy sidles up between them.

"Where'd you go last night?" he asks Ron.

"Magical Mystery Tour," Ron answers, obliquely.

"What'd Dennis's bonito do?"

"Seven-seventy-seven," Ron says.

The wharf is an information bazaar, and everybody's a buyer and a seller. Magical Mystery Tour, I come to learn, is not another code name for a spot but slang for a journey: start here and cast and walk and cast and walk and maybe when you get your fish you're three miles from your car and you've got to drag it back. Ron got a couple of bass in the twenties last night. He's been putting in twenty hours of fishing a day. "Everybody looks at us like we're completely and totally insane," he tells me, "and we are."

All the while, Ron's casting and retrieving. Suddenly he gets a hit.

"I'm on! I'm on!" he shouts. "Get the net!"

In about twenty seconds—really—a little albie is on the dock. Ron quickly gets the fish back in the water, then keeps casting.

The ferry has just started to run from Chappaquiddick, bringing back fishermen who went over yesterday before dark and spent the whole night fishing. Sherry's husband, Roland Perreault, is on the boat. He hasn't slept in a day and a half (he thinks). He stops off at the weigh station, then appears on the wharf, still wearing his waders. "We got a blue and a bass," he announces, "and it only took fourteen hours. Hey, there's only seven, eight days left in the derby. Gotta give it hell." Roland takes me over to his friend's Jeep and pops open the trunk. "Cookies, toilet paper, some popcorn, peanuts, peanut butter, marshmallow, some bread." He picks up each item, shows it off, and tosses it back in. "That's the survival kit."

Sherry brought twenty-five jars of pickles for the derby. The juice calms her stomach when they're out on the boat.

Fishermen are milling around the waterfront, eyes glazed. Some of them fish for bait. Others make phone calls. Cars are parked three deep in front of the wharf, soggy waders hung over the doors to dry. Another Rat shows up with his brother and reports that he got a bluefish last night, but no sleep. His brother has the thousand-yard stare to prove it.

Annette Cingle and her two-and-a-half-year-old daughter appear. The little girl is wearing pink shoes and a green dress that's patterned with dragonflies and bees. One of the Rats gives her a fish quilt made by his wife and she thanks the woman over his cell phone. She plays on the picnic table while Annette fishes, but in a minute she's on the dock among the anglers. Her mother keeps watch while reeling in her lure. "Annalee," she says, "please take your Barbie off the dock."

Finally, Dennis, he of the first-place bonito, turns up. "I'd just told Ron there weren't any fish here," he says, launching into the story without prompting. The thing took off to the north, right into the path of the *On Time*. "It's a ten-pounder!" somebody screamed. Ron yelled at the ferry to stop. Dennis said his heart stopped for thirty seconds. Somehow he got the fish to the dock, and that night it took over first place.

He got three hours of sleep last night but he says he's feeling great. "That'll keep you going for a day and a half!" Ron calls out. When you get this sleep deprived, the Rats explain, you can't really sleep much anyway. You might as well just stay up. A few days later, I see Dennis wearing a tattered red sweatshirt with a picture of a skeleton holding a fishing rod. "One More Cast," it reads.

Down the dock, an angler hooks into a big fish, and he draws a crowd as he races back and forth, lifting his arcing rod tip over the pilings. "If you've got a bonito," Dennis says, "I'm going to have to cut it." A dozen people watch and coach.

"Watch the corner!" somebody calls out.

"Come on, pull him up!" Dennis grouses, impatient to see what's on the line. "You're a man, he's a fish!"

Out it comes and Dennis can breathe again. It's just an albie.

Desperation has brought Janet Messineo to the wharf. She was a Rat once, but she gave it up because she didn't want to fish in a crowd. What she really wants out of the derby is to be alone. But there's this overriding fact: she still doesn't have a bonito. She pulls up at nine one morning in her Blazer (bumper sticker: "the BLUES Have got ME!") wearing jeans, boots, two sweatshirts, and a gold fish necklace. Her derby hat this year reads "Property of Alcatraz"— no significance, other than the fact that it fits—and it's festooned with derby pins and a costume-jewelry horseshoe. She greets me with a hug and then gets a line in the water.

Janet is the daughter of an English war bride and a thorough-bred jockey, and she inherited her father's slim build. When she was born, the family lived in the attic of a tenement building in Lawrence, Massachusetts. She spent her early years in the housing projects. She loved living among people of all nationalities speaking different languages. When she was eight, her parents moved to Salem, New Hampshire, and by fourteen she was paying rent out of her earnings as a hot dog vendor at the horseracing track across the street. She wanted to go to art school but her parents had something more traditional in mind. She wound up working on the assembly line at a shoe factory, attaching reinforcements to the toes, one after another after another. She'll never forget: a woman and her daughter who worked across the line from Janet won an in-house contest—a Caribbean vacation—and they didn't go. They cashed it in because they needed the money. For young Janet, it was an object lesson in how she didn't want to live. "You know what I did?" Janet recalled. "I punched out and never went back."

At eighteen she blew out of Salem. It was 1965, and she went to Cape Cod and fell into the sixties scene. Bob Dylan, bohemians, LSD, in about that order. A couple of guys she met in Hyannis asked her if she wanted to go to Martha's Vineyard. This being four years before Ted Kennedy and Chappaquiddick, even a New England girl didn't know a thing about the place.

"I said, 'What's that?' They said, 'It's an island.' I pictured monkeys and bananas. 'An island! Oh, cool, palm trees. Like, yeah, I'll go to an island.' I was pretty naive." Janet was part of a hippie invasion of the island. She left before the authorities broke up the drug scene and she ended up in Haight-Ashbury in psychedelic 1968 with her first husband and a gang of friends, David and Frank and Freckles.

She found her way back to the Vineyard by 1971 and for $33,000 she purchased an acre and three-quarters of land and a shack—it had plywood floors but no interior walls nor electricity nor indoor plumbing. One day she bought her boyfriend a fishing rod. (She and her husband had parted.) When he didn't use it she decided to try it out. She begged other fishermen to take her. Somebody finally did: Tim White, the guy whose 56½-pound striper would finish second to Dick Hathaway's 60 in 1978. With Tim's help, Janet caught a 16-pound bluefish and a new addiction jolted her system. She started fishing with a hardcore gang that included Steve Amaral and Whit Manter. They taught her how to catch stripers and how to keep a secret. She was out on South Beach alongside Steve and Whit murdering bass after the derby in 1979. She and her partner, Jackie Coutinho, landed 1,747 pounds of stripers in six days.

The guys called her "Mess"—a perfect nickname in those wild years. Janet was struggling to kick the drug and alcohol habits she picked up during the sixties. She would wake up in the morning and have to think hard to remember where she'd left her car. She would abandon the old yellow Scout if she drank too much, fearful that if she wrecked it she wouldn't be able to get out to the beach. Looking back, she thanks the higher powers that she took up the sport. It saved her life. Her moment of clarity came after an encounter with an eleven-year-old boy on the Oak Bluffs pier one morning. "I must've been up for about three days," she says. "I wasn't even speaking English half the time." The boy turned to her and said, "You know what, Mess? You're not only an alcoholic, you're a real pain in the ass."

"Ohhh," Janet thought, "maybe I better go home."

She did a stint in rehab in 1984 and fished the derby sober for the first time. She wound up landing the biggest bass she's ever caught, a 45-pounder during a bass blitz on bunker at Tisbury Great Pond. She took second place. (Her partner Jackie won that year with a 48.) She fell off the wagon, went back to rehab in March 1985, and returned to have the best derby of her life. "I was on a roll," she remembered. "That's when I had a huge bluefish. I was leading the grand slam. My name was everywhere." She caught the first-place albie and the second-place bonito in the resident divisions and, after it ended, she stayed sober. She got married and took in a special-needs Wampanoag child and started the taxidermy business. Her fish are real works of art that sell in Vineyard galleries for mind-blowing prices. Although she's managed to stay clean for two decades, the horseshoe pin on her ball cap is accented with two amethysts, reputed to protect alcoholics from relapses—just in case. These days, fishing feeds her craving. "The derby for me is an excuse to get out of my life. Normally during the year I'm working and trying to balance family and work with doing a little fishing. But once the derby starts, it's derby time. I'm going fishing, leave me alone, don't bother me. It's just my chance to kind of jump off."

She is driven by her two fishing goals: to catch a striped bass over 45 pounds and to become the first woman to win the derby shore grand slam. The first aspiration is complicated by the fact that the fish don't run as big as they once did. As of this year, the last shore bass winner over 45 pounds came in 1997, when Dick Hathaway caught his 50. As for the second goal, she'd have to repeat the slam she let slip through her hands in 1998, when she came in second place by a pound after letting a heavy bass go toward the end of the derby. She thought she'd get something larger that day. When you caught a fish back then, anglers thought, *They're here!* "It meant there was a school of fish," she said. "That has changed." Now it might be the last one you see that night, that *week*. After she let that heavy bass go in 1998 she didn't get another fish. Not one.

"I hate to hate myself, but there are mornings when I wake up and I'm like, ohhh, that was my fish! To be the first woman ever! Now I'm like sixty years old and I cannot catch a fucking bonito!"

Her bonito losing streak does not end on the wharf today, but Janet will always have her first love, bass fishing. Tonight she's headed over to Chappy with Ed Jerome and she invites me along. I meet them at the ferry line, clip my rod onto her roof rack, and jump in the backseat, shoehorned among the fishing gear. They've picked the spot we're heading toward by deduction: (a) Janet has been out there during the derby and done well, (b) she's not catching anything anywhere else, and (c) the leaderboard guys all fish this spot. She's optimistic as the *On Time* docks at the Chappy side and she drives off the boat. "This is good. We're gonna get some fish tonight."

The road turns from asphalt to dirt and then we're on the beach, bucking over the sandy trail down to the water. It's a perfectly clear night and a zillion stars dot the sky. Fireworks go off in the distance for some unknown celebration, adding to the feeling of being cut off. We're on an island's island, two ferries from the mainland.

A handful of SUVs are on the beach, their owners out working the surf. We tie on plugs and start fishing. We're getting snarls of weed on every cast, but we can hurl the lures out past the weeds and get a few clean cranks. Janet and I switch plugs every few minutes in hopes that the fish might hit a different shape, or something with different action, or a different color—if there are fish here at all. Ed, huffing and puffing, had reeled in a giant slug of concrete on one of his early casts and now he's sitting on the tailgate of the Blazer watching and waiting.

Two hours into the night I hook up with a striper and release it. Moments later, a second fish hits and rips out line but quickly escapes. Then Janet gets one too. "We weren't doing anything wrong," she shouts over the roar of the surf, "they just weren't here! Let's catch 'em! Let's catch the hell out of 'em!" She practically runs to the water.

But soon it's almost midnight, when the ferry stops running, and she and Ed aren't planning an all-nighter. Janet is antsy as we leave the fish in the rearview mirror and pickups roll past us in the opposite direction. They'll be out there for the last few hours of the tide, and if they slam the fish we'll regret leaving. "We'll know tomorrow," Janet says. (A couple of twenties arrive the next day but nothing that alters the leaderboard.)

She and Ed talk strategy as we rumble back onto the asphalt. Some years, they've located fish at the end of the derby and kept the school to themselves. They need to find that kind of spot. "We're down to the wire," Janet says. "No time to do anything stupid. Like chasing bonito."

"That *would* be stupid," Ed says.

Janet thinks they should come back to the same spot tomorrow night, stay on the school, and hope for something bigger mixed in. Ed thinks the right move is to go to one of their proven big fish spots and hope for a miracle.

"We only have five nights," Janet frets.

We make it onto the last ferry and a well-dressed couple is riding over to Edgartown on foot.

"Catch anything?" the man asks.

"A couple," Ed says. "Not the big one."

After I drive down to the weigh station empty-handed night after night for several weeks, Louisa Gould takes to taunting me. The official derby photographer and art gallery owner is well on her way to a fourteenth place finish in the boat grand slam standings with an impressive four-fish total of 54.08 pounds. All I've weighed in is a lone bluefish—and a relatively petite one at that—caught a month earlier on Ed's charter boat, the *Wayfarer*. Louisa doesn't seem to be buying my story about the 30-pounder I got with Lev on *Wampum,* or the 8½-pound albie I landed on Lobsterville jetty, or the albies and bonito I caught on the *Wyknot* with Patrick Jenkinson. By not weighing in these fish, by not putting them on the record, it's as if I have passed up a basic civil right. This is how it works: if you catch a fish that's big enough to make you wonder about weighing it in, then you should. You might win a daily pin. You might need it for your grand slam down the road. When in doubt, weigh it.

I spent one morning on the beach with a retired businessman named Ron Domurat prospecting for bluefish in the darkness just before dawn. Ron is a dyed-in-the-wool surfcaster, the sort of man who speaks about the mystical beauty of long nights as a lone sentry beside the sea waiting for the fish to arrive. He is also a serious competitor, and this year his goal is to finish in the top three of the grand slam standings. He cherishes the derby pins that go to daily winners, collects them like other men keep matchbooks to remember all the fine restaurants and hotels they've visited. He likes to have something he can hold and display, something that says he put in his hours. Ron has more than forty derby pins attached to the passenger-side visor of his fishing truck, which explains the conversation we had on the beach at four that morning.

"You gotta get a pin," Ron said, leaning against the side of his SUV in his waders, watching the rods for signs of bluefish.

"You know," I said, "I caught a thirty-pound bass on somebody's boat that I didn't weigh in."

"Why?" Ron cried. He almost shouted the question.

"I was racing to get on the ferry," I answered. I had needed to get home to New Jersey for a couple of days to see my family.

"Oh my God!" he said. "That was your pin!"

"But I did make my ferry, which was good."

Ron was silent. He didn't seem to agree.

As the derby nears its conclusion, it seems I'm relating less and less to the hardcores and more to the guys who aren't quite so intense—fishermen like the newspaperman Nelson Sigelman and his friend Tom Robinson. They're accomplished anglers. Nelson holds the derby's boat fly-rod record for bonito (10.81 pounds) and Tom caught two 50-pound bass when the giants ran thick on the Vineyard. They're just not as serious as they once were. These days, they have a running comedy routine that basically revolves around them not catching fish. Tom's wife tells me they have bad karma, and he admits that lately he's been able to relate to the cartoon on his refrigerator: two men are in a boat, beer cans piled high, and one of them is holding up a fish.

"What am I supposed to do with it?" he asks.

The other one says, "Don't ask me. This has never happened before."

They've resorted to the easygoing approach after years of driving themselves crazy, running all over the island in the classic sleep-deprived haze. Nelson devolved into one of those people who yell at Joeys who get too close to their fly-fishing back casts. Tom became preoccupied with getting to the exact spot he wanted. If he arrived at five in the morning and somebody was there, he'd show up at four the next day, or three. Some fishermen who find themselves becoming excessively intense or angry decide to stop fishing the derby altogether. Nelson and Tom just dialed back. "Perhaps when you're younger, you crave recognition," Nelson says. "You want to see your name up in lights—derby lights. But later on that's not as important."

My evening surf trip with Nelson comes together in typical fashion: on a whim at the last minute. After telling me he needed to finish writing a story, Nelson calls back a few minutes later. "Let's go fishing. It's too nice out."

Half an hour later we pull into the driveway at Tom's house in Vineyard Haven. Tom is scraping the last of a sloppy joe off his dinner plate when we walk in. Nelson folds his lean frame into a straight-backed chair tucked in the corner of the dining room and he and Tom mull over where to fish and what to use. Nelson brought four eels he found in a cooler in his backyard, left over from an earlier trip. Tom is dubious about their viability. "How long have they been there?" he asks. They hem and haw as Tom pulls on his shoes and gets his fishing gear together. Nelson needles him sarcastically for fussing over his tackle when he knows they probably will come home fishless again. "We could just basically go out and stand there for three or four hours and then come home," Nelson says. "I can tell Norma we went fishing and the end result will be the same."

I can't say I expect to catch anything and I'm not disappointed. We fight the wind at a beach on the Atlantic, a spot they've been prospecting for a giant striper because it sits between two known big-bass haunts.

"Good theory," I say as we wade out to cast.

"We're loaded with theories," Nelson says.

This one remains unproven as we depart for a private spot on the North Shore where they have standing permission from the owner, a retired drug company CEO, to drive through his expansive property and park fifty feet from the beach. The new location is dead calm, and we cast and retrieve in peaceful contemplation. I don't get a bump on Nelson's three-day-old eels, but he hooks a 16-pound striper, which demonstrates to me that his bait was fresh enough and will prove to his wife that he really did go fishing. As he brings the fish to shore his reel seizes up. True to his latter-day slacker approach, Nelson had ignored early warning signs that his gear needed an overhaul. Instead, he relied on the duct tape of fishing: he doused the reel with WD-40 and tempted the fates to send him the fish of a lifetime.

Some of Nelson's laid-back habits evidently rub off on me. A few days later, the alarm goes off next to my bed and I haul myself out to the car and down to the Edgartown lighthouse at six in the morning. It's Bonito Saturday. The anglers who catch the biggest bones from shore and boat will each win $500. Already, a picket fence of fly fishermen and spin casters are on the point reaching out into the harbor. I say hello to a couple of familiar faces and step up to the water and fire a cast. As I reel in I look down the beach and see more people arriving by the minute. I cast again, and my lure hits the water and stops, then goes in the other direction, fast, for two heart-stopping seconds. *Zzzzzzz,* the drag screeches. I feel a pop, and I reel up to examine my line. Where there used to be a knot, there's a loop of line that looks like a pig's tail. The fish, no doubt a $500 bonito, had yanked loose my knot. I think for a minute and can't remember when I'd tied the lure on. Probably weeks ago. I rig up another lure and make another cast and—*snap!*—off it flies to Chappaquiddick. The nearest angler just looks at me and goes back to fishing. I can read his mind. *Joey.*

Surrendering to the shame, I retreat to my car and drive to the Man Mall, where I find someone just opening up Larry's Tackle Shop. He winds new line on the reel and I pull some new lures off the wall and return to the beach. I pass a woman who's clutching a fish wrapped in a T-shirt and speed-walking—frantic, out of breath—toward the weigh station. She's just caught an albie right where I was standing. It's her first, ever. I offer her congratulations through gritted teeth, return to the beach, and flail away without success for another hour.

Three days later, my odds of winning the derby continue to shrink. I ride the ferry over to Chappaquiddick in the morning to check out the beach. I find a gang of fishermen who have been out all night. Most of them are sitting in the sand or fiddling with their fly-fishing gear, but one of them is out flogging away at the surf and he hooks into a nice albie. In a flash, everybody is up and casting. I really put my shoulder into a cast and—*snap!*—my rod breaks in half. This I have never seen: a rod breaking on a cast. The top half flops around lamely as I try to reel up the line. I make another retreat to another parking lot and happen to run into a salesman from Larry's. He has a perfect replacement rod in mind. I follow him to the shop and, $250 later, I have a new rod, fresh line, and some more lures.

With the new gear comes newfound confidence, and suddenly, in this last week of the derby, I'm finding a rhythm. I call up the derby pin accumulator, Ron Domurat, and hitch a ride out on East Beach, where Ron puts me on a pair of thoroughbred albies. The fight is electric as always, and Ron pulls out his camera and snaps some photos, but neither fish is big enough to take any prizes and I toss them back.

The day before they close the weigh station for the season, I decide it's time to take what I've learned about the Vineyard beaches and relieve the Great Fish Gods of one decent striper to bring to Edgartown—if only to answer Louisa's jeers. A friendly fisherman suggests I try Cape Poge Gut. I stop in at Dick's Bait and Tackle, where Mark Plante is razzing thirteen-year-old Chris Morris about his first-place bluefish and vowing to catch a bigger one. I buy some eels, stop in at a bar in Oak Bluffs to stuff myself with a burrito, then ride the *On Time* over to Chappaquiddick under the setting sun. It's dark by the time I turn down the dirt road leading to the parking lot at the Gut. I pull a fleece over my sweatshirt and climb down the steep staircase that leads from the top of a cliff to the beach.

To the west, the lights of Edgartown flicker in the distance. To the north, Cape Poge Bay is enclosed by a long sandy arm, the fist of which ends across from where I'm standing. A river of saltwater and baitfish and stripers flows in and out according to the whim of the tides. The wind is in my face, a bracing taste of late fall.

I open my bucket and, using Steve Amaral's trick, toss an eel on the sand and let it batter itself. Then I take it by the head and hook it through one eye. The thing writhes and corkscrews as if it's receiving a jolt of electricity. I wade out and cast before it can wrap its body around the hook in a slimy knot, as eels tend to do in a frantic, futile bid for escape. I start cranking it back as slowly as I can, concentrating so I can feel the flutter of eel terror if a striper swims close to investigate. I work for an hour. Nothing. Crunching over the sand to try a different stretch of water I run into a couple of fishermen.

"You looking to leave?" one of them asks.

"Huh?"

"The stairs are behind you," he says.

I'm not sure if he's giving me a polite hint to beat it before he sucker-punches me, but I discover that the man's friend is none other than Ron Domurat, and he's reeling in a striper. We exchange greetings and I walk upstream from them and start anew. Line in the water, I crank the reel at an achingly slow speed. After a few minutes I discover I've let the gusts wrap my line around my reel handle, and as I free it a fish hits and hooks itself. I reel it in: just a short striper.

A few minutes pass. The current slacks as the tide begins to turn. My mind wanders. I'm thinking about other surfcasters on other beaches. Then I'm thinking about home and how strangely different my life will be in four days when I'm back to the everyday grind. And then, without any warning from the eel on the end of my line, I feel the solid punch of a striped bass and I'm on. The fish yanks out line, swims off for thirty yards, pulses in the current for a minute, then gives up and comes right ashore. I drag it up on the beach and measure it with my outstretched fingers. It's four hands, about thirty-six inches.

Ron starts to walk over. "Good fish?"

"Not bad."

He stands beside me and we study it. "That's a good fish, Dave. You should weigh it in. That'll get you a pin!"

I pile some wet seaweed on the fish and get my line back in the water, hoping for more. I see the third fisherman get a bass and head to the weigh-in. I look at my watch. It's nine. I grab the fish under the gill plate and climb up the staircase to the parking lot. The man is stowing his gear away, then he walks over and peers at me from under his sweatshirt hood. "Don't tell anybody where you got that fish," he hisses.

I laugh.

"I'm serious!" he says. "There'll be forty people here tomorrow night."

When I arrive at the weigh station Louisa is there. "I've got to get a picture of this," she says, snapping away as I lay the fish on the table. It comes in at a respectable 17.82 pounds. People had described to me what they felt as they brought a special fish into the weigh station: their hearts raced, or their hands shook, or they felt faint. (One dude felt so light-headed after he brought in a big bonito that EMTs had to transport him from the weigh station to the hospital.) I think about those stories as I pick up my official weigh-in slip and feel an upwelling of pride. Looking back, it's hard to understand why. It's a fine fish but it's not the biggest I've ever caught. And other than Louisa, no one in the weigh station takes notice or claps me on the back. Still I have the crazy idea that I've proven something.

Charged up, I decide to drive all the way across the island to Squibnocket to try a spot I'd fished with some guys earlier. It's a perfect night there—perfectly dead. I return down-island and try another spot. I've learned enough in a few short weeks that I can think of a tide to try at every point on the compass. With eels at the ready and the rod rigged up and the water right there, it's hard to resist. I fish until one in the morning, and as I crash into bed I have a flash. If I moved to the Vineyard I might very easily slide into the hardcore fishing game.

I checked the Web site before I went to bed. My fish landed me in third place for the day. At 10:05 p.m., five minutes after the results were posted on the Internet, Patrick Jenkinson shot me an e-mail: "Nice job on that bass." The next morning, I swing by the weigh station and pick up the envelope waiting for me. Inside, there are two $5 checks and a bronze pin in the shape of a striped bass.

14

"Menemsha Rules!"

Menemsha can be a tough place to fish.

Day thirty-five. Tonight at ten, they'll erase the blackboards, ring the bell on the sixty-second Martha's Vineyard Derby, and shut the big sliding door for the winter.

It's a cloudless, blustery day, and everybody on the shore is try-ing to catch a 7.78-pound bonito. Dennis Gough's 7.77-pounder is the low-hanging fruit on the leaderboard. At the Lobsterville jetty three fly fishermen flog away. At East Chop a clutch of spin fisher-man keep watch. At the Big Bridge in Oak Bluffs, Dave Skok is whipping a fly into the channel, his clinical precision unhampered by the weeks of tireless casting. At Larry's a couple of guys gossip about a dude who's shopping for a mail-order bride.

The outgoing tide is starting late in the morning at Menemsha, and Geoff Codding and Lev Wlodyka are there for it. With the wind blowing hard for the second straight day, they don't see much point in taking *Wampum* out. Yesterday, they caught bait and dumped it into a livewell bucket, then eased the boat up to the Lobsterville jetty and hoisted the tank onto the rocks. They sat at the tip huddled against the wind in their foul-weather gear, hoods up. Geoff reeled in a little bonito and a very fat albie.

His 9.14-pound boat bonito still leads the board, but Geoff of all people knows better than to bank it. He came in second place *six times*—three times with the boat bonito, twice with the boat albie, once with the boat bass—before he won last year with an albie. His fish is on the small side for a championship bonito, but it wouldn't be the smallest to bring home the prize. He swears he's not even thinking about it. If the bonito holds, it holds. If not? He'll always be a derby champ. Nobody can wrest *that* away from him.

Drinking coffee in the parking lot, he watches Lev try to catch bait again at the water's edge. But then the albies break on the beach and Geoff runs to the Titan, snatches his rod, and races out to cast at them. Lev jumps off the dock, tugs on his orange foul-weather gear, picks up his rods, and scrambles out to the jetty tip, screaming, "*Yah boy!*"

The albies burst through balls of baitfish, their assaults rattling across the waves like *pip-popping* strings of Chinese firecrackers. Fishermen send their hooks flying into the frenzy, grimacing and cursing at the fish as they reel at a frantic pace. But the albies are merely average, and the ones unlucky enough to be hooked are granted final-day dispensation. There are no derby winners here.

"It's all over but the crying and the lying," Lev says.

"And the drinking," Geoff chimes in.

The mood is festive, like the last day of the Tour de France when the winner has the yellow jersey locked up and the world's greatest cyclists are drinking champagne on the way to the Champs-Élysées. Geoff brought sandwich bags full of his smoked bonito. He brined the filets and smoked them all day yesterday, and now he offers them up to the crowd. A six-pack of Budweiser materializes from the trunk of somebody's car. A guy recites a bawdy little ditty, then delivers the punch line: "A nursery rhyme my parents taught me."

Fly fishermen are working the Lobsterville side and Lev is keeping watch of who's catching what. When somebody lands a fish on Menemsha, he starts taunting. "Go Menemsha! Menemsha rules!" He's slipping into screeching silliness.

Lev loves this jetty. It's where he first tangled, unsuccessfully, with a large fish on a very small rod. Some guys won't fish Menemsha because they're made to feel uncomfortable by the jetty regulars, who aren't always particularly friendly. Fine with them: more casting room. Somebody remembers having a discussion on the jetty about installing a chain-link fence to keep out lousy fishermen. You would have to demonstrate some skill and knowledge of fishing and local customs before you could walk out and fish the tip.

A fly rodder on Lobsterville hooks up, then another.

"Gay Head sucks!" Lev yells.

Two guys on Menemsha hook up.

"Three to two! Menemsha rules!"

Around 1:30 p.m. Geoff calls it. This will be his last cast of the derby. Out it goes, in it comes, and true to his word the defending champ picks up his bag, shakes some hands, and walks off.

Lev is not going anywhere. He's done it all this derby, and he still can't claim a grand leader. Hours on *Wampum*. Hours on the jetty. At least one trip to a beach with his infant son along for the ride. He's not about to give up now. "I'm going to stay out here all day," he announces to no one in particular. "And eventually, I'm going to catch a fish. It's inevitable."

As the afternoon wears on, he gets bored and launches his own contest, "Lev's Derby." He reaches into his jeans for his wallet and pulls out the prize, one of the $5 checks that come with daily derby pins. He pokes the treble hook of a lure through the check and hangs it on the rusty tower. Next fish wins the prize, he declares. Within minutes, a pod of albies appears in front of the jetty and somebody hooks up. "I'm on!" the man cries. As he unhooks the prize from the tower, the lure slips out of his hands and drops down into the rocks. Fishing stops while they get on their hands and knees and try to find it—worrying all the while that they're hunting in a place desperate fishermen use as a toilet. Lev initiates a sequel, attaching another derby check to the navigational aid, but he reneges on the deal and instead gives the check to somebody who's going to the Texaco for cigarettes. A fisherman's girlfriend pads onto the freezing rocks barefoot and delivers a brown bag filled with cheeseburgers and french fries. As they are handed out Lev professes his undying love for the girl.

The sun starts to drift toward the horizon, and Lev's wife, Jen, arrives. She parks in the handicapped spot at the end of the jetty and sits in her silver pickup and watches. Lev digs in. "I won't go in. She knows."

He leaps up and throws a cast. The end of the derby is at hand and he is determined to catch a fish. He has not lost hope. He will not lose hope. Ten minutes pass, twenty minutes, a half hour. Jen gets out of the truck and pulls the baby into a backpack and walks out onto the jetty. It's time to go home, she tells him. Lev protests briefly. Her look does not invite negotiation. He packs up his gear, grabs his rods, and heads home.

The other fishermen, windburned, exhausted, trickle off after him until the jetty is empty.

"All the fish are going, '*Whew!*'" somebody says.

"I'm going to sleep for a month," his friend replies.

It's officially all over but the—

Wait! No! It's not over. It can't be over. There are still fish to be caught! Leaderboard fish! There's the evening tide, one last-second Hail Mary for bass and bluefish. Somehow, Lev escapes his house, meets a friend, and takes to the beach for a few more hours of fishing.

But no one defies time and as ten p.m. looms and the final minutes of the derby tick away—50,277, 50,278, 50,279—a crowd descends on the weigh station.

Men and women cram the rooms of the rod and gun club. Dead stripers lay in a heap under the pool table. The guests ignore the refreshments and speak so quietly that you can hear feet shuffling as the clock ticks toward the end of the derby. "The hands of the big wall clock moved, but slowly. But they moved, creeping toward the hour of the deadline," the *Gazette* would report. "The eyes of the crowd followed them as they drew nearer and nearer to the hour. Followed them, until the silence became so intense that the ticking of the clock could be heard."

That was October 15, 1947, the end of the second derby. Today, there is none of that time-stopping silence during the final minutes of the competition, but great drama still thickens the atmosphere. Spectators and fishermen convene at headquarters by the dozens— especially those with fish on the leaderboard—because there's always the possibility of a photo finish. In a tradition that stretches back six decades, young William Kadison, Wyatt Jenkinson's archrival, waits with his father to make sure nobody knocks him out of first place in the junior boat bonito and bluefish divisions. "I think you're okay," his father says, trying to pry his son away from the chalkboard and back home.

Kris Kiehn, who is clinging to second place in the boat bonito division, is positively terrified that the heavy hitters will walk in with something bigger tonight and knock her off the leaderboard. "The big guns haven't shown up yet," she says. After a month of fishing, she's traded in her surfcasting sweatpants for her night-out jeans. She holds her cell phone in a death grip as she watches the door. Kris has one of those quintessential derby stories, and though she can barely carry on a conversation in her current condition she gives me the high points as the minutes tick on toward ten p.m.

She took up fishing for the first time five weeks ago. She'd been laid off earlier in the year and she was spending a lot of time at the family home on the Vineyard. A few days before the derby started she had a crazy idea: Why not enter? "Seriously, it was like, 'If I can catch a fish, it'll make me feel better,'" she said. At Dick's Bait and Tackle, somebody showed her how to tie a knot, and she fished for fifteen hours her second day out. Yet all she had to show for nine days of wall-to-wall casting was a four-inch striper. Unraveling, she went into Coop's and described her plight. "I gotta catch a fish, you've gotta help me catch a fish," she'd rattle. Finally, Dan Gilkes, Coop's son and a fishing guide himself, offered to take her out on his boat. He put her on an 8.64-pound bonito and Kris found herself on the board just behind the bonito-fishing professional himself, Geoff Codding. But Kris is right to quake. No derby lead is safe until the closing bell has been rung. Though he's calm and collected this year, Geoff knows what ails Kris. "For a couple of years there," he told me, "I was so stressed out, having the worst heartburn at the end of the derby."

The stories of derbies won and lost at the wire are legion. Here's one from 1983. Steve Morris, age twenty, not yet running Dick's, went out with two friends on a little boat in weather he'd never brave now. They plowed through rough seas, brutal enough that the Coast Guard stopped them on the way out of Menemsha and asked them not to go. But it was the last day of the derby, and they were young, so they went. It took them an hour just to get to the Gay Head cliffs, another hour to get down to their spot around Nomans Land. They waited for the tide to turn and started fishing at eleven p.m. Their boat was so tiny that they had to take turns, two men fishing, one guy waiting. Steve solved that problem with his first fish: a bass that looked pretty close to 50 pounds. Steve went to the bow and fell asleep while the others continued fishing. They stayed out all night, and at dawn they lumbered back to the harbor. In those days, the derby ended at ten a.m. They grabbed breakfast, even though Steve was itching to weigh his fish. His friends had dramatic flair in mind. They didn't get to the weigh station until 9:45 a.m. A fisherman had just come in with a 48-pounder when Steve appeared. His striper went on the scale, which stopped at 49.98 pounds. Not a 50 but good enough to win.

Hundredths of a pound matter. Just yesterday morning, I had been down at the weigh station when fly-fisherman Brice Contessa zoomed up in his truck, still wearing his waders, and carried in a bonito by the tail. He'd caught it on a fly from shore and he needed to beat 5.86 pounds to take over first place. When weighmaster Roy Langley put the bonito on the scale it ticked up to exactly 5.86 pounds.

"Five-eight-six," the weighmaster said.

Brice spun around in disgust. "Weigh it again!"

Roy turned around and looked at the readout again. Like magic, it ticked up by one one-hundredth of a pound. He hadn't touched the fish. He hadn't done anything. Maybe a mote of dust fell on the scale.

"Five-eight-seven," Roy called out.

"Yes!" Brice exulted. "Can you believe that?"

A few hours later I spoke to a heartbroken Dave Nash, the hard-core fisherman/ex-bureaucrat whose bonito got knocked out of third place and off the leaderboard by Brice's fish. "Now it might as well be a non-fish."

When it comes to tales of woe, however, no one, and I mean no one, can beat Morgan Taylor this year. As the clock nears ten, he has every right to go back to his house and destroy something to vent his anger and frustration. Morgan caught the bonito he wanted and needed and had pursued like nothing else.

Then he threw it back.

It all went down on Bonito Saturday at the Edgartown lighthouse beach—the same morning my equipment malfunction cost me a nice fish and sent me fuming to Larry's for new monofilament. Morgan and I watched Dave Nash catch a 5-pound bonito on a fly rod, and when Dave left for the morning weigh-in Morgan slipped into the spot. He let his lure sink in front of a moored sailboat, the *Aurora,* and then jigged it up and down and hooked a bonito. He fought it to the shore and, to his horror, saw that it was foul-hooked: snagged in the side, not in the mouth. He was crestfallen. He was almost certain that the derby's rules prohibited weighing in a foul-hooked fish. He asked the other fishermen and they confirmed his understanding. (I thought: *Of course* they did.) So he tossed it back. His boss, cruising through the harbor after a fishing trip, spotted him pacing and talking to himself on the beach like a man who'd come completely unglued.

Only later did Morgan learn his grievous error. It's illegal only to *intentionally* snag a fish. Morgan estimated that his bonito weighed about 6 pounds. If he had kept it he probably would have won the $500 bonito day prize that Dave Nash won instead. Morgan also would have finished second in the shore grand slam, worth perhaps a couple grand in cash and prizes. It was sickening.

Now the last minute of the competition has arrived, and it's time to switch off the scale at the weigh station. Three thousand ninety-nine fish weighing 33,013.94 pounds—sixteen and a half tons, almost a thousand pounds a day—have been carried up to the table over the past five weeks. Derbyites gather around the sliding door and cheer as a junior angler rings the closing bell. Hugs and congratulations go around. When the final leaderboard is posted online, the brothers Tilton lead the striped bass divisions, Zeb with his 56 from the boat, Zack with his 40 from shore. Chris Morris, Steve's thirteen-year-old son, wins a shot at the Boston Whaler with his 11.70-pound bluefish. (It comes out later that a guy who didn't register for the derby caught a bigger bluefish. It happens every derby, though this year's most unfortunate angler can take solace in the fact that he didn't screw up like Harry Beach did in 1993. Harry had come down for the day to fish with Buddy Vanderhoop, but he didn't bother to enter the derby—it was just a day, right?—and then proceeded to catch a huge striper. He took it into Larsen's fish market and it weighed 61.2 pounds. It would have topped Dick Hathaway's record. It also would have made a nice trophy, but $1,000 for the mount sounded like a lot of money so his family ended up eating the giant instead. Ah, well, Harry says. It still makes for a hell of a yarn to tell on sales trips.)

Nobody beats Geoff Codding's 9-pound boat bonito, nor Kris's second-place bonito. "I did it!" she screams to her father over her cell phone as the weigh station shuts down. "I can't believe it! I'm so excited!" Tom Rapone is a winner himself, taking the fly-rod boat bass division with his 29-pounder. (Dave Skok is nowhere to be found on the leaderboard this year.) Dennis's smallish bonito from the wharf holds on. "Hey, Wharf Rat!" yells Ron McKee, giving Dennis a hug. "Congratulations!" I shake Dennis's hand and say, "Lucky dog!" His leader seemed sure to fall in the final days but, as it turned out, more than three-quarters of the bonito were caught in September. Dennis shoots me an annoyed look. "Lucky? Yeah, I'm lucky. I can't open and close my hands." He's right. He spent a month fishing. That's not luck. That's called putting in your hours.

"What you've got to do is find out the mystery of that key," a fisherman had told me the last week of the derby.

Apparently, even the mechanics of the awards ceremony are grounds for debate. The four men who caught the biggest of each derby fish from boats will draw for the key that opens the padlock standing in for the Silverado, and the four men—actually, three men and a teenager—who caught the grand leaders from the shore will draw for the Boston Whaler.

Last year, when Geoff's turn came to pick a key from the box, he lingered and felt around. "Wait a second," he joked. "Let me find the right one." He got it, and when he handed it over, Ed Jerome put it in the lock and it turned. But his curious key-drawing behavior sparked a minor controversy. Why did Geoff take so long? Isn't a key just a key? Or did he know something nobody else knows? Lev had gotten up on the stage four times between 1999 and 2002, finally picking the right key in 2002 to win the grand prize. Had he memorized the bumps and ridges on the winning key and told Geoff how they felt? "I don't know if they change the lock every year," said the skeptical fisherman who had urged me to investigate, "but I think they should." He assured me he was not accusing Geoff of trafficking in inside information. But the prospect that somebody would, or could, had him thinking.

Silly conspiracy theory though it is, I notice that this year the derby brass has tucked the grand-prize keys into little envelopes.

At one p.m. the day after the derby ends, hundreds of people show up at the Outerland, a nightclub by the island's airport, to munch on wings and pasta salad, swap stories, and drink a few cocktails. Winners and hangers-on sit in rows of folding chairs that face the stage. Behind a curtain are bags and bags of prizes that derby chairman John Custer meticulously assembled at his house and trucked over today. Lev and Geoff and their families find a booth far in the back. Zack and Zeb sit near the bar.

After some preliminaries on the stage it's time to hand out the awards. Steve Amaral receives one for heaviest bluefish—that 8.54-pounder he got the night before I went out with him—caught by a resident senior citizen. Wyatt Jenkinson got bumped to third place in the junior boat grand slam, but he hung on to second place in the kids' bonito and albie divisions. He and Patrick win the award for top father-and-son fishing team. (It's given in the name of the two fathers and sons whose boat sank during the 1993 derby.) Skipper's son, Quint Long, wins second place in the junior shore albie division with an 8.78-pounder. Quint's award *almost* makes up for the fact that he'd blown off his homework the week before coming to the derby, and his teachers had called his mother and his mother had called Skipper, who had to come down hard on the kid and force him to spend the last few days of the derby in the truck or at the house or in the library catching up on his studies. He's ready for a long and distinguished derby career, having already figured out how to drop everything for fishing.

Lev shows up wearing his Miller High Life ball cap, and it seems somehow appropriate. After surviving the weirdest up-and-down derby of his life, he walks up to the stage to accept the award for heaviest boat grand slam, the title that hardcore fishermen value above all others. Lev caught a 10-pound blue in the final days while fishing with his father at one of the hot spots they used to work when Lev was a kid. With a combined weight of 86.90 pounds, he took back the grand slam record that Zeb had briefly seized—a mark that Lev wanted more than anything. It's a kind of vindication after all he went through.

The energy in the room builds as the eight grand leaders take the stage and shake hands and nervously shift from foot to foot. In the past, the experience has made men sick to their stomachs. Last year, when Geoff finally got on stage after so many near-misses, he wanted to throw up. "I've never been so friggin' nervous and stressed out in my life. It was awful."

The room gets quiet as Bob Clay takes the stage. His family donates the Silverado, but he reminds the crowd that the derby is more about camaraderie than the grand prizes to come. "While I was thinking about what to say, I wondered what really made this derby something special and my conclusion is that it's you guys. It's the people. It's all about the people. The thing is, we all picnic together, we all kibitz together, we all tell each other stories together and that's all good and that's all fun and that's what makes this derby so very special."

Somehow, I doubt this is how they put it at most big fishing tournaments. The audience gives Bob a round of warm applause and people begin to shout and cheer for their favorites as the grand leaders select their keys. The spectators are calling out like bettors at a horse track, screaming as if their voices can have some influence on the result. But the fishermen have picked their keys, and now it's settled.

First up is the truck. Ed tries the first key. Nothing. He tries Zeb Tilton's key. Nothing. He tries a third key. Nothing. By process of elimination, the winner is Geoff Codding—again. Two years, two big fish, two trucks. So much for the key controversy. The audience erupts but Geoff just gives a big smile. No fist pumping like Mark Plante in 2000, no arms to the sky like Lev in 2002, no visible show of emotion like probably every other winner in derby history. In the back of the room, Lev stomps his feet and spins and hoots and hugs Geoff's father. "Yeah!" he screams. "Yeah, Geoffrey! Wooo!" Geoff takes the microphone from Ed. "Wow," he says. He thanks Lev for being his fishing partner (he forgot to do that last year) and steps aside. "I don't know what else to say."

Then it's the shore anglers' turn. The junior among them, Chris Morris, is the obvious crowd favorite, and his is the first key Ed puts into the padlock. "Come on Chris!" people shout. The noise builds and then resides as Ed holds the microphone up to the padlock and wiggles the key. *Click*. It brings down the house. Chris looks stunned. His father, Steve, nearly has a heart attack and rushes to the stage to give him a bear hug. Moments later, Ed hands Chris the microphone. It seems impossible that he could give a shorter speech than Geoff's but, then again, he is just a teenager. "Thanks Dad," he says, and that about says it all. He's the first junior ever to take home the grand prize in the derby. Chris and Steve climb into the Whaler outside and pose for pictures and giggle about the idea of an eighth-grader with a $30,000 boat. When Steve won the derby in 1983, he took home a sports coat, a rod and reel, a couple of plane tickets and some spending money.

"*Yah boy*," Lev says, rubbing his fingers together as the ceremony starts to break up. He and Geoff had made a deal this year. If either of them won the truck, they'd sell it and split the proceeds. "Greenbacks!" he tells me as he walks outside for a cigarette. "I tell you, the kid is touched. That was awesome. That's one of the best things I've ever seen." The rest of Geoff's friends are acting goofy. A man who is filming a derby documentary gets Lev and Geoff together in front of his camera, and Lev tells him he's going to Las Vegas with a lock of Geoff's hair. Geoff is asked about the lucky bonito and what he used to catch it.

"Bait," Geoff answers.

His friend Zack Tilton catcalls from off-camera: "He was fishing with luck and reeling in reality." (Huh?)

And then Geoff and his fiancée and Zack pile into the Titan— last year's grand prize—and drive back to his little apartment above his family barn. Geoff's parents and a knot of friends arrive in ones and twos to join the celebration. Lev nails the new plaque up on the wall next to all the others, and Geoff spends the evening just laughing and laughing and laughing.

Epilogue: Winter

"Just to show the level of dedication": Brad Upp.

One hot Thursday afternoon during the derby I came upon Brad Upp—the tattooed recovering addict—lying spread-eagle on the rocks by the beach at Menemsha. Like he'd been crucified, like the derby had just about finished him. He rose up and staggered over to his truck and chomped into an apple. Sweat coated his body and he looked like he hadn't shaved in a couple of weeks. It was time to think about how he was going to decompress before he drove home, put away his fishing gear and went back to work. Though there were still two weeks left in the tournament he and Skipper had to leave.

He had reentry fears. He would have no time to ease back into the real world. "Post-derby depression is a real, real thing," he said. "You're like, 'The derby's over for this year.' And nothing excites you." After one derby Skipper had so much trouble returning to normal, everyday life that his wife called Brad and asked what had happened on that island. "I'd come home and I couldn't talk," Skipper told me. "Not for a day, not for two days. For months."

The next day—their last day of fishing—Brad and Skipper switched things up and went to the Lobsterville side of the channel. They encountered the biggest albie blitz they had ever seen. Everybody caught fish. That night, they held their "closing ceremonies" at a restaurant called The Wharf in Edgartown with a gang of friends. The guys bought the others a few rounds of drinks, and on Saturday morning, their gear stowed away, they drove to the ferry terminal and headed back to the world—Brian and the boys to Logan International Airport, Brad back to Pennsylvania in his truck, the hula girl on the dashboard swaying with every bump.

Brad stayed overnight at a friend's house in the Poconos, and on Monday he found himself back at the grind of running the business he took over when his father died a year and a half earlier. (He also started a diet: no more two-large-pizza lunches.) "There's nothing better than the fantasy of being there," he told me a few months later. "Everything and anything is okay. There's no schedule. You can do anything you want. Your best day post-derby can't come close to your worst day at the derby. It could be the smoothest problem-free day, but you're still convalescing internally."

I ask him to imagine not going this year, and he reels off one of his incisive, metaphoric answers. "You know what that would feel like? Let's say I required a heart and I was in my last five minutes and the little organ truck or whatever gets into a car accident. *Truck crashed, sorry, it's going to be over.* I would feel like that. And I don't know why. Listen, man, let's bring this right down. To the outside observer it's like, 'You're going on a trip. You guys go out there and screw around. What's the big deal?' And I don't know that I can answer in a way that would satisfy their question. I don't know that I could explain it."

Two weeks after Brad and Skipper left, the derby ended for every-body else. The weather turned and the island emptied. Hunters took to the woods for the start of deer season. People began rigging their boats for scalloping. A few days after the contest ended, a bunch of guys got into a massive bluefish blitz, and Lev's friend Mike Holtham caught what would have been a definite leaderboard blue. The albies stuck around later than usual, until almost November.

Then came a winter pastime: rehashing the fishing season. The biggest story of the derby provided great grist. People never really stopped talking about Lev and the giant bass full of lead. It spawned an endless stream of jokes, the best having to do with ridiculous things you could stuff inside a fish. (That night I had spent with Nelson Sigelman and Tom Robinson, Nelson suggested that if he got a big fish he might pack his friend inside to add weight. "Hey, Tom's in that fish! How'd that happen?") The whole situation also stoked Dick Hathaway's bitterness. How could they throw him out on other competitors' word and *not* toss a guy who caught a fish that was crammed with lead? He took to calling derby headquarters a smelting factory.

Privately, people who didn't know much about yo-yoing before this episode were intrigued. Kib Bramhall, a paragon of derby sports-manship, cornered Lev at a New Year's party and quizzed him about the tactic. "I think it's absolutely fascinating," Kib told me. "I want to do it myself. It sounds very challenging and very effective."

In November the derby committee called for Massachusetts to outlaw the practice. Ed Jerome wrote a letter urging the Division of Marine Fisheries "to address this potentially dangerous health issue for all of us in the Commonwealth who eat these fish. If lead is banned in paint, toys, birdshot and many other products, one can only imagine the potential health hazard it could cause if lead goes undetected for an extended period of time in the millions of pounds of Massachusetts striped bass eaten each year in the Commonwealth."

Children who accidentally swallow sinkers or pellets have displayed elevated levels of lead in their bloodstreams, and swans, loons, and other waterfowl have died from lead poisoning after eating small weights. Although the digestive processes of humans, birds, and fish are not identical, fisheries biologists and toxicologists say a lead sinker could be broken down over time by the stomach acid of a striped bass, which could harm the fish and taint its meat. In experiments, researchers fed rainbow trout pellets that were laced with lead nitrate; within days, the fish showed elevated levels of lead in their intestines, bones, kidneys, livers and white muscle— the meat. More research would be required to prove the same effects in stripers swimming around with guts full of lead weights. Testing filets from derby stripers that contain sinkers may shed some light on that question.

The public move against yo-yoing brought an old derby critic out on the hustings: Scott Terry, the maverick who was thrown out in 1992 after Buddy accused him of fishing in a boat out of bounds. He sent a letter to *The Martha's Vineyard Times* that took the tone of a guy who is pretty sure he knows more about the topic of striped bass than just about anybody else. "In view of the fact that I am already considered by many in the 'sport' fishing community as one of those dirty commercial bass fishermen," he began, "it will do little to hurt my reputation to shed some light on the history and practice of yo-yoing that has been conveniently overlooked in the knee-jerk and poorly considered reaction to lead weights being found in several Derby fish this year."

He applauded the derby for its decision to deduct the weights from the fish Lev and Glenn caught. But he took shots at the committee's argument for a yo-yoing ban, calling it "sensationalism." The real danger, he argued, was not lead but rather industrial pollutants such as PCBs. These compounds are known to collect at dangerous levels in fish flesh, which is why some public health agencies advise children and pregnant women not to eat striped bass and many other species. He suggested that the fish Lev and Glenn caught were anomalies. In most cases, he believes, fish will pass or regurgitate lead weights that they swallow. (He hypothesizes that a sinker could have turned sideways and blocked the digestive tract of the giant Lev caught.) He wrote that, contrary to their image as greedy practitioners of a dirty technique, it's in the interest of the commercial fishermen who yo-yo to protect small bass because their livelihood depends on a healthy striper population. At the same time, Scott explained, fishermen are experimenting with ways to ensure weights do not come detached from the hook, or substituting other materials for the lead sinkers. That would effectively negate the arguments against yo-yoing.

The derby ignored Scott's letter, leaving it to my erstwhile guide Ron Domurat to reply. He is a member of the Martha's Vineyard Surfcasters Association and the former executive director of the Coastal Conservation Association of Connecticut. "I don't know about anyone else, but I wouldn't knowingly consume a striper whose digestive system contained lead," he wrote in a rebuttal the *Times* printed two weeks later. Ron argued for a straightforward approach. The state should bar "any method of fishing that forces lead, cement, spark plugs, wood, steel, or any unnatural substance into a bait that could potentially wind up in the stomach of a striped bass."

Beyond the environmental implications, derby officials would rather not have weights dropping out on the floor of the filet station every year. They don't want to spend future tournaments adjudi-cating a docket of "foreign matter" cases. This fall, Martha Smith retired as weigh station coordinator after two decades and looked forward to fishing the derby seriously again. She wondered: What if I get lucky and catch a giant striped bass? "We're going to have to take the fish to the courthouse now? Have the fish X-rayed be-fore we bring it in because we don't want to be accused of doing anything illegal?" Martha hopes some good comes out of those few traumatic days of debate during the 2007 derby. She hopes regula-tors will be forced to outlaw yo-yoing. "It needs to be corrected," she said.

One day in the heat of the debate I talked to Dick Sevigny and asked what he thought about the possibility of the state prohibiting the technique he invented. Dick is not one to be cowed by those who criticize commercial fishermen for plundering the seas. ("I didn't pass up a nickel out there," he told me. "I grabbed every-thing I could.") The old fisherman gave me a characteristically un-varnished answer: "I don't care. I'm retired." He can understand the critics' point, even if he harbors no regrets about his creation. "I can see it destroying bass. But there are too many bass. They've been overprotected. They're eating lobsters, they're eating every-thing. There are *swarms* of bass. There are millions and millions of bass." Government fisheries managers agree that the population is healthy and sustainable, but more than 30 million pounds of strip-ers are now removed from the oceans annually, and conservation-ists cite anecdotal reports that fishermen are catching fewer big fish. People who lived through one striper population crash worry about witnessing another.

State fisheries officials did not rush to the derby's rescue. In-stead, they announced in early 2008 that they would research how often the sinkers are found in fish bellies and "consider possible rule-making to restrict this activity later next year." In its 2008

"Responsible Angler Practices" brochure, the state advised against the tactic unless the weights are somehow attached to the hook or the line.

As for Lev, he thinks he was lucky the committee didn't bounce him out for ten years like it did Dick Hathaway and Scott Terry. He can't get over what happened to him.

"Seriously," his wife Jen says one afternoon in their living room, "the chance of Lev catching a fish that was bigger than Zeb's—"

Lev talks over her. "And then having a bunch of lead in it? Are you kidding me? 'Cheater!' If I went before a grand jury, I'd be in jail right now, on death row, accused of something I didn't do. I'd be one of those guys like, 'No, I'm innocent, I'm innocent!' They'd be like, 'No, you're going to the chair, buddy.'"

The fact that Lev's fish put yo-yoing on the front page of the newspapers makes him exceedingly uncomfortable. He has no interest in being dragged into the debate over it, and he dreads the inevitable explosion in yo-yoing that he sees on the horizon. He predicts that the number of fishermen using the technique will double within the year. He sounds practically apocalyptic. "It's all over. It's going to be the worst thing that's ever happened to bass fishing."

I get the impression that his mind is already racing ahead to figure out some different twist, some new technique, so that he and his gang can continue to separate themselves from the mob of fishermen—and separate the biggest fish from their watery homes. With the Menemsha gang, it's only a matter of time.

I took the first ferry out the morning after the awards ceremony, as burned out on fishing as just about everybody else. The ferry docked at Woods Hole and I wound through the two-lane roads of Falmouth. Then I hit the first highway and, with a seventy-mile-per-hour *whoosh*, returned to reality. Back to the planet where people don't watch the waves during their commutes, where people don't skip work to bomb out onto the seas, where you don't see a fish around every corner. I scrubbed the bluefish blood out of my jeans and gathered up my battered reels to send away for professional overhauls. I'd had my fill.

Yet I knew that, like the fish wintering offshore, I'd be back to the island and back to the derby. No, I didn't expect to win it, even after thirty-five days at the feet of some of the island's fishing greats. Restlessness, not relentlessness, is my nature, and it is a great enemy to proficiency. I'd spent hours watching professionals at work, like a schoolchild getting a peek at the answer key. I learned new skills and discovered some mistakes I'd been making for years. But for all the talk of secret spots and trick tactics, I saw that ruthless single-mindedness—yes, obsession—is the currency that buys angling glory. The rest of us are left to rely on those other staples of the derby: bullshit luck and camaraderie, superstitions and sarcastic self-deprecation.

One day as I tried to make sense of these people and their curious competition, I came across a book published in 1976 by the island's first resident psychiatrist. *People and Predicaments* is a lengthy study of the Vineyard's psyche by Milton Mazer, a Philadelphia-raised clinician who moved to the island in 1961. His book aimed to explain the social problems and needs of his adopted community. It also seemed to explain the Vineyard's annual fishing fixation.

The islander, Mazer wrote, "is willing to earn less as the price of freedom." The flexibility of being a freelancer is what gives them the opportunity to fish their brains out. An angler with one steady, full-time job, instead of three more casual arrangements, might not be able to escape when the albies are breaking. Lev, the part-time fisherman and part-time home-repair jack-of-all-trades, would never let a work schedule get in the way of derby fishing. "The relationships of individuals are best visualized not as the branches of a tree or of a genealogical table, but rather as a fishnet," the psychiatrist wrote. I thought of Dick Hathaway and his unforgiving history, and Mark Plante turning in his wife's uncle. And I thought of Patrick, Wendy, and Wyatt Jenkinson and the gilded safety net that caught them in their hours of need. In July 2008, Wendy died in her home with Patrick by her side. "It has been the most amazing fight I have ever seen," he wrote of her thirteen-month battle with cancer in a letter to the *Times*. "Her strength and courage were inspiring and unmatched." One afternoon a week later, friends and family gathered at a farm in Chilmark to celebrate her life.

"If he has inherited land," Mazer wrote, "he values it more than the things its sale might permit him to have, for the possession of land gives him prestige and deference from his neighbors, and its sale is felt as a betrayal of his past." Steve Amaral is a man rooted to the island not so much by the land he owns but by the precious bits of real estate he is authorized to tread upon in pursuit of fish. These permissions are worth more than money to him. "Access to the oceans," the psychiatrist continued, "which they once thought of as theirs by right, though they recognized that its title was held by either God or the Commonwealth of Massachusetts, they now find effectively owned by off-islanders whose caretakers are busy tacking up 'No Trespassing' signs, while their own police enforce, often reluctantly to be sure, the new order against them." I thought of them all, every fisherman staking a claim to the seas.

I once asked Steve Amaral why he still does it. After all, the 50-pounders don't swim as thick as they once did, and he's already caught his share of great fish. "It just turned into a way of life for me. It's a part of me. I don't know," he said, suddenly turning gruff and exasperated, as if he could swat away my question with his voice. "It's mystifying. I've been doing it so long." Zack Tilton is a generation removed from Steve, but he used the same words to explain the Menemsha gang. "It's an identity for all of us," he said. "We can do what other guys can't. We've been doing it so long."

Late one Saturday night during the derby, I climbed into Cooper Gilkes's truck and rode with him and his brother-in-law into Edgartown. They had spent all day out on a boat, and he walked into the crowded weigh station holding a 33-pound bass by its bloodied gill plate. Cooper is a legend in the island's outdoor community, a guy who has caught his fish and made a life of passing on what he knows. I had heard story after story about the man's sporting prowess. "He's like *God* as far as stripers go," one fisherman told me. As we approached the weighmaster, it felt like walking with a star athlete through a mass of fans onto the playing field. People seemed to take special notice when Coop arrived with a fish.

"Look at that one," a woman said.

"Nice fish, Coop," somebody called out from behind the rope line.

Like a ballplayer grown accustomed to fan appreciation, he didn't acknowledge the comment. Instead, he went straight back to the truck. He was exhausted but he had more work to do. Every year in the middle of September, Coop runs the derby's one-day fishing contest for kids. Though it takes place in the midst of the main tournament, it's a stand-alone event. At six the next morning, a few hundred kids would show up with their parents on the steamship wharf in Oak Bluffs for two hours of fishing before the boats started to run. The kid's day rules are simple: longest fish wins. It can be a little baitfish, like a scup, or an eel, or a sea bass, or even a bonito. Coop supplies the bait, so after we left the weigh station we went out to a pond and seined enough silversides to fill a cooler four inches deep. The next morning, the kids caught a mess of scup. Donald O'Shaughnessy Jr., eight years old, caught the winner—it measured a bit over fourteen inches—and went home with a trophy scup mounted by Janet Messineo. "He's been fishing hard since he was four," said his dad, Donald Sr. "He's nuts. He'll have a charter boat by the time he's eighteen." Nelson Sigelman asked the boy if he'd share his secret of success. "Never," came the reply. Everybody laughed as the O'Shaughnessys made their way back to their car. "Okay," father said to son, "let's go win the other derby."

As I thought more about those weeks I spent on the island, it struck me that the derby could never be transported to a different place. Only on the Vineyard could a fishing contest become something more than a bunch of fishermen flogging the water, another time slot on ESPN2's weekend schedule. Its people are clinging to their island's history and its status as a place apart, even if they can't help but worry that their grasp is slipping. Six decades is a long time, though, and the derby has a momentum that's not likely to be slowed anytime soon. For some people, it's one of the few things that haven't changed about the island. *Gazette* writer Mark Alan Lovewell says the tournament has grown into something akin to a historic building, like the Tabernacle in Oak Bluffs or Edgartown's Old Whaling Church. It is an institution not to be trifled with. It connects past and present on an island where the new is relentlessly erasing the old. "I just think we're really lucky that the fish are still in the ocean," he says, "that the stories still get told, that the memories of what this island is about are still getting told. That makes the derby even more important."

It's one long Vineyard tale that stretches as far as the mind can see in both directions, from the first Wampanoag bone-hook anglers of antiquity to the kids who tried their luck on the Oak Bluffs wharf and who, in a few years, will no doubt stride into the weigh station gripping winners by the gills—that next generation of ordinary islanders mainlining the sea and taking their measure by it.

Acknowledgments

I'm grateful to the anglers in the book who gamely let me tag along and document scenes from their derby lives. Lev Wlodyka and his wife, Jen, were especially patient as he evolved into a central figure in the story. They put up with a year's worth of phone calls, e-mails, and unannounced visits to their home. Pat, Wendy, and Wyatt Jenkinson also deserve special thanks: They had every reason to tell me this wasn't the year to ask about fishing but they didn't and I appreciate that more than they know. My deepest sympathies to the family for their loss.

I ended up with far more material than would fit in one book, but every outing with Vineyard fishermen broadened my understanding of the island and the hold the derby has on its devotees. Though I didn't write about our trips, I'm grateful to Ed Jerome, Charles Ogletree, Dave Nash, "English Pete" Bradshaw, Steve London, Don MacGillivray, Bob and Fran Clay, Geoff Codding, Nick Warburton, Zack Tilton, and Casey Elliston for taking me out on the water.

Nelson Sigelman, managing editor of *The Martha's Vineyard Times,* not only took me fishing but also shared contacts, old newspapers, and his sound counsel. *Gazette* reporter Mark Alan Lovewell handed over his files, while Eulalie Regan and Cindy Meisner opened the *Gazette* library to me. Nelson and Mark reviewed parts of the manuscript and made valuable suggestions.

In addition to the many individuals mentioned in the book, others deserve thanks for their time and contributions: Michael Bamberger, Charlie Barr, Helen Binns, Marica Cicoria, Bo Christensen, Jennifer Clarke, Larry Curtis, John Custer, David Flood, Christine Flynn, Jim Fraser, Al Gale, Nancy Gardella, Sherm Goldstein, Sgt. Pat Grady, Tom Gralish, Joe Healy, Edward Houde, Wayne Iacono, Bob Lane, Linsey Lee and the staff at the Martha's Vineyard Museum, Chris Kennedy, Wilson Kerr, Carol Koser, Karsten Larsen, Louis Larsen Sr., Gary Look, Matt Malowski, Jonathan Mayhew, Scott McDowell, Chris Megan, Carys Mitchelmore, Don and Marian Mohr, Gary Nelson, Scott Patterson, Vic Pribanic, Kathi Pogoda, Pia Post, Dan Purdy, Stan Richards, James Roberts, Bill Roman, Dick Russell, Alberto Salvini, Jeff Sayre, Daniel Schlenk, Tyson Schmidt, Chris Scott, Tim Sheran, Dick Sherman, Greg Skomal, Hollis Smith, Paul Strauss, Rick Sylva, Dicky Vincent, Dave Warburton, Ted Williams, Chris Windram, and Chris Wood.

Thanks also go to Mark Plante, Ally Moore, Dick Hathaway, and Scott Terry for speaking about their roles in derby controversies.

Cynthia Riggs and Jonathan Revere volunteered pungent observations about island life during my stays at the Cleaveland House, Cynthia's peaceful bed and breakfast in West Tisbury. John and Laurel Chapman in Vineyard Haven provided a comfortable place to crash. Keeping my tackle bag stocked and my eel bucket full were Steve Purcell and the guys at Larry's; Steve Morris at Dick's; and Cooper Gilkes at Coop's.

Chris McDougall introduced me to my literary agent, Larry Weissman, who convinced me I could tackle a book. Larry made it a reality and enthusiastically championed the project to the end. Annik La Farge, my first editor, buoyed my morale when I needed it most and came to my aid even after leaving her publishing house. At Grove/Atlantic, Morgan Entrekin and the rest of the house gave me a warm welcome. Jofie Ferrari-Adler's incisive editing improved the manuscript in countless ways and I'm grateful for his unflagging passion.

My parents Richard and Barbara Kinney put me through the University of Notre Dame and I can never thank them enough for that. More to the point they took the time to review early drafts, as did my sisters, Kate Galyon, Jeanne Villahermosa, and Pat Ross, my brother-in-law Geoff Ross, and my friend Bill Reynolds. My daughter, Jane, unwittingly started me down the road to becoming an author—just one in the multitude of reasons I have to be thankful for her. I'm counting on her little brother, Owen, to launch me into my next project. I would never have made it to the Vineyard at all if not for my wife, Monica, who agreed with some apprehension to become a single mother for the many days and nights I was away. She juggled our little girl and her job for endless weeks. When I returned she read draft after draft and with loyal and loving encouragement helped me through the long winter of writing in my freezing attic office.

Notes

I consulted scores of newspapers, magazines, and books to comple-
ment my firsthand reporting during the 2007 derby. Most indispensable were the *Vineyard Gazette* and *The Martha's Vineyard
Times,* which offered detailed briefings on all the stuff of island
life: overdevelopment, affordable housing, celebrities, everyday
citizens—and of course fishing. Their coverage formed the frame-
work for sections in the book about the nascent derbies of the
1940s, the dispute over striped bass in 1984–85, Dick Hathaway's
banishment in 1999, and tournament controversies in other years.
Pieces in *The New York Times, The Boston Globe, The Boston
Herald, Boston Magazine, The Baltimore Sun, The Standard-Times*
of New Bedford, the *Cape Cod Times, The Grapevine, The Star-
Ledger* of Newark, New Jersey, and *Salt Water Sportsman* also
provided useful background.

In researching derby mania and island fishermen for chapter 1,
I turned first to *Reading the Water* by Robert Post and *Fishing the
Vineyard* by Ed Jerome and Ray Ellis. Also helpful were stories in
On the Water magazine; "Astronaut Training on Martha's Vine-
yard" by Joe Healy in *Saltwater Fly Fishing;* and the documentary
Feeding the Water by David Flood. Background on the fish of the
derby came from *The Striped Bass* by Nick Karas, *Striper* by John
Cole, *The Striped Bass Chronicles* by George Reiger, *The Fishes of
the Sea* by Dave Preble, *On the Run* by David DiBenedetto, *Blues*

by John Hersey, *False Albacore* by Tom Gilmore, and from government reports. *Bass Madness* by Ken Schultz is the last word on the history of fishing competitions. Letters in *The Writings and Speeches of Daniel Webster* detail the statesman's bluefishing trip to the island.

For stories about the Vineyard in chapter 2 and elsewhere, I drew from *Gazette* compilations published in 1967 and 1996 and comprehensive histories of Martha's Vineyard by Charles Banks and Arthur Railton. Cornelia Dean's *Against the Tide,* Polly Borroughs's *Guide to Martha's Vineyard,* pieces in *The Dukes County Intelligencer,* and reports from the Martha's Vineyard Commission also aided my research. A story for *Salon* by William Mullins helped crystallize for me the Vineyard's love-hate relationship with celebrity and fame. Jane Carpineto's *On the Vineyard* offered an outsider's perspective. I depended on the reporting of *The Boston Globe* and *Martha's Vineyard Magazine* in describing the island's closed beaches. I also found answers to my questions in the island magazine's features about erosion and the 1977 secession attempt.

Of the many books about the collapsing fishing industry in New England, I relied most on *Cod* and *The Last Fish Tale* by Mark Kurlansky and *Against the Tide* by Richard Adams Carey. Series in the *Gazette* and *The Times-Picayune* of New Orleans also documented the crisis. Much of the history of the Vineyard fishing industry in chapter 3 is drawn from accounts in the *Intelligencer.* I found useful nuggets in *The Fisheries and Fishery Industries of the United States* by George Brown Goode, *The Maritime History of Massachusetts, 1783–1860* by Samuel Eliot Morison, *Mutiny on the Globe* by Thomas Farel Heffernan, *Letters from an American Farmer* by J. Hector St. John de Crèvecoeur, *Zeb* by Polly Burroughs, *Vineyard Voices* by Linsey Lee, and the documentary *Striker's Passing* by Jeremy Mayhew.

Dave Skok's quote in chapter 4 about winning the derby came from a 2001 interview on the Web site Saltwaterflies.com. For my description of the first derbies in chapter 6, I used some details from contemporary reports in *The New York Times* and *The Boston Herald,* and from a brief history of the tournament by Mark Alan Lovewell. In chapter 7, the description of President Clinton's 1998 press conference at the Edgartown School came from *The Washington Post. Striper Wars* by Dick Russell and *Something's Fishy* by Ted Williams navigate the fault lines between recreational and commercial fishermen. Stories by the Associated Press and *The Boston Phoenix* shed light on the Fort Hill Community. The sentiments of John Cole and Brad Burns about the crashing striper population were drawn from a piece they wrote for *On the Water* magazine in 1999. Ray Scott's remark about fishing contests is quoted in Schultz's *Bass Madness.* Details of the cheating incidents in Louisiana and Texas were reported by the Associated Press and *The New York Times. Boating* magazine's piece on dishonest anglers, Jeanne Craig's "Cheating For $$$$$," ran in November 1992. Shirley Craig's recipe for albies appears in a book she wrote with her husband, Phil, titled *Delish!*

In telling stories of the famous visitors in chapter 10, I relied on Railton's history and stories in *The New York Times, The Boston Globe, The Washington Post, People* magazine, and *Entertainment Weekly.* Some details of the brawl over the proposed links in Oak Bluffs came from Steve Kemper's "The Golf Wars" in the October 2004 issue of *Yankee Magazine.* The wreck of the *City of Columbus* is recounted in Dorothy Scoville's *Shipwrecks on Martha's Vineyard.* Barbara Blau Chamberlain's *These Fragile Outposts,* Paul Schneider's *The Enduring Shore,* and Helen Manning's *Moshup's Footsteps* tell the stories of the Gay Head cliffs. I found accounts of Native American fishermen in *Changes in the Land* by William

Cronon, *Indian New England Before the Mayflower* by Howard Russell, and *Coastal New England: Its Life and Past* by William Robinson. Articles in *The New York Times, Smithsonian, Time,* and *The New Yorker* provided underpinnings for my account of the lives and art collections of Joseph and Olga Hirshhorn. In chapter 12, I relied on pieces about John of God in *Men's Health* and on the ABC News show *Primetime.*